Global Mexican Cultural Productions

# Global Mexican Cultural Productions

Edited by

*Rosana Blanco-Cano and*

*Rita E. Urquijo-Ruiz*

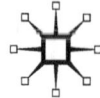

GLOBAL MEXICAN CULTURAL PRODUCTIONS
Copyright © Rosana Blanco-Cano and Rita E. Urquijo-Ruiz, 2011.

All rights reserved.

First published in 2011 by
PALGRAVE MACMILLAN®
in the United States—a division of St. Martin's Press LLC,
175 Fifth Avenue, New York, NY 10010.

Where this book is distributed in the UK, Europe and the rest of the world, this is by Palgrave Macmillan, a division of Macmillan Publishers Limited, registered in England, company number 785998, of Houndmills, Basingstoke, Hampshire RG21 6XS.

Palgrave Macmillan is the global academic imprint of the above companies and has companies and representatives throughout the world.

Palgrave® and Macmillan® are registered trademarks in the United States, the United Kingdom, Europe and other countries.

ISBN: 978–0–230–12047–1

Library of Congress Cataloging-in-Publication Data

    Global Mexican cultural productions / edited by Rosana Blanco-Cano and Rita E. Urquijo-Ruiz.
      p. cm.
    Includes bibliographical references.
    ISBN 978–0–230–12047–1
      1. Mexican Americans—Mexican-American Border Region—Intellectual life. 2. Mexicans—Mexican-American Border Region—Intellectual life. 3. Mexican Americans—Mexican-American Border Region—Ethnic identity. 4. Mexicans—Mexican-American Border Region—Ethnic identity. 5. Mexican-American Border Region—Intellectual life. I. Blanco Cano, Rosana. II. Urquijo-Ruiz, Rita.

F790.M5G56 2011
973'.046872—dc23                                                                2011017333

A catalogue record of the book is available from the British Library.

Design by Newgen Imaging Systems (P) Ltd., Chennai, India.

First edition: November 2011

*To the global immigrants who transgress many real and imaginary borders. To the new generation of transnational scholars:*

*Maya Isabel Ruedas-Blanco*

*Génesis Gabriela Rodríguez Arias*

*Santiago Páramo*

*Scarlet Ahumada Chávez*

# Contents

| | |
|---|---|
| *List of Illustrations* | xi |
| *Foreword* <br> Arturo Madrid | xiii |
| Introduction: Transnational Transgressions: Multidisciplinary Approaches to Global Mexican Cultural Productions <br> *Rosana Blanco-Cano and Rita E. Urquijo-Ruiz* | 1 |

### Part I   And What Are Transnational Mexican Border Cultures?

| | |
|---|---|
| 1. Wet Minds, Bookleggers, and the Place of Borders and Diasporas in U.S. Academic Circles <br> *Javier Durán* | 19 |
| 2. *Fronterizo* [Border] and Transborder Existences: Binding Megascripts in a Transnational World <br> *Carlos G. Vélez-Ibáñez* | 31 |
| 3. Transnational Mexicano Cultural Production: *El Otro Lado* [The Other Side] <br> *Ellie D. Hernández* | 49 |

### Part II   Voices and Literatures in *Las Fronteras* [The Borderlands]

| | |
|---|---|
| 4. *Dos Mundos* [Two Worlds]: Two Celebrations in Laredo, Texas—*Los Matachines de la Santa Cruz* and The Pocahontas Pageant of the George Washington's Birthday Celebration <br> *Norma E. Cantú* | 61 |

5. Transnational Narratives, Cultural Production, and
   Representations: Blurred Subjects in Juárez, México  75
   *María Socorro Tabuenca Córdoba*

   **Part III   Performing Borders: *De Aquí y de Allá*
   [from Here and from There]**

6. Performing Borders: *De Aquí y de Allá* (Preliminary Notes on
   Mexican and Chicana/o Transnational Performance Art)  97
   *Laura G. Gutiérrez*

7. *Aquí y Allá* [Here and There]: Distance and Difference in Monica
   Palacios's *Transfronteriza* [Transborder] Chicana Performance  119
   *Marivel T. Danielson*

8. Selena's "*Como la Flor*": Laying the Sound Track of
   *Latinidad* [Latinness]  139
   *Deborah Parédez*

   **Part IV   *De Imágenes y Sueños* [Of Images and Dreams]:
   Transnational Border Visual Cultures**

9. *De Imágenes y Sueños* [Of Images and Dreams]:
   Transnational Mexican Visual Culture  157
   *Tomás Ybarra-Frausto*

10. Coming and Going: Transborder Visual Art in Tijuana  175
    *Norma Iglesias-Prieto*

    **Part V   Young Voices at the Crossroads:
    Student Artistic and Scholarly Interventions**

11. Petition  199
    *Analicia Sotelo*

12. Self-Portrait  201
    *Analicia Sotelo*

13. Socialized into "Whiteness"  203
    *Roxana J. Rojas*

14. From My Street to Main Street  213
    *Miguel Guerra*

## Part VI  Interviews with Transnational Mexican Artists

15. Interview with Yolanda Cruz, April 16, 2008,
    San Antonio, Texas                                    223
    *Rosana Blanco-Cano*

16. Interview with Rosina Conde, March 10, 2008,
    San Antonio, Texas                                    231
    *Rosana Blanco-Cano and Rita E. Urquijo-Ruiz*

*Bibliography*                                            239

*List of Contributors*                                    253

*Index*                                                   255

# Illustrations

| | | |
|---|---|---|
| Figure 2.1 | Border Crossing Card | 34 |
| Figure 2.2 | Border Crossing | 40 |
| Figure 2.3 | Modular Housing | 41 |
| Figure 2.4 | Chon | 42 |
| Figure 9.1 | "Minerva Valencia from Puebla," by Dulce Pinzón | 166 |
| Figure 9.2 | "Vocho (Paprika-Red Orange)," by Margarita Cabrera, 2004 | 168 |
| Figure 9.3 | "Unblock Your Chimichanga," Part of the *Lupe & Juan Di from the Block* Project, Fulana 2003 | 172 |
| Figure 10.1 | "Don't Be a Man for a Minute, Be a Man Your Whole Life," by Marcos Ramírez Erre, 2007 | 187 |
| Figure 10.2 | "Proyecto Jardín Zen," by Jaime Ruiz Otis | 190 |
| Figure 10.3 | "Gordas," by Tania Candiani | 192 |

# Foreword

*Arturo Madrid*

Over the course of the past five decades the Mexican-origin population of the United States has been generating cultural practices and developing art forms that constitute a departure from what has traditionally been defined as "Mexican." In the literature, for example, English and Spanish alternate and integrate in both the narrative and in the dialogue and textual references, and allusions are drawn from U.S. as much as from Mexican popular culture. From the perspective of Mexicans who see themselves as traditionalists, these new forms of expression are not "authentic" and are seen as "transgressive" in that they violate accepted cultural practices and/or artistic standards. These "transgressions" no longer are limited to the Mexican-origin population of the United States but in fact have become a transnational phenomenon.

This very provocative phenomenon was the subject of a semester-long seminar carried out under the auspices of Trinity University's 2008 Lennox Seminar. Over the course of the spring semester of the 2007–2008 academic year, Trinity University faculty, students, invited artists and scholars, and community members (cultural workers, artists, and critics) examined the nature, character, and range of this evolving cultural production. The seminar, titled "Transnational Mexican Cultural Production," involved scholarly presentations, seminar discussions, films, as well as artistic performances and presentations. This volume is a compilation of the presentations made as part of that seminar and constitutes a pioneering and provocative discussion and analysis of a vital, dynamic, and significant cultural phenomenon.

The "transgressions" referred to above have an important and interesting history. They involve the existence of two (or more) Mexican historical experiences. Shortly after being established as a nation following its War of Independence with Spain, Mexico lost half of its national territory to its northern neighbor. Mexicans, unlike Americans, have remained mindful of the rupture that created two Mexicos: a Political Mexico and a Cultural Mexico. Political Mexico, the nation-state, is highly defined geographically and has sharply demarcated borders. Cultural Mexico has defied geographical definition and has existed beyond the borders of the nation-state. The latter is determined by the presence of Mexicans, whether historical or contemporary.

The Mexican American scholar Américo Paredes referred to a component of the latter as Greater Mexico. For Don Américo, Greater Mexico also had geographical definition, although he was principally concerned with its cultural dimensions. Greater Mexico consisted of those Mexican territories the United States appropriated in 1848. Don Américo challenged scholars who denied the Mexican roots of Texas and denigrated its Tejano culture. He documented the existence and authenticity of Tejano cultural expression, demonstrated its profound connection to Mexico, and confirmed its vitality and significance. Unlike his scholarly brethren, Paredes affirmed the historical experience and the cultural expression of Mexicans in the United States, rather than a romanticized Spanish colonial heritage.

\* \* \*

Mexican scholars and political figures have historically paid lip service to Cultural Mexico, known to them as *el otro Mexico*. That other Mexico comprised the territories that were lost to the United States and included the descendants of the *mexicanos* who remained in those lands after the signing of the Treaty of Guadalupe Hidalgo. In truth, however, the elites and traditionalists of Political Mexico did not consider the "Mexicans" of that other Mexico to be truly "Mexican." They scorned the identity and expression of Mexicans residing outside the nation-state. These erstwhile "Mexicans" had allowed English to inform their discourse and had taken on U.S. values and modes. Their cultural expression was not authentic and was not really Mexican. A popular song of the first half of the twentieth Century, "*Puro Mexicano*," emphasized that difference.

The gulf between the two Mexicos widened in the middle of the twentieth century as the percentage of U.S.-born persons of Mexican origin surpassed that of foreign-born Mexicans. These new generations were shaped not only by the institutional culture of their historical communities but also by the culture promulgated by the institutions of U.S. society in which they were deeply immersed. Understandably, their U.S. culture moved them further away from their ancestral culture and made them ever more suspect from the perspective of the residents of Political Mexico and the traditionalist Mexican population living in the United States.

The Chicano Movement of the 1960s and 1970s reaffirmed the cultural "mexicanness" of the U.S.-born population. In addition to acknowledging and promoting traditional cultural forms—most notably the Spanish language, folkloric dance, and popular Catholic religious expression—Chicanos created a syncretic cultural expression that was deeply Mexican in its origins and character but profoundly American in its presentation. It appropriated static, sometimes iconic, Mexican cultural expression and imbued it with new forms and meanings, even as it adapted and redefined U.S. forms of cultural expression. From a traditional point of view, this expression was transgressive. It violated the norms and values of "traditional" Mexican cultural and artistic expression; it was considered trashy, kitschy, and, of course, not "true" or "real" or *authentic*.

The phenomenon of globalization has further complicated the matter. Contemporary discourse refers to the existence of a transnational Mexican population; that is, a population that is identified, or identifies itself, as Mexican, whatever their national context. It is a population that extends beyond the borders of the Mexican state, even beyond the historical political space that Américo Paredes labeled "Greater Mexico." Mexican immigrants once again constitute the majority of the Mexican-origin populations of the United States and have revitalized the historical cultural traditions and expression present among U.S.-born "Mexicans." But immigrants, particularly their children, are in turn being inescapably shaped by U.S. culture, even though they might live out their lives in a "Mexican" cultural context, whether in San Antonio or Seattle. Globalization has furthermore called into question the matter of authenticity as regards cultural production and artistic expression. Not unlike commerce, culture and art respect no boundaries or rules. Artistic and cultural expression are as fluid as other globalized products, and they can be produced (and reproduced) anywhere and by anyone. Factors distinguishing artistic production in this environment are social context (location, situation, language), cultural specificity (forms and referents), and quality. "Mexican" artistic and cultural production has been occurring both inside and outside Political Mexico. Traditional and transgressive artistic and cultural expressions coexist, have currency both within and outside of the nation-state, and even feed off each other.

Mexican cultural and artistic expression produced outside Mexico may differ from that produced within the nation-state, but the difference is not one of kind. The two have their roots in the same cultural and historical milieu and are shaped by the same global forces, but because of the context in which they find themselves, the artists of the transnational Mexican community have not been as bound by tradition as those of the national community. This artistic freedom has permitted expression that is often transgressive, but it ultimately has served to enrich the foundational arts and cultures of Mexico.

# Introduction

## Transnational Transgressions: Multidisciplinary Approaches to Global Mexican[1] Cultural Productions

*Rosana Blanco-Cano and Rita E. Urquijo-Ruiz*

The city of San Antonio, Texas, historically has maintained close artistic, political, social, and economic relations with Mexico. Because it embodies the complexity of transcultural and transnational exchanges in everyday life, in 2008 it became the site of a series of academic and artistic exchanges, out of which this text on global Mexican cultural productions emerges. A variety of artistic and theoretical perspectives were conceptualized to reflect the multiple transcultural dynamics of San Antonio and also other transnational Mexican areas physically and metaphorically located on both sides of the border.

In order to create such dialogues, we considered it crucial to include scholars, artists, and academically advanced undergraduate students who, through their complex subjectivities and innovative analytical approaches, enriched the understanding of cultural productions and negotiations within transnational Mexican communities. Using various academic standpoints such as cultural studies, anthropology, folklore, and performance studies, insightful discussions ensued, in which the intersections of class, race, ethnicity, sexual orientation, gender, and national origin, among other factors, were considered in the production of *nuevos saberes*/new understandings. We wanted to open spaces for the historically marginalized Chicana/o and Mexican voices in the field of cultural interpretation. In addition, we expanded on the traditional academic canon by conceiving transdisciplinary dialogues from which students, artists, activists, and scholars could reflect on the discourses permeating exclusion and strategies of cultural resistance. As the exchange of ideas occurred, it became clear that in order to do justice to these emergent cultural and critical reflections from all participants, the publication of a coedited volume with articles, interviews, and cultural interventions is imperative.

The discussions on the topic are framed under the following parts: (I) And What are Transnational Mexican Border Cultures? (II) Voices and Literatures in Las Fronteras [the Borderlands]; (III) Performing Borders: De aquí y de allá [from Here and from There]; and (IV) De imágenes y sueños [Of Images and Dreams]: Transnational Border Visual Cultures. Furthermore, such topics became an integral part of the academic curriculum in two classes (one in English/one in Spanish). Later, we selected the work of two students whose voices reflected the rich exchanges among a diverse group of critics, scholars, activists, and artists devoted to these themes. Although such students are the incipient critical voices in these discussions, we considered it significant to incorporate their perspectives among established scholars in the field.

This volume aims to enrich and expand the fields of cultural, transcultural/transnational, Chicana/o, gender/sexuality, and Latina/o studies by incorporating a multidisciplinary approach that examines cultural productions through a variety of analytical perspectives. Transnational identities in the Américas have been examined, for several decades, in the fields mentioned above as well as in traditional fields such as history, sociology, and anthropology.[2] Nevertheless, we propose a new multilayered reading of contemporary transnational cultural manifestations in which it is possible to recognize challenges and cultural strategies that transnational Mexican communities conceive in order to claim cultural, political, and social agency. In this respect the chapters included here elaborate on the creation of new forms of citizenship that reshape the long history of exclusion that has marked the experiences of these particular groups not just in the United States and Mexico.

In her work included in this volume, Norma Iglesias-Prieto provides very clear definitions of "transborder" and "transnational" dynamics. She defines the former as symbolic and material exchanges that occur in spaces situated on the Mexico-U.S. border. Additionally, she argues that "transnational" refers to similar exchanges, except that these could be situated anywhere within the two countries. Both processes are crucial in order to understand the characteristics and tendencies related to globalization and neoliberalism. On the other hand, Carlos Vélez-Ibáñez's chapter serves to further complicate these terms by conflating them at times. He states: "When I use the word[s] 'transnational' and 'transborder' at one level, I include activities, events, behaviors, transactions, networks, and relationships in which persons on both sides of the border participate in mutual fields and arenas in Southwest North America and beyond. These may be symmetrical or asymmetrical, open or close ended, and certainly political, economic, and social." Although these "material and symbolic exchanges" have historically existed between the two countries, it is indispensable to examine the unequal relations of power in these cultural, economic, and social practices.

## Transnational Mexican Historical Context

In spite of the fact that the history of these two neighboring countries has been interrelated for over a century and a half, little has changed in terms of their relations of power at the economic, political, and social levels. As such, their histories continue to demonstrate a subordination of one country's people and resources to the other, resulting in persistent exploitation and exclusion that, in turn, create an array of contesting cultural productions. Although such historical interventions have called into question these marginalized voices, they have not, however, incorporated a gender and sexuality framework that in turn perpetuates the traditional/patriarchal critical model. Our attempt is to incorporate and privilege the previously silenced voices.

According to Gilbert Paul Carrasco (1998), since 1848 and throughout its history, the United States has requested and utilized cheap labor from its neighbor to the south during times of economic growth and has rejected it during economic recessions. The first wave of Mexican immigrant workers into this country occurred during the Gold Rush era, adding to a population of Californios who had settled in the region with the expansion of the Spanish colonial frontier (Castañeda 1993). Anglo miners benefited significantly from the skills, tools, and techniques of Mexican immigrants, other longtime settlers, and Chinese miners.

But there was no gratitude shown toward any of these workers, instead, given the racism of the time, such miners became victims of discrimination, threats, violence, and restrictive legislation. Throughout the nineteenth century, Mexican labor continued to be exploited, especially in the areas of ranching, agriculture, and building railroads. At times they were held captive and at other times they were left to fend for themselves after finishing a labor season. Similar to the treatment suffered by the miners, other Mexican workers, seen as "foreigners" and an economic threat, also continued to be victims of violence and terror even when their labor was much needed (Carrasco 1998; Acuña 1972).

The U.S. invasion of Mexico in 1846, which in turn challenged the formation of the Mexican nation, was an opportunity for Mexican indigenous groups to reclaim the communal lands taken away from them.³ Alongside, they were also reclaiming their political autonomy, which continues to be one of their major struggles in the twenty-first century. However, such community land and communal living were considered a threat to the nation and its notion of private property. As the Mexico-U.S. border became geopolitically redefined throughout the nineteenth century, such as after the Gadsden Purchase following the Mexican-American War, people of all ethnicities living in the borderlands experienced violent, contradictory, and complex redefinitions of the limits of their cultural and social experiences. Chapter 2 by Carlos Vélez-Ibáñez narrates these occurrences and reflects on his childhood experiences in relation to Irish and Jewish families who migrated from the East Coast and became "mexicanized," given that they lived most of their lives in his Tucson neighborhood.

In the process of nation building, major economic advances were implemented in Mexico, and none of them was more violent and imposing than Porfirio Díaz's national development plans. The process of Mexico's modernization was accelerated with his coup in 1876. His dictatorship lasted until the beginning of the Mexican Revolution and was responsible for displacing the country's peasants and the poor who, in turn, migrated to industrialized cities and as far north as the United States (Acuña 148). Thanks to foreign capital from England, France, and the United States, Mexico invested heavily in the agriculture, mining, and railroad industries. According to Acuña, such investment produced a "reserve labor pool of unskilled labor" (12) for the industrialized cities in Mexico and for its neighbor to the north. Adolfo Gilly states that Mexico has thus become a servile colony for the United States, as it provides the United States with an inexhaustible reserve of cheap labor, which began with the Porfiriato (Gilly et. al. 29).

A primary reason for the United States needing cheap labor, in particular from Mexico, during the end of the nineteenth century was that it passed the Chinese Exclusion Act of 1882, which prohibited further migration from China. Racist and nativist sentiments against the Chinese (many of whom later migrated to northwestern Mexico) led to increasing Mexican migration of unskilled laborers. But regardless of the racism of the time, the agricultural industry (as well as others) had one concern: "... [i]f you drive the Chinese out now, who is going to gather the fruit and the harvests next summer and fall?" (Saxton 209). The answer was simple: invite more Mexican workers to continue to develop the U.S. industries that needed them. Acuña indicates that by 1917 the United States had also limited migration from Europe (especially from eastern Europe), and that most immigrants had to clear reading, writing, and medical exams and had to pay an eight-dollar fee. Mexican workers were exempt from these requirements until 1921 (Acuña 142; Sánchez 55, 57). However, once the law changed against them, historical records confirm the increased racism regarding the treatment of Mexican immigrants at the border, given that they were considered "dirty" because of their high rate of poverty and illiteracy. A demeaning example of this racism was that immigrant Mexican workers had to bathe at the border and their clothes were washed and fumigated before they entered the United States (Sánchez, 56).

As if such humiliation were not enough, some of their own compatriots of Mexican descent born in the United States also humiliated and disdained the new arrivals. David Gutiérrez indicates that the feelings of mistrust were mutual and that one group considered the other unworthy of whatever cultural values they held in high esteem. This created a rivalry between the "recién llegados/recent arrivals" and the "pochos/culturally deprived" (Gutiérrez 57, 63). Nevertheless, the opposite also occurred among some parts of these communities: "...the increasing flow of immigrants into the Southwest was welcomed by some Mexican Americans because the immigrants helped to rejuvenate Mexican culture, customs, and the use of Spanish in their communities..." (40). But it is important to recognize that such responses, whether positive or negative, were not merely due to cultural nationalism; they were fueled, instead, by economic and material conditions. By the mid 1920s the immigrant Mexican population had surpassed its U.S.-born counterpart. It is estimated that as many as 1.5 million Mexican immigrants entered the country between 1890 and 1929. Such high numbers of immigrants threatened some Mexican Americans, who felt they had to compete with the immigrants for the same or similar jobs in a racist economic system that constantly offered them very few job opportunities (Gutiérrez 40, 60).

Although initially the majority of Mexican immigrants into the United States were male, in the 1920s, according to Pierrette Hondagneu-Sotelo, Mexican women and children joined the workforce and were used by employers as a stabilizing and exploitative tool, given that "...when accompanied by their families, men more willingly endured harsh working conditions" (Hondagneu-Sotelo 1994, 21). However, by the time of the Great Depression in the 1930s, hundreds of thousands of women, men, and children, even those who were U.S. citizens, were deported/expatriated (Hondagneu-Sotelo 1997, 117; Ruiz 1998, 29–32; Acuña 1972). By 1942, amid the economic prosperity brought on by World War II, another big wave of Mexican laborers was sponsored under the Bracero Program (Calavita, Gutiérrez, Acuña), which was intended to last a few years but was expanded until 1964. Although this program offered work permits to 5 million men, another 5 million were in the country without documentation (Hondagneu-Sotelo 1994, 23; Sánchez 1993; Gutiérrez 1995). During the 1950s, after the Korean War, yet another economic recession prompted labor unions' complaints that called for the control of undocumented immigration. This "control" measure was better known as "Operation Wetback," because it entailed the human rights violation of over 1 million people of Mexican ancestry who were deported within a few months in 1954 (Acuña 1972; Gutiérrez 1995).

But as soon as the recession ended, the United States, true to its pattern, requested a reinstatement of the Bracero Program to bring back cheap Mexican labor (González 2000, 203). In 1965 the United States initiated the Border Industrialization Program (BIP), also known as the Maquiladora Program, which was designed to reduce undocumented immigration by taking the factories and jobs to Mexico and locating them along the border region (González 2000, 233–45). However, this program has had the opposite effect.

According to Michael Huspek (1998), the United States contributes to the large-scale migration of Mexican undocumented workers by establishing commercial agricultural firms in Mexico that eventually drive peasants and indigenous families to the cities and across the border where they in turn obtain exploitative jobs at Maquiladora plants. The U.S. employers who hire such undocumented workers are rarely punished (*San Diego Union Tribune*, November 5, 1998). Such programs became even stronger after the 1982 near collapse of the Mexican economy, which was dependant primarily on the U.S. market for import and export of raw materials (such as oil) as well as human capital, such as the immigrants (documented or not) who send billions of dollars to their native country while working in the United States.

The culmination of the Maquiladora Program was the signing of the North American Free Trade Agreement (NAFTA) in 1994, which has failed to stop undocumented migration and instead continues to facilitate the exploitation of Mexican workers on both sides of the border (In Motion Magazine 1997; González 2000). As Luis Méndez discusses, NAFTA was pursued and implemented by the Mexican ruling class who was looking to solidify the economic, neoliberal system from which the consolidation of the Mexican political right could be possible. The result is that the Partido Acción Nacional (National Action Party) gained control of the country's political system at the national and state levels in 2000.[4] NAFTA is also the result of transnational unequal economic and political dynamics between the Mexican and U.S. elites. It is no coincidence that the agreement was ultimately signed in the city of San Antonio, which has historically been a point of transnational and transborder relations. Given the current nativist and racist attitudes across the United States after the election of Barack Obama, the first African American president, these sentiments still exist. Immigrants, as well as people of color in general, often receive the blame for the economic crisis, which causes them to live in a state-produced terror.

When NAFTA went into effect on January 1, 1994, it was no surprise to the critics of this agreement that the Ejército Zapatista de Liberación Nacional/Zapatista Army of National Liberation (EZLN) took up arms against the Mexican government in Chiapas, one of the poorest states, to denounce five centuries of annihilation as well as the economic and cultural exploitation of indigenous peoples in Mexico. One of the main goals of EZLN was to challenge NAFTA's notion of aggressive development and implementation of global agribusinesses that in turn eliminated governmental subsidies for indigenous and peasant communities. As June Nash indicates: "The integration of Mexico into [the] global economy is correlated with the shrinking of national controls affecting the redistribution of wealth and the direction of development" (78). However, even a grassroots movement, like the EZLN's, has been criticized for marginalizing indigenous women within it and negating equal rights to them because of their gender while demanding their rights as men from the Mexican government. It is well known that the BIP and NAFTA have targeted young women as the main employees in the Maquiladoras and other gendered industrialized sectors. Since NAFTA's implementation, the human rights violations and murders, especially of young women in the Ciudad Juárez/El Paso border region, have increased dramatically. As shown, the twentieth century was marked by an opening and closing of the southwestern border to Mexican labor, a trend explained since the 1970s by the "push-pull factor" of immigration, as previously discussed by Acuña and Gilly, among other authors.

Gerald López's analysis has complicated this earlier proposal even further by stating that as long as the United States continues to be more economically advantaged, migration north from Mexico will persist given that immigrants will continue to believe that this country will provide them with better-paying jobs than those available or unavailable at home (López 1988, 93). However, migration north is often that of undocumented immigrants, a source of contention between the two countries: although they fulfill the demand for cheap labor, they are also readily blamed for the United States' economic problems during times of recession. Unfortunately, racist sentiments disseminated by the press and public figures have resulted in hundreds of immigrants being physically brutalized (*In Motion Magazine* 1997, 2–4; Avilés 1999). Therefore it should come as no surprise that the border between the United States and Mexico has been a site of continued human rights violations against immigrants in general and women in particular. The most recent example of these xenophobic attacks is Arizona's State Bill 1070, which criminalizes the immigrant and produces terror for all people who do not fit into the U.S. white model/imaginary of citizenship. Furthermore, the Texas Board of Education, a leader in the development of textbook materials nationally, has decided to enact similar xenophobic and racist endeavors by eliminating marginalized voices from history textbooks. It is no coincidence that such erased voices are those of women of all ethnicities and people of color in particular. After the 2010 midterm elections where Republicans gained a majority in the House of Representatives, other state officials have proposed similar discriminatory legislation, moving the country as a whole into further conservatism.

## Theoretical Framework on Global and Transnational Dynamics

There are countless critical interpretations of the various manifestations of transnational/transborder Mexican cultures not only because of the broad scope of theoretical approaches that critics have been using for several decades but also because of the many forms in which Mexican identities are experienced on both sides of the Río Bravo/Rio Grande. For decades the existence of various *Mexicos* has been considered by the national Mexican elite as a symbol of *entreguismo* or betrayal and, to some extent, a Pocho-incomplete Mexican identity. However, for the diverse populations that represent the many *Mexicos* and live throughout the United States (as well as in other countries), embodying a cultural difference, this has implied a dynamic of empowerment that contests exclusionary discourses derived from the negative connotations associated with Mexican cultural identity.

Following Ana Sampaio's reflections (51), the chapters included in this volume consider the urgent incorporation of complex theoretical approaches in which transnationality works as the common thread. Such chapters also expand this discussion by reflecting on the transnational and multisituated critical approaches from which critics discuss local and global dynamics that affect and transform cultural productions and every day lives of Latina/o, Mexican, and Chicana/o communities. As Raymond Rocco argues, due to the complexities that exist within Latina/o communities in the United States, adopting interdisciplinary theoretical approaches—such as poststructuralism, cultural studies, and Chicana-Latina feminisms, among others—serves to disentangle social practices and to foster agency related to "the historical disempowerment and exclusion of Latina/o communities" (91). It is vital, as Rocco also suggests (93), to use critical standpoints that underline the complexity and specificity of the visible and invisible borders that, based on Eurocentric and patriarchal discourses, mark everyday life for Latinas/os, since their subjectivities break with dominant notions of ideal citizenship, ethnicity, national origin, gender, sexuality, social class, and education.

Thus, this volume includes critical interventions that contribute to the theoretical corpus that examines visible and invisible borders from a historical perspective. Adopting a complex historical analysis reveals the many layers associated with colonial and postcolonial societies—both in the United States and the rest of the Americas—in which unequal relations are still articulated among the colonizers and the colonized, the oppressed, and the exploited. Examining hybrid spaces—borders, limits, margins—and dynamics produced in that in-between space enlightens not only the complexity of exclusionary discourses toward nonideal subjects but also the multiple forms of resistance and renegotiation they establish against the power structures. It is from these in-between spaces that new political, social, and economic agents emerge, transforming dynamics of exclusion in the local, national, transnational, and global arenas.

Borders/Fronteras, as determining categories of analysis in this volume, have been one of the most powerful tropes for the understanding of cultural and historical connections present in quotidian experiences in the transnational *Mexicos* through personal, collective, and institutional practices. Gloria E. Anzaldúa, as a radical queer feminist voice, argues that the political borders between Mexico and the United States affect both the social position and agency for Mexican transnational communities. Furthermore, she expands and incorporates a broader concept of the border—a psychological, metaphorical, and spiritual one—that refers to exchanges among groups that have experienced exclusion and oppression from the dominant discursive matrix that determines those borders:

> The actual physical borderland that I'm dealing with [...] is the Texas-U.S. Southwest/Mexican border. The psychological borderlands, the sexual borderlands and the spiritual borderlands are not particular to the Southwest. In fact, the Borderlands are physically present wherever two or more cultures edge each other, where people of different races occupy the same territory, where under, middle and upper class touch, where the space between two individuals shrinks with intimacy. (Anzaldúa, preface)

In this regard, theoretical perspectives on transculturality are relevant because this critical approach reminds us of "the confrontation and entanglement that occur when different social groups relate to each other" (García Canclini, 15).[5] As Néstor García Canclini suggests, the multi-layered process of identity creation goes beyond a romantic and static notion of identity politics (2004, 21–22). Using transcultural theoretical approaches helps, in turn, to elucidate social practices intervening—either in facilitating or obstructing—in the (re)construction of political identities. The chapters included in this volume establish a discussion on the social practices that prevail in the construction of identities as processes. Such identity formation takes into account differences—ethnicity, gender, sexual orientation, national origin, and language, among others—social inequalities and a lack of access to cultural spheres and resources that facilitate or obstruct the development of a cultural, economic, and political agency for transnational Mexican communities.

Global, transcultural, and transborder exchanges prevalent in spaces marked by visible and invisible borders will be central in the critical reflection these chapters present. By focusing on these three types of exchanges, the voices included in this volume establish a dialogue with Mary Louise Pratt's "contact zones," defined as "space[s] of colonial encounters, the space[s] in which peoples geographically and historically separated come into contact with each other and establish ongoing relations, usually involving conditions of coercion, radical inequality, and intractable conflict" (6). Furthermore, the chapters also elaborate on Anzaldúa's concepts of borders, margins, and hybrid spaces, identifying practices of empowerment that help to reconfigure the oppressive connotations associated with the implementation of borders, claiming these fronterizos [border] spaces as third spaces that break with the narrow notion of national specificities, cultures, identities, and citizenships.

Dislocating binary constructs and social practices that base their exclusionary mechanisms on the imposition of one term over the other—male/female, heterosexual/queer, American/Mexican, documented/undocumented—can serve to reveal new spaces of power in which emergent identities transform social landscapes immersed in complex and somewhat contradictory global exchanges (Rocco, 101). As Anzaldúa discusses: "Living in Nepantla, the overlapping space between different perceptions and belief systems, you are aware of the changeability of racial, gender, sexual and other categories rendering the conventional labeling obsolete" (2002, 541).

The many shapes of (trans)border and (trans)national identities, as Ramón Saldívar suggests in his examination of the concept of transnationalism proposed by Américo Paredes, are constituted through symbols and social practices that emphasize "the language of citizenship in which claims of belonging, community, and rights are formulated and expressed as a discourse of citizenship" (62). This language of citizenship also embodies multiple forms that should be considered not only by projects of historical preservation of communities inscribed in hybrid spaces. At the same time, such language must be examined from a complex theoretical framework that incorporates powerful manifestations of the language of citizenship that bridge the examination of social and institutional practices such as the notion of "lived identities":

> The "lived identities" and realities of these hybrid and third spaces, margins, borders, contact zones and spaces "in-between" are not random, epiphenomenal, or transient. They are institutional spaces, structures of cultural, economic, and political practice that determine conditions, strategies and options for social and political actions. And their quality as spaces of the hybrid, border, or margin is directly linked to a variety of changes in the nature of the relationship between territory, space, identity, and community that have resulted from the processes of transnationalization. (Rocco, 100)

If "lived identities" also refers to the need to reconfigure the use of public spaces and institutions to create new spaces of power, it can be said that transnational cultural dynamics also offer the possibility of "reterritorializations" (Varese/Escárcega, 16) that bring, in consequence, the reconfiguration of traditional concepts of nationality. As Yolanda Cruz explains in her interview, included in chapter 15, binational Oaxacan indigenous groups participate in processes of reterritorialization by creating new social, economic, and political spaces of power and identity both in Mexico and the United States. Despite the fact that identity has been traditionally associated with a specific territory for its constitution, transnational communities immersed in processes of reterritorialization make explicit a new form of identity that is not necessarily formed by its association with one space, but instead with multiple and transnational spaces. Hence, it is now possible to conceive multisituated subjectivities that establish affective relationships with more than one geographic space and, in many cases, with metaphorical spaces. As Anna Sampaio suggests, "immigrants continually build familial and social networks that bridge the boundaries of multiple nations which situates them in a transnational space between countries" (56).

The way in which transnational Mexican communities articulate new cultural, political, and economic citizenship is one of the main themes this volume presents through the chapters included. These new identities—still in formation and transformation during the first decades of the new millennium—have based their social and cultural strategies in the established manifestations of various social movements, institutions, and cultural texts. Chicana feminisms, student activisms, grassroots interventions, Chicana and Latina cultural productions, and binational indigenous organizations are examples of such entities that, in many ways, have been creating discursive channels of expression for negotiating the historical marginalization that Latinas/os have experienced in the United States. In this regard, we are currently experiencing new forms of empowerment for citizens with more than one affective or political national affiliation. In José Manuel Valenzuela's words, we are facing "New ways of legislating citizenship" (Valenzuela Arce, 25)[6] that to some extent allow more fluidity and exchange within the multiple hybrid spaces in which transnational identities are constructed and lived.

## Contributors

This volume includes academic and artistic contributions from Latina/o scholars and artists as well as two visual artists' interviews. The first section includes a broad multidisciplinary perspective on the definition of transborder/transnational cultures and identities.

"Wet Minds, Bookleggers, and the Place of Borders and Diasporas in U.S. Academic Circles," by Durán, reframes the concept of *mojado*—wet back—in order to produce a critical examination of practices and discourses that mark the experience of both academicians and cultural producers of Mexican origin working on border and transnational spaces. In his "anti-paper," Durán examines rigorously not only the asymmetric cultural exchange that takes place in American universities in relation to Mexican, Chicana/o, and Latina/o Studies but also demonstrates that Mexican national perspectives of cultural identity insist on marginalizing the transborder subject—and the knowledge produced beyond the Eurocentric notions of culture.

Vélez-Ibáñez questions unilineal megascripts of assimilation and daily experiences, exchanges, and cultural transformations of fronterizo life in his chapter entitled "Fronterizo and Transborder Existences: Binding Megascripts in a Transnational World." This chapter presents a short biographical account on the Sonora-Arizona border as well as an analysis and criticism of the model of assimilation as related to border lives and border peoples, whether they belong to white or Latina/o communities. His rich narrative critically demonstrates the several layers that comprise the transborder experiences in relation to ethnicity, social class, gender, and nationality, among other factors.

In "Transnational Mexicano Cultural Production: *El OtroLado*," Hernández reevaluates traditional definitions of transnational/transborder cultures by examining not only spatial, capitalist, and socioeconomic relations but also the intersection of factors such as gender, sexuality, race, and cultural differences in the production of transborder/transnational subjects and discourses. Reading contemporary cultural media phenomena under the light of an Anzaldúan critical discourse, Hernández demonstrates how traditional concepts of transborder/transnational subjectivities break with rational and Eurocentric notions of the "rational subject."

In the second section, scholars reconsider the meaning of textos fronterizos/border texts by means of analyzing cultural texts embedded in the everyday social practices that constitute border identities. In "Dos Mundos: Two Celebrations in Laredo, Texas—Los Matachines de la Santa Cruz and The Pocahontas Pageant of the George Washington's Birthday Celebration," Cantú examines the complexity of celebrations on the border cities of the "Two Laredos," spaces that are marked by the confluence and, as the author states, "seemingly contradictory behaviors." Reflecting on historic and sociocultural dynamics of resistance, Cantú highlights the cultural hybridity among border cultural productions such as the Laredo celebration of Washington's birthday and the Matachines de la Santa Cruz, an indigenous celebration about the Day of the Cross. Cantú posits that "textos fronterizos/border texts" establish a new cultural relationship across the border of Laredo/Nuevo Laredo: a cultural relationship that enables the "performing of what has been suppressed" by colonial, nationalistic, and patriarchal discourses and practices along the Mexico-U.S. border.

"Transnational Narratives, Cultural Production, and Representations: Blurred Subjects in Juárez, México," by Tabuenca Córdoba, examines narratives on the femicide in Ciudad Juárez, Mexico, as a "fundamental expression of transnational economy." She critically examines cultural circuits that in conjunction with Eurocentric and neocolonialist discourses mark nonideal subjects—people of color, women, and those with nontraditional sexualities, among others—as disposable/replaceable subjects with no access to economic, political, or cultural citizenship in the global machine that operates in border spaces like Ciudad Juárez. In her complex analysis she proposes that the murdered women have been represented as "blurred subjects" that both in life and death are unrecognized, stigmatized, and discriminated against.

The third section reflects on the rich scope of cultural manifestations that examine the performative nature of cultural identities and practices. In "Performing Borders: De aquí y de allá (Preliminary Notes on Mexican and Chicana/o Transnational Performance Art)," Gutiérrez presents a nontraditional scholarly overview of performance art from a (trans)national Mexican perspective that includes questions regarding the main artistic preoccupations of multisituated and transborder performance cultural producers. Using her own transnational, bicultural, bilingual, and performance-like academic standpoint, Gutiérrez proposes the concept of unsettling comfort as one of the key features in Mexico-U.S. transnational performance practices. Her rigorous overview opens academic innovative spaces that serve to understand not only the complexity of transborder cultures and subjectivities but also transborder critical standpoints from which she produces new definitions of academic knowledge.

Danielson's "Aquí y Allá: Distance and Difference in Mónica Palacios' Transfronteriza Chicana Performance" focuses on the work of Chicana lesbian artist Monica Palacios as representational of the "transfronteriza experience and performance" by utilizing Anzaldúa's and Laura Gutiérrez's transborder and transnational theories. Danielson highlights the Latina lesbian body on stage as representational of the "de aquí y allá" transfronteriza subjectivity. The author analyzes strategies of resistance by queer, gendered, and racialized subjects within the local and global perspectives.

Parédez's "Selena's 'Como la Flor': Laying the Sound-Track of *Latinidad*" focuses on Selena Quintanilla's performances of "Como la Flor" [Like a Flower] to examine how "selenidad" produces critical questions "about the tensions that disrupt and affiliations that enable Latinidad." Parédez reflects on how this song—rhythm, lyrics, and performance features—affords us the opportunity to understand the mechanisms that permeated the staging of racialized sexuality, charting the emotional and cultural codes of Latinidad through Selena's performances. Parédez's analysis considers the contradictory practices that permeate the spectrum of Latinidad in Selena's body: a space for Latina/o working class empowerment in the midst of legislations against Latina/o bodies in the United States.

Section four revises the complex and rich set of visual manifestations developed in transnational and transborder Mexican areas. In "De Imagénes y Sueños [Of Images and Dreams]: Transnational Mexican Visual Culture," Ybarra-Frausto analyzes the work of various visual and performance artists beginning from the 1920s to the present. The author contextualizes and situates such works on both sides of the border in order to exult the notions of transfronterizo/transborder art as ubiquitous throughout the United States and Mexico, not just in the border region. In addition, the author highlights the importance of examining what he defines as the Latino imagination, cultural and artistic dynamic that provides new and expanded narratives of the American experience.

In "Coming and Going: Transborder Visual Art in Tijuana," Iglesias-Prieto discusses some of the most significant features that characterize contemporary visual arts in Tijuana, Mexico, conceiving art as a radical space from which Mexican and transborder artists reimagine practices and discourses that deny border subjects the power of critical enunciation. Iglesias highlights the multiple transborder dynamics—unequal exchanges in relation to money, power, services, labor, people, and ideas—as factors that contribute to the formation of a complex visual cultural production in places such as the Tijuana/San Diego border.

Section five consists of works written as a result of, or in response to, the discussions at the Lennox seminar; ethnic, gender, and linguistic identities by Mexican-American students are presented in this section. As editors, we firmly believe in democratizing academic spaces by recognizing and validating such vibrant and emerging approaches. This section opens with Sotelo's poems, entitled "Petition" and "Self-Portrait," in which she explores her identity as a young, Latina writer living in the Texas borderlands. In "Socialized into 'Whiteness,'" Rojas examines her Illinois elementary school's attempt at assimilating her into mainstream—read white, middle class—society in order to remove any trace of her Mexican cultural descent. Rojas details the linguistic and cultural assimilation traps laid by the educational system and her struggle to maintain and sustain her Mexican cultural pride. In Guerra's "From My Street to Main Street," he details his effort to survive racial, ethnic, and linguistic bigotry in a white-dominant university environment after previously spending his entire life in the predominantly Latina/o areas of the Rio Grande Valley in South Texas.

Section six details the work of Yolanda Cruz and Rosina Conde. Cruz is a Chatino indigenous film maker who presents critical reflections in relation to immigration, trans(national) indigenous cultures, and gender transformations within Oaxacan transnational communities. On the other hand, Rosina Conde is a writer, singer, and performance artist. In her interview, Conde reflects on the cultural politics that permeate the Mexico-U.S. border cultural production.

This critical volume thus presents an opportunity to encounter and examine, at one place, various aspects of contemporary transnational Mexican cultural productions from artists, filmmakers, academics, and scholars. It is our hope that the readers will encounter in this volume established and emerging voices on the topics presented from both sides of the Mexico-U.S. border and from across each country. Additionally, we hope that this text contributes to the enrichment of scholarship on Transnational/Transborder studies.

## Notes

1. In this volume, the term "transnational Mexican" refers to Mexicans as well as Chicana/os.
2. See *Dark Sweat, White Gold* (1994); *Stages of Life* (2001); *Border Women* (2002); *Transnational Latina/o Communities* (2002); *Por las fronteras del norte* (2004); and *An Impossible Living* (2010).
3. Particularly in the Yucatán. See Florescano's *Etnia, estado y nación*.
4. See Luis H. Méndez, "Neoliberalismo y derechización."
5. Original in Spanish, translated by the editors.
6. Ibid.

Part I

# And What Are Transnational Mexican Border Cultures?

# Wet Minds, Bookleggers, and the Place of Borders and Diasporas in U.S. Academic Circles

*Javier Durán*

No me critiquen porque vivo al otro lado
No soy un desarraigado, vine por necesidad
*"El otro México"* Los tigres del norte

In a 1998 conference on Mexican literature held at UC-Irvine, Mexican writer and critic Carlos Monsiváis took a long look at the line for the buffet luncheon and noticed that all of us lined up there were relatively young, mostly U.S. trained Mexican or Chicano scholars.[1] At one point he said to no one in particular: "Mira, los wet minds" [Look, the wet minds]. His comment did not seem to be made (or taken at the moment) in a derogatory manner, but rather in a festive tone commenting on how much the composition and membership of academic gatherings in U.S. universities was changing. We thought that he used the term to refer specifically to the growing number of professors from Mexico and of Mexican origin currently working in U.S. colleges and universities. When later I told this anecdote to a colleague working in another U.S. college, he thought that Monsiváis' remark was disrespectful and out of place. It was obvious to him that Mexican academics working in the United States had not yet achieved the level of respect and recognition that they deserved in Mexican high cultural circles, and this would qualify them to be considered as "wet backs or wet minds," or cheap academic labor. Moreover, he mentioned that this might be due to the often precarious positions held by Mexican or Chicano faculty in literature and language departments where professors were assigned to teach language courses, survey classes, and, sometimes, "culture courses." When a graduate program existed, he said, these professors were rarely assigned graduate courses, and almost never courses on theory. In addition, most of the time they are known for being well versed in Chicana/o Studies, because, after all, they were "all" Mexican. My colleague's comments made me think about the real (and perceived) position of this group of scholars in both countries. His observations also problematize the controversial topic of the Mexican diaspora. This anecdote raises a number of important issues and questions. This chapter examines the following questions: what is the profile of the "wet mind"? Why did Monsiváis call us "wet minds"? What was he trying to say?

This reflective chapter, or, rather, this *anti-paper*, seeks to open a conversation concerning a group of academics known as "Wet Minds." As borders and migrations seem to become interchangeable topics in academic and nonacademic circles, it is important to point to their differences, since as objects of study they are not necessarily synonymous. I began this chapter with an anecdote, trying to contextualize its plot to shed light on the role of what has recently been called "La otra migración": Mexican academics in U.S. colleges and universities.[2] In what follows, I frame the story within an auto-ethno-biographic lens in order to problematize a series of critical issues that I see emerging from it.[3] In this context, I posit some questions suggesting lines of inquiry on the *"mojado"* issue under what is known in U.S. academic circles as "post-critical ethnography." Finally, I engage in a brief discussion of a music video and a group's manifesto tightly connected to all of the above.

My colleague's reflections made me think about the real and imaginary situation of this group of academics, amongst which I include myself. His remarks also made me speculate if Monsiváis' comment, apparently innocent and descriptive, was a manifestation of a subaltern position that these academics face versus two metropolitan poles: the U.S. academic circles and Mexico's high culture. In the same fashion, his observations made me rethink the notion of cultural citizenship and its consequences as they relate to the study of Mexico and of things Mexican in the United States.[4] On the other hand, I am persuaded that the negotiation between cultural citizenship and belonging not only emerges from this binary but rather also arises from flexible mechanisms of citizenship (Ong 1999) that regulate such a negotiation.

At this point, it seems that an exploration of the broad dimensions and critical implications of the term "wet" could be productive to engage in a theoretical reframing of such a denomination on both sides of the

BORDERS IN U.S. ACADEMIC CIRCLES 21

border. Chicano anthropologist Enrique Murillo (2004) uses the notion of "Mojado ethnography" to problematize the place of enunciation of the ethnographer versus globalization and cultural studies. Murillo's work falls within the critical trend called "post-critical ethnography," and it attempts to revise the "positioning" of the researcher investigating cultural phenomena. Moreover, as Kathy Hytten has argued: "The basic concern of critical ethnographers is that by not explicating how the local contexts they study are situated within larger social and historical structures, traditional ethnographers contribute to simply reproducing the status quo, including its constitutive asymmetrical relations of power" (2004, 97).

I find it interesting that for Murillo the Spanish word "mojado" [translated literally as "wet," and typically used to label undocumented immigrants as "wet backs"] represents and describes

> both the current socio-political and academia distresses, as well as the heroic yet costly successes of ethnographers who are Chicano/Mexicano, pan-Latino, womanists, feminists, working-class and other scholars of color. It refers principally to an inequality of mobility and movement across borders, be it the larger research setting, the classroom, the dominant Euro-centric theoretical conversation, or in the university policies and practices of admission and faculty tenure. (2004, 169)

Perhaps more important for my own work here is the fact that Murillo uses the term because "it reflects a processual and agentic celebration of the irony of reversal" (2004, 170).[5]

Furthermore, if the notion of "wet" (be it a mind or a back) is usually associated with the notion of (non)documentation and, by extension, of "(il)legality," the issue of documented versus undocumented becomes a piece of the argument. In this context, documentation as it pertains to academic settings is also part of the conversation. But how do we document anecdotal material that may include hearsay, rumor, or even gossip? How do we make sense of these ephemera, as José Esteban Muñoz (1996) has called it? How do we begin theorizing what mainstream academia may see as non-rigorous scholarship?[6] I admit that I do not have answers for these questions, but this exercise will begin to articulate some possibilities that can eventually be taken into account in future maneuvers to try to create some responses.

With that in mind, let us return to the Monsiváis affair. Years later, some members of this so-called group of *Wet Minds* attempted to establish a dialogue with Monsiváis in order to clarify the genealogical nature of the term as well as to open a conversation with a broader audience. To that end, Juan Carlos Ramírez-Pimienta and I organized a roundtable/ workshop discussion entitled "Wet Minds, Bookleggers, Mexicanistas, and the Place of Borders and Transnationalism in US Academic Circles." The panel was held at the 2006 Latin American Studies Association conference in San Juan, Puerto Rico, and it gathered six colleagues, plus Monsiváis as the respondent.[7] Perhaps the most interesting feature of the session was the distancing that Monsiváis seemed to show from the group. This was reflected during three particular moments during the discussion. First, his reluctance to be recognized as the "Godfather," the instigator, or the creator of the term *Wet Minds*: "Yes, I was in Irvine in '98, but I do not remember saying such a thing," he confided privately. Second, the visceral reaction by some Mexican colleagues from Mexico in the audience who found problematic, and even insulting, that we, the panelists, resorted to the use of the "I" as a locus of enunciation to present our position papers. Hence we were accused of blasphemy, transgression of academic conventions, and of breaking academic etiquette, whatever that meant.[8] Finally, a third moment was by way of Monsiváis' comments and his apparent incapacity to recognize and contextualize the difference between manual and intellectual labor within the broader referent "Mexicans in the United States," comments made in reaction to some images presented in the video *The Bookleggers* (Tijuana: Caltranzit, 2004), which was shown as part of my intervention[9] in the panel:

> Y lo que más me llamó la atención, es que es un trabajo académico que nunca está lejos de la experiencia de trabajo, es una labor académica que nunca está lejos de la experiencia del trabajo. En México la experiencia del trabajo físico ya quedó convertida en una, pues una fachada teórica o un complemento de la alimentación cubicular pero lo que es cierto es que, lo vimos en lo del Nortec o los que hicieron esto...Castellanos...en fin. La experiencia del trabajo físico, la legitimidad del trabajo físico, la grandeza del trabajo físico está muy presente, y eso en México desde la colonia que se comenzó la demonización del trabajo físico desaparece...(Monsiváis 2006)[10]

In other words, for Monsiváis—consciously or unconsciously—the critical difference between *Wet Minds* and *wet backs* was not significant since both groups seem to be framed around the referent "labor" and even perhaps, as what Chicano anthropologist Carlos Vélez-Ibáñez has termed, a "commodity identity."[11] In fact, in another article entitled "De las comunidades fronterizas," Monsiváis seems to argue this very same perspective, even citing Vélez-Ibáñez's work, although in my view this is again done without fully grasping the scope of the Chicano anthropologist's project, and in particular the notion of what he calls the "distribution of sadness," which discusses the historical and statistical overrepresentation of Mexicans and Chicanos in social topics such as poverty, criminality, low education levels, scarce access to health programs, and the impact of military recruitment in those communities.[12] In other words, despite his rhetorical efforts, Monsiváis' border vision seems intrinsically linked to a dated and rather centralist view of the border and of the "México de fuera," demonstrating that *Wet Minds* continue to be a complicated theme that has still not been fully incorporated into the agendas of both Mexican high culture and mainstream Eurocentric cultural studies. While it was possible to recognize "manual labor" as part of the "wet" part, "intellectual labor" did not receive the same recognition during the discussion, hence it is my assumption that he didn't seem to understand the role or notion of "wetmind" in our panel.

Of course, I do not intend to create a polemic with Monsiváis himself about this issue. Unfortunately the fact that he has recently passed away complicates this further.[13] After all, he had been a consistent spokesperson for marginal and minority discourses during his distinguished trajectory as a public intellectual. Rather, what I want to point out is the existence and the prevalence, despite historical, economic, and demographic changes, of particular viewpoints in central Mexico about the border and about representations of Mexicans in the United States. It was thus ironic, perhaps as a sort of "irony of reversal" a discursive strategy that Monsiváis himself has mastered in his writings, that as part of his response Monsiváis also seemed to indirectly question the group's intellectual project as well as its legitimate right to be there [at the conference] through some comments on our relationship to the "community."[14] In other words, I found it rather curious that at a point when we were precisely in search of a space and a collective identity in U.S. academic circles, the immediate response from our alleged "padrino" was, instead, to send us back to the *barrios* and to the *comunidades*:

> Está muy bien situar lo que tiene que ver con las posiciones académicas, lo que el…ostracismo, el arrinconamiento, lo que se quiera, está muy bien, pero lo otro, es, pienso yo, igualmente de importante. ¿Qué presencia tienen en las comunidades? ¿Cuál es el rango de efectividad de diálogo que tienen con las comunidades?…Se ve, no hay tal cosa como abandono de ideas, siempre están presentes de un modo u otro y yo quisiera, ahí sí, no sé, ¿cuál es la presencia de ustedes en las comunidades respectivas? Y es lo que no tengo claro o lo que no pude establecer así, con claridad. (Monsiváis 2006)

Thus, it is interesting to see the connections established by the author of *Los rituales del caos* with a prevalent view of Mexicans in the United States:

their deep rooting in the notion of community. Yet, as María Socorro Tabuenca (2007) reflecting on the nature of the *Wet Minds* project states:

> El grupo lo componemos un puñado de mexicanas y mexicanos de corazón quienes, a excepción de mi persona, se encuentran trabajando en universidades de los Estados Unidos de forma documentada, o gracias a la ventaja fronteriza de poseer la doble nacionalidad legal o ilegalmente. Nos autonombramos "fronterólogos" y nos consideramos una comunidad desprestigiada por nuestra posición geográfica y preferencia intelectual. Bautizados por Carlos Monsiváis como *WetMinds* nuestras reflexiones han girado en dos direcciones: (1) El papel que tenemos en la academia mexicana desde el llamado "México de afuera" y (2), el rol que jugamos en la academia norteamericana como mexicanos, méxicoamericanos, chicanos o fronterizos.

Tabuenca's comments succinctly summarize the overall positioning of most members of the group and clearly locate the academic setting as its locus of enunciation. This is not, however, the first time that Monsiváis's centralist views about the border have been discussed. Tabuenca has engaged in a critical analysis of these views in several works, including *Mujeres y fronteras. Una perspectiva de género* (1998), and *Border Women: Writing from La Frontera* (2002). Her basic argument is that Monsiváis' vision of the border reinforces a stereotypical view of the region as a place where "culture," or rather high culture, has difficulty in "developing" a sustained presence and impact on the communities themselves. In a sense, this view will embrace one of the ways the border has been represented in the national imaginary as argued by border critics Eduardo Barrera (1995) and Víctor Zúñiga (1999), that of the border as a "cultural desert." As Monsiváis noted in another article (2007):

> Ciudades de paso, eso han sido Tijuana en Baja California, Matamoros, Reynosa y Nuevo Laredo en Tamaulipas, Nogales en Sonora, Ciudad Juárez en Chihuahua. El fugitivo de las regiones o de la capital llega a la frontera y modifica sicológica y socialmente la provisionalidad del medio, y procura carecer de reacciones ante el narcotráfico y ante la violencia, la señal más trágica de la urbanización. En las últimas décadas la movilidad espacial en la frontera norte detiene su aceleramiento y aparecen las señas de la perdurabilidad (instituciones, personas, vida cultural, historia recuperada, centros de enseñanza superior, localización de orgullos locales).

In the final part of this chapter, I discuss Monsiváis' misreading of the notion of *Wet Minds* in the context of the video *The Bookleggers*, created and produced by Octavio Castellanos and Omar Pimienta of Tijuana's

BORDERS IN U.S. ACADEMIC CIRCLES    25

Caltranzit group in 2004. Caltranzit is a collaboration between various artists living in Tijuana (Yonke Art, La Línea, Omar Pimienta) and UCSD Visual students. As stated on their website:

> The goal of the project is to find ways to intersect our communities, as well as to open alternative spaces for dialogue through collaborative projects. This project focuses on a car (1975 Chevy Malibu) that is currently being passed among the artists involved. The car, a perpetually transforming multi-media sculpture shared by the artists, acts as a binding vessel for our collaboration.[15]

The video very much influenced people conceptually and technically (as Monsiváis observed in his first quote) by the Nortec project,[16] and it crystallized an interdisciplinary dialogue between several types of *Wet Minds*, visual artists, and critical thinkers, all suspects of conspiring in the manufacturing of a border intelligentsia. The piece incorporates the song "Still Balling" by the late rapper Tupac Shakur and the *norteño* classic hit "La banda del carrorojo" by Los Tigres del Norte.[17]

If we agree with Tijuana's critic Heriberto Yépez (2004) when he states "La frontera y su estética no se definen por sus síntesis sino por sus contradicciones" (34), the result of this "contrapunteo" signals not so much to a "fusion," as many critics have characterized border culture, but rather to a clear tension between dissimilar elements. Yépez has analyzed Nortec's aesthetic project in the context of border culture and found a "tensorial" relationship suggesting that:

> Nortec es algo más inteligente que lo que el discurso imperante ha postulado. Nortec construyó un sonido donde lo que se escucha no es sencillamente una fusión de música popular norteña y tecnología digital. Construyó algo más interesante: un sonido tensorial, un sonido en que se perciben las tensiones provocadas por los desencuentros culturales, un sonido donde se escuchan las intermitencias y las alternancias propias de una policultura donde reina la dinámica de acercamiento y distanciamiento entre Culturas. (46)

Thus, *The Bookleggers* also interrogates and challenges centralist notions of the border and dialogues with several loci of enunciation, as well as with the above-mentioned ideas by Murillo, Vélez-Ibáñez, and other *Wet Minds* who are currently working underground on a book about the topic. As Murillo has stated, *Mojado* [wet] "reflects a processual and agentic celebration of the irony of reversal" (170), the video also plays with the idea of culture as a clandestine activity and smuggling as a fact of life among border communities. Moreover, this "irony of reversal" engages, disestablishes, and projects some possibilities for other readings and repositioning. This is perhaps best reflected by the textual incorporation of the "*booklegger manifesto*" in the video:

> Border scholars Javier Durán and Juan Carlos Ramírez-Pimienta have theorized the notion of "educated" Mexicans residing in the United States, Mexicans who have migrated to the United States as well as to U.S. education during their formative years and who are referred to as "Wet Minds." The natives of the Mexican northern border states, many of whom have been pushed abroad by centralist education, cross the border on a daily basis. Since this phenomenon of the "Commuter minds" first occurred, the U.S. immigration officers have been on the lookout for books as incriminating evidence for the crime of getting educated. Many imprudent prospective "Commuter Minds" get caught and their rights to cross the border are taken away. Our job is, as Capone once stated, to supply a demand. We are the bookleggers.

The images in the video center around two lines of action: first the placement of reading materials by an unidentified individual (called "Clavo" in the credits) in several hidden compartments of a red car, and second, the transit of the red Chevy across the Tijuana-San Yisidro border crossing checkpoint. What I believe produced Monsiváis' misreading was precisely the fact that Clavo is portrayed as a mechanic, a manual worker, in an automobile shop using a number of tools to be able to insert the reading materials that in some instances may look like a different type of object (drugs or just contraband) in the car. The images in the video go back-and-forth between Clavo's actions at the shop "somewhere in Tijuana" and the red car traveling into the border crossing checkpoint. What seems to be missing in the Mexican writer's interpretation is the ultimate goal of the "manual labor" Clavo is performing: the smuggling of that material into the United States.

Smuggling then becomes the quintessential act of border crossing. Simulation and deceit substitute "legality" and the official discourses sanctioned by the state. Simulation can also be a negotiation to imitate, to copy, or to mimic something without internalizing it. We could even talk about a certain degree of mimicry, a cultural attitude to amalgamate with the landscape, fully conscious and skeptical of any outcome this may bring.[18] In the many ways in which the border has been represented, it is clear that materiality is an important element of border culture and life. Exchange, commerce, and trade are privileged nouns in border discourse, and so is trafficking. In this trafficking of simulations, we can also see a trafficking of knowledge and wisdoms, of ideas and readings, of "*saberes y leeres*." It is in this particular position that I would like to locate the late border writer and critic Ricardo Aguilar as a paradigmatic *booklegger*.[19] He was not only an intellectual mediator but also a "commuter mind" between two countries, two cultures, two languages, and two worlds, a *traficante*, a smuggler, of readings and knowledge. But maybe more than a "*contrabandista*," or a "*coyote*," Aguilar was a smuggler of border culture, a sort of academic *fayuquero*, as he represented himself in his narrative works, as a border crossing free spirit eventually appropriated and represented as a Chicano character [José Francisco] by Carlos Fuentes in his novel *La frontera de cristal*.[20] Aguilar seems to effortlessly merge with the following border vision provided by critic Fernando García Núñez:

> The border is the meeting place for the images that one nation creates about another, yet do not result in identification with either. Again, this ambiguous situation necessarily leads to continuous deception or simulation, for the permanent confluence of opposites on the border prevent the setting of any limits or definitions of being: existence on the border implies continuous change. (Quoted in Aguilar ND, 4)

As a way of conclusion, I want to express my concurrence with Murillo when he discusses the (re)positioning of the *Mojado* academic, in this case the *Wet Mind*, and his or her research agenda:

> The defamiliarization and alienation experienced through a Mojado positionality (real, imagined, temporary or otherwise) can serve as pedagogical resources to create alternative and diverse discourses and models, what Villenas (1996) has named to be "our own paradigms and languages"... Mojados create the need for *coyotes* and *fayuqueros*, for border guides and smugglers. They present an opportunity to invent and re-imagine new *coyote* strategies and pedagogies, where we can better band and learn from each other's struggles through renewed horizontal and reciprocal associations. (Murillo 2004, 173–174)

In the end, my hope is to see this conversation continued at several levels. It is also within this context that I see *Wet Minds* articulating a new and productive intellectual relationship between center and periphery, between nation and border, between high culture and popular expression, and most importantly between two nations sharing a common space: la frontera. This chapter begins with an epigraph from the song "El otro México" by the Tigres del Norte as a way to establish and define a cultural and economic distance between the "Mexican lettered city" (center) and the "otro México" (periphery). The lyrics should also be a wise reminder of the trials and tribulations that many "wets" undergo trying to gain access to a better life in the United States: "No me critiquen porque vivo al otro lado. No soy un desarraigado, vine por necesidad." As for our search for critical space in the Mexican and U.S. academic circles, we are, to follow Tupac Shakur, "still searching."

## Notes

1. Carlos Monsiváis (Mexico City, 1938–2010) was one of Mexico's most popular and prolific writers, cultural historian, independent scholar, and an intellectual known for his chronicles of life in Mexico and in Mexico City. He documented the changes in the educational, cultural, and political landscapes of his country in journalistic and editorial venues. His published works range from political writings, Indigenous rights, multiculturalism, globalization, gender issues, popular music, photography, painting, the language of the streets, the short story format in Mexico, other eminent Mexican authors, religion, and national idols.
2. See Ana Lalinde's "La otra migración: 100 mexicanos que enseñan en universidades de Estados Unidos" (2007) for a discussion on Mexican academics teaching in the United States.
3. I follow Sidonie Smith and Julia Watson's reflections on "autobiographical acts." I am also in dialogue with Chicana writer Norma Cantú who has developed the notion of auto-ethno-biographical writing. Another influence was Luis Alberto Urrea's *Nobody's Son*.
4. For a reflection on the role of Chicano Studies and Mexican Studies as they converge in U.S. academic circles, see Rolando Romero's article "Troublemakers."
5. Murillo explains his positioning: "I choose to use the real-life metaphor as an experiential and culturally-genealogical tool to make meaning of my cultural, racial, ethnic, discursive, political, theoretical, and even class crossings into ethnography and academia" (2004, 167).
6. See Muñoz (1996), "Ephemera as Evidence."
7. The participants in the panel were Ignacio Corona, Javier Durán, Laura Gutiérrez, Juan Carlos Ramírez-Pimienta, José Pablo Villalobos, and María Socorro Tabuenca Córdoba.
8. Muñoz sees such dynamics when scholars engage in nontraditional approaches to scholarship (1996, 6). Moreover, Muñoz's discussion of "rigor" in his article helped me to make sense of these reactions by these members of the audience, since there is a clear performative dimension connected to challenging established ways to cultivate knowledge (1996, 10).
9. Durán, "Los Wet Minds."
10. Monsiváis associates the production of the video "Bookleggers" to the Nortec collective, but that is not the case. Castellanos here refers to Octavio

Castellanos, a Tijuana video producer who is the coauthor of the video along with Omar Pimienta. It is a video that is part of the Cal Tranzit art project.
11. Vélez-Ibáñez conceptualizes this term as a historical and economic consequence of a neocolonial relation between the United States and the Mexican population inhabiting the Southwest after the Treaty of Guadalupe Hidalgo, in particular the industrialization period in the late nineteenth century. It basically argues that the notion of Mexican identity is tightly connected to the idea of labor. See also *Border Visions*.
12. See *Border Visions*, 57–87.
13. Sadly, Carlos Monsiváis passed away on June 19, 2010, as revisions to this article were being made.
14. There is another element that I do not discuss in this chapter due to space limitations, but that I am developing elsewhere: the systematic neglect of Chicano Studies in Mexican academic settings. Perhaps with the exception of the UNAM, Chicano Studies as a field of study has never been fully developed in Mexican academic institutions. Ironically, even at UNAM, the marginal status of Chicano Studies was represented by its location not at the Centro de Estudios para América del Norte (CISAN) [Center for North American Studies] but at the Centro de Estudios para Extranjeros (CEPE) [Center for Foreign Students].
15. For an explanation of the project, see http://omarpimienta.blogspot.com/2004_03_01_archive.html and http://amarantacaballero.blogspot.com/2004_03_01_archive.html.
16. Nortec (from the combination of "norteño" and "techno") is an electronic musical genre from Tijuana that first gained popularity in 2001. Nortec music is characterized by hard dance beats and samples from traditional forms of Mexican music such as *Banda sinaloense* and Norteño, unmistakably Mexican horns are often used. Nortec has become a collective project (www.nor-tec.org) and its popularity has transcended borders. For more, see Yépez (2005) and Valenzuela Arce (2004).
17. For a version of the video on the web, see http://www.youtube.com/watch?v=uax9jnVKqLU.
18. Simulation and mimicry in border culture are thus a common strategy, as Homi Bhabha indicates (Bhabha 1994, 88). I will not get into this particular discussion, which is the subject of another paper, but I wanted to call attention to the ways in which border subjects project themselves textually while constructing their own representations.
19. Ricardo Aguilar Melantzon (1947–2004) was a border writer and academic. A native of Juárez-El Paso, Aguilar was a narrator, poet, translator, and essayist. Considered by some critics as a Chicano writer, Aguilar is in my view a clear example of the trials and tribulations of creating and performing border culture and literature in both sides of "la línea."
20. As Aguilar convincingly argued in his article "Life as Fiction, Fiction as Life":

In the novel, as on the border, the concepts of geography, personal history, politics, social issues, even the act of writing are, as García Núñez asserts, in continuous flux and in a never ending process of definition. The process of simulation is a necessary element of survival. Changing countries, languages, customs, ways of presenting oneself, of acting in all kinds of situations, even of thinking, are a daily aspect of living. You must change so often that, after a period, the very process becomes so internalized, such a constant occurrence, that you do it unconsciously.

2

# *Fronterizo* [Border] and Transborder Existences: Binding Megascripts in a Transnational World

*Carlos G. Vélez-Ibáñez*

### Introduction

When I use the word "transnational" and "transborder" at one level, I only include activities, events, behaviors, transactions, networks, and relationships in which persons on both sides of the border participate in mutual fields and arenas in southwest North America and beyond. These may be symmetrical or asymmetrical, open- or close ended, and certainly political, economic, and social. Here is one example of the limited definition in which Mixe-speaking Zapotec indigenous families migrate to Tijuana from Riverside, California, which is their permanent home. In Tijuana they will rent a home next to a relative, usually a brother or sister, and here the heads of households will work in one of the maquiladoras while children are being cared for by the elders or another female relative. A month later, after much visiting and celebrations of birthdays and other parts of the ritual cycles, they will drive all the way to Oaxaca and participate in local ritual obligations and activities. These are especially important in that they maintain membership in communal groups and access to land through continued membership in the Cargo or mayordamia systems.[1] A month to two months later they will drive back to the north, but this time through Mexicali where they will rent a house nearby to yet another relative and work in a maquila. Thus, it is this transnationalization of work and ritual function together with children, not only learning the geography as they move in these distances but also the religious and ritual spaces, that are crucial to the reinforcement of non transnational Mixe identities.

In addition, I also mean those activities carried over as very useful practices and unseen ideas from their points of origin and introduced in a new national setting to persons already accustomed to their use, ideational analogs, or as new knowledge learned in the new setting. Also, there is a spatial sense that is not located in a single space, which is that many people live out "transnational and transborder lives" in that their "citizenship" is not the main locater for their existential sense of self but rather tied to myriad points of cultural and physical spaces, emotional places, and cultural references on either side of the "border." For Mexican-origin populations living in the United States and those migrating to northern Mexico on the border, the transnational "living" phenomenon has been an increasingly important one, especially since the great demographic transitions between Mexico and the United States took place after 1980 and continues to the present, much of it being the aftermath of NAFTA.[2]

## Historical Dimensions of Transborder and Transnational Identities

Culturally and historically, we have in fact been living transborder, transborder lives that cannot be reduced to a category of citizenship or to the engagement of persons in the transnational networks described above. In Ramón Saldívar's fine book on Américo Paredes, he quotes Américo Paredes as regarding himself as "a sociological phenomenon" because of his double cultural presence in both nations. Saldívar, extending his position, expands this as "a preposterous oddity existing both inside and outside of two discrete national realities" (161).[3] But I think it not as preposterous as either Saldívar or Paredes would suggest. Put simply, events and history have prevented the development of a single-tracked citizenship-based personality development in which our beings are tied only to an American civil life. The acculturation model has been pretty much devastated by the recognition that there are multiple dimensions of cultural personalities that cannot be reduced to simple unilineal identities. We live American civil lives, but our lives are contextualized within multiple transnational and transborder points of reference. Therefore, culturally we amass and discard layers of cultural skins that simply do not refer to only a simple cultural referent such as citizenship. We do live that life, but we as well live within and on many bordered aspects of ourselves that are historically penetrating of our very beings and beyond the reach of an imposed or acquired citizenship. We gather in the midst of social relations that are as old as the Romans, worship in religions that are older, and from told and lived experiences we participate and are reminded of our transnational and transborder selves on a daily basis, and we simultaneously die in American wars. It's been this way since the nineteenth century. However, there have been huge contradictory megascripts that often led us in different directions and created filters over our minds.

### Megascript Uno: The Single-Culture Citizenship Premise

Among the various identities is certainly the famous acculturation model that citizenship is based on a single cultural referent in which cultural erasure and being swallowed is normative with language, social relations, ideology, and kinship moving unilineally from one group to another. Since the American Mexican war to this minute, an often repeated and juridically and institutionalized established framework was established for its articulation. For this framework, the border was a dividing line demarcating the Mexican from the American, and simply a choice for *lo Americano* could be made to become good "citizens." Complex transborder Mexican cultural narratives, however, have often countered this notion, and actions that were often expressed daily in our homes, and different versions of these, are told and projected today. For some, the preposterous metaphor of simultaneous participation in dual nations was somehow so contradictory that cultural choices had to be made of one or the other. But our daily courses of economic regional life did not permit such easy cultural removal. As the following example of a simple border crossing card of the 1920s makes apparent, there was no intended or unintended loss of cultural reference in stepping from one side of the border to another and back again. It details where the person lives, her personal particulars, and place and date of crossing. There is no linguistic insistence and much less one regarding citizenship. The border has been a place to cross and recross with limited information provided and few restrictions of any kind indicated on the card itself as to length of stay or reporting requirements. And for those born in the transborder context, such processes were frequent and constant, and although still restricted by institutional frameworks, cultural histories often countered the unilineal megascript.

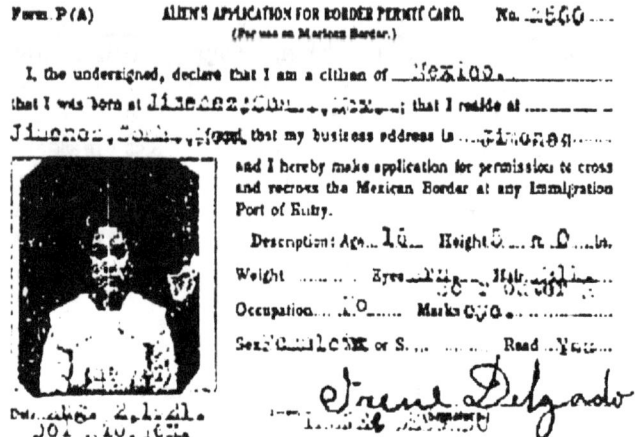

**Figure 2.1**   Border Crossing Card (Archive: Carlos Vélez-Ibáñez).

## Being Transbordered y lo de Antes [What Comes from the Past]

I was first "transbordered" by birth. That is, I was born by accident in Nogales, Arizona. My parents who lived in Tucson were visiting relatives in Magdalena, Sonora, 60 miles south of Nogales, and on our return I was born. My mother always said that I was always *"muy inquieto,"* and so I was born in St. Joseph's hospital, which was situated a few feet north of the cyclone fence that separated the two Nogaleses. My mother said that my bassinet for the next 12 hours or so was placed with my feet almost touching the window that looked out to the cyclone fence itself before we all returned to Tucson where I was raised, going back and forth for most of my formative years between there and Sonora. For my father, these were the same trips that he, his father, and his grandfather had taken since even before the Gadsden Purchase, when my father's granduncle saw the last Mexican troops leaving Tucson in 1857.[4]

But the creation of that border where my feet almost touched the window that separated the two sides was not only transparent but in fact depended on continuous flows across—that is, a transnational flow of material, ideas, people, and institutions. The point here, that *un poco después* of the Mexican troops leaving Tucson, is that great changes transpired in our region as it did throughout southwest North America with the influx of many Anglos, the penetration of railroads, large land corporations, and the extraction, on a large scale and manner, minerals, land, animals, and, most importantly, the labor value of men and women. These large changes of economy ushered "*lo moderno*," and with it as well the large-scale use of Mexican people from either side of the border that was convenient. Therefore, there has always been an inherent contradiction between the national lines created by war and the reality of a regional economy dependent on non-bordered transnational and transborder populations and the transborder culture-bearing populations that made it up.

## Lo Transfronterizo/The Transborder Experience

For many of us especially from the states of Arizona, Texas, and southern New Mexico, and certainly for many in southern California, we lived the lives of Fronterizos on both sides of the border. As a Sonorense (or as my father referred to our southern Arizona and northern Sonoran region, "La Pimería"), I inherited the stories of Apache raids, revolutions, and strikes in the copper mines, and I thought nothing of visiting relatives in Magdalena, Sonora, or going to school there in the summer months, or of cousins visiting us in Tucson and going to high school to learn English. We lived as Fronterizos hearing stories of how my mother fled floods from Santiago, Nayarit, to live in Magdalena, Sonora, with her sister and brother-in-law and there at a dance met my visiting father from Tucson. We learned early on of how death visited both sides of the border by disease, wars, revolutions, expulsions, mine cave-ins, railroad accidents, construction falls, and sometimes just accidents or simple vendettas from cross words at a wedding or baptism.

We learned a lot about women and many little things. We learned about my *Tía abuelas* [Great Aunts] who fought hand-to-hand combat with Apache warriors from Magdalena to Tucson for many years. One Tía is said to have killed a warrior as he crept into her kitchen window. She evidently was adept with lance, bow and arrow, rifle, and with the stone *mano*, which she used to kill him. There was nothing passive about my mother, who was the daughter of a Mexican cavalry colonel killed in the revolution, in comparison to my father, who was a softie and whose big brown eyes often welled with tears when he spoke about his childhood in Tucson and recalled how his aunts with whom he lived never bothered to give him soap to wash his lice-ridden hair. My mother, on the other hand, was the mover in the family who, with only a third-grade education, taught herself to play concert-quality piano, learned to read, write, and speak English on her own by listening to the radio and reading the newspapers, and at one time sold clothes to *braceros* and native peoples in Marana, Arizona. She was the major decision maker and accountant for the $75 per week mechanic's salary that my Dad earned. And when he came home exhausted, it was she who soothed his brow in spite of her own hard day at work at home.

And there were other little things learned, like the killing of my Tío Lauro's compadre by one of the revolutionary Colonels, but when the Colonel fell out of political favor and was not protected, my Tío hunted for him for months until he learned, with the help of Yaqui friends, that his quarry was traveling down from the Bacatete mountains toward Nogales. My uncle waited at the border, which at that time had no cyclone fence but only a yellow line that divided the two Nogaleses. He noticed that one of the covered ice wagons that used to cross the border from the Mexican to the American side for delivering ice was not dripping water from its back gate as it normally did. He stopped it, found the Colonel, and while he begged for his life on his knees, my Tío placed his gun barrel in his mouth and shot him. His body landed straddled on the yellow line.

The grand array of human behaviors of alcoholic uncles and fathers, of murders in the street, of mass on Sunday, of Irish or Spanish missionaries in our churches even though we had been Catholics for 500 years in this land, of having one's hair pulled in elementary school for speaking the only language one knew, of crossing back and forth between borders of many sorts—all of these were part of the lived processes we knew to be true. But, of course, none of this was included in any text, with the only texts being in conversation and platicas and experiences. Yet these are the aspects of transborder culture, and there were others that contradict many cherished American beliefs about culture and its preposterous unilineal acculturation, citizenship-based model, and its arrangements.

### The Mexicanization of the Irish and the Krugers

There were preposterous arrangements that the acculturation model could never contend with, such as Irish and Jewish families moving into our neighborhood in the fifties because this was the most affordable for the fathers and mothers working in the defense plant assembling planes for the Korean War. Our transborder lives were enriched by their presence and we certainly enriched theirs, but not at first.

At first the Irish boys thought we were Italians, since they came from south Boston and were separated from Italian immigrants in the north, so they called us Wops, and we wondered "Qué es esto de Wops?" ["And What is Wops?"]. But we knew it wasn't good and so we sought each other out with fists and feet, and they were very good fighters, but eventually one of the Irish priests from our parish, Father James Murphy, who had been a missionary in the Kalahari Desert in southwest Africa among the Pygmies, founded a series of boys and girls clubs, and we started meeting each other's sisters and brothers. I met Shelia Campbell as a ten-year-old and fell madly in love. My sister Lucy who was seven years older met Brendan Flannery. My sister's real name was Luz del Socorro, but in Walnut Creek, California, where she was born, the birth certificate was filled out as "Lucy" because the administrator didn't know Spanish.

When my mother told my Sonorense father that Brendan Flannery was coming to see my sister, he protested and said that "No quiero irlandeses en mi casa" ["I do not want Irish men in my house"]. My mother said, "Oye viejo, que no te acuerdas que peliaron con nosotros?" ["Don't you remember that Irish men fought with us?"].[5] My dad looked at her puzzled and then brightened up and said, "Ay sí, de veras. Que venga el muchacho" ["Oh, yes, that is true. Let the young man come"].

And so to this day there are Mexican Irish couples whose children had amazingly rich phenotypes of red hair and brown eyes and freckled skin, and others with olive skin and blue eyes and thick, dark Yaqui hair like some of our ancestors.

But the most telling transborder phenomenon is that to this day in Tucson there are Los Coxes, y Los Callahan y Los Murphys, y Los Daley since our transborder social structure and cultures are like black holes, so that the nearest non-Mexican being close to their rims are swallowed up culturally, just as the Irish kids become Mexicanized. Friends such as Jackie Cox, whose father taught me about the Sinn Féin and the IRA, fought against the British in the twenty's, and spoke with a Mexican accent until he took his Ph.D. in American literature.

It was also during those childhood transborder days that my first introduction to a Jewish family, Los Kruger, took place. We Mexicanized all family surnames with the plural Spanish article so that they would seem more like us. But they weren't, or so we thought. Los Kruger had moved from New York, and since they did not have much money they rented the house next to us, as did many other east coast families who moved to Tucson in that period. But Los Krugers were special, Betty was this outlandish, smart, independent woman who scandalized the neighborhood by hitching a ride to work in the morning, in contrast to Leonard, her husband, who always wore a tie and was a kind of mousey man who worked in a drug store. Leonard Jr. and Irma were eight and four, and we became friends. Betty would often tell us in an offhanded manner, while we played in their house, stories of her dead parents and grandparents who had been lost in the holocaust, of strange places called Palestine, and of Jews fleeing the Holy Land. Leonard quickly became a member of our neighborhood troop of Mexican, and some Irish, kids—all Catholic and bigoted. Leonard, eventually as did the Irish kids, acquired a Mexican accent and on Sundays we took him to mass with us where he peered confusedly through what we now consider as Harry Potter glasses.

He had to shift all the time from going to Shabbat and Saturday services reciting Hebrew to Sunday mass where he listened to the Latin mass and the fiery sermons of Father Murphy who lambasted apostate protestants and heathen Jews in Irish-English. We would elbow Leonard and we would stifle our giggles and laughter and roll over from our attentive positions on the last pew of the church. Los Kruger moved to the other side of town a few years later.

I lost track of Leonard until much later as a graduate student while I was reading a newly authored book of the "I'm Okay, Your Okay" type. The author on the back cover who peered out through Harry Potter glasses was Leonard, who was now a psychiatrist in Beverly Hills. But the tale did not end here. About ten years later, I read that one of the more notorious Swamis in Oregon had become a controversial figures for not only driving his Rolls Royce up and down a single street while his followers heaped garlands of flowers as he passed, but also for having his followers engage in sometimes questionable political activity in one of the towns nearby.

The spokesman for the Swami was one Darilama Contishepra, formerly known as Leonard Kruger Jr. I think this may have had something to do with his journey toward self-discovery. So the "Irish and Kruger Effects" illustrate that this transborder population is a culturally powerful one in which acculturational masks have been long used to confuse the multiple domains in which we participate. And all these are very much associated with, connected by, and glued to the border in a transnational and transborder sense.

## On Transborder Cultural Consciousness and Existences of the Border

In general, then, we live the border, whether on it, by it, near it, or distant from it, and this is a constant for most Mexican-origin populations and also for many non-Mexicans. Here lies the great mega contradiction in that while it is a line that divides, it also ensures its own crossing, its own violation, and its own transborder dynamic. Whether a person is estranged and distant or crosses it daily to work on one side and live on the other, the Mexico-U.S. border is like a permanent dye marker on someone's clothes, no matter how many washings, its presence may fade from the conscious cloth, but in a thousand ways the color will remain and become resurrected by economy and polity—accentuating and making permanent and sometimes directing our cultural directions. The border is the persistent and dynamic presence that becomes "transnational" and transgenerational, and it becomes a transcultural phenomenon that permeates the region's historical shape and memory.[6] Its creation and continuance is a part and parcel of its institutionalism; it is not just an imaginary or a "cultural artifact" but entails lived and experientially supported objective realities.

Whether it is a third-generation school teacher in Mecca, California, in the middle of the Coachella Valley, or *colonos* in southern New Mexico in the Hatch Valley, or migrants in the south Valley in Texas, or a fifth-generation anthropologist or a recently graduated undocumented computer specialist from Mexico City working as a painter in Phoenix, Arizona, the border is carried and becomes an unthought-of constant presence in and around us all often as a masked actuality. It becomes "normal" except when reminded of how abnormal it is. Here are some reminders.

Consider the internal borders placed strategically to interrupt migration from northern Chihuahua to southern New Mexico. Located about 20 miles south of Las Cruces on Highway 25, the sign reads: Alien Removals: 2,749; Narcotics: 5,092 lbs; Value: $8,014,348. The equating of all three, of course, provides one aspect of the internal contradictions in that (1) the border point is in the United States, (2) removals and narcotics are equivalent, and (3) it is not clear as to whether both are measured in value. In either case, such enforcement messages clearly support the national presumption of control based on citizenship and legal institutions.

In contrast, let us consider the colonias in the same region.[7] At present there are over 2,000 rural, largely impoverished, federally recognized colonias of approximately a million persons in Arizona, California, New Mexico, and Texas made up largely of makeshift housing that is mostly clandestine and not zoned for residential use.[8] Colonias will vary between "settlements" and communities.[9] In their entirety, they make up part of the larger regions of refuge, but the colonias are especially characterized by inadequate or nonexistent water supplies, sewage, electrification, and surface drainage systems. The populations themselves have been largely poor, about 40 percent being Mexico-born, with the rest born in the United States and with sizeable families of five to six members sustained by a combination of local and migrant agricultural work, including dairies and field labor that are often located in areas such as El Recuerdo. These particular populations in the 1980s migrated to towns and settlements developed originally by Anglo and Mexican homesteaders in the nineteenth century. But many of these were vacated by populations moving to larger urban centers in New Mexico or elsewhere.

**Figure 2.2** Border Crossing (Archive: Carlos Vélez-Ibáñez).

Yet this description says little of the cultural creativity and development effort of the populations themselves and the organized efforts of these very communities to gain basic infrastructure, access to schools, medical care, and basic amenities. This in fact is transborder culture in the making and the emergence of mostly well-organized and culturally healthy nodes of human creation and development of "modular" housing, as shown in the figure below, in which persons begin with a trailer and then add on permanent rooms adjacent as well as surrounding the original

Figure 2.3   Modular Housing (Archive: Carlos Vélez-Ibáñez).

mobile structure until, in some cases, the trailer is lost and, except for the cardboard-like walls, little is recognizable of the original.

Undoubtedly, there are also multiple issues of health, abuse, low income, narcotics, poverty, border patrol harassment, judicial deportations, and miseducation. But for the most part these are in fact vibrant communities living out their lives mostly in a manner that provides stability and sound social platforms for the generations that follow and are the transborder cultural and physical manifestations of the failed attempt by national institutions to control transnational economic dynamics especially in agriculture, but also in construction, services, and in sundry other economically productive activities. That is because these economies are integrated (asymmetrically) institutionally through production chains without any reference to the accompanying labor necessities that require basic amenities; little in these colonias initially resembles any type of planned or rational settlement. It is as if economic policy institutions such as banks, corporations, and other major trade, production, and assembly players all forgot that human beings through their labor actually must also move between borders to fulfill the required production demands.

Yet these colonias also have within them previous generations, such as Chon below, whose predecessors arrived as agriculture workers in the 1920s, purchased the surrounding land, raised cows, grew crops, suffered through the depression, and were targets of repatriation. Their children fought in World War II and raised two more generations, including Chon. This transborder and transnational personality surrounded by the desert

**Figure 2.4**   Chon (Archive: Carlos Vélez-Ibáñez).

and adobe walls is a case in point of the way in which our references are multiple and not tied to a single citizenship referent, even though Chon has paid a terrible price for the privilege of this inclusion by serving two tours in Vietnam, during the second of which he fought as a sniper, was wounded seriously by a rocket, and spent the next seven years getting treated and suffering from extreme posttraumatic stress. Yet he lives next door to the colonias and within one that had been mostly a Mexican village prior to its redesignation as a colonia by the Federal Government.

When these generations all live within the same geographical spaces and yet occupy varying cultural spaces, then we can barely begin to appreciate the density of cultural systems being learned, utilized, distributed, and discarded in this huge transborder and transnational arena. Yet they have a commonality: they are also driven by a second megascript—the drive for success.

### Megascript Two: Racialized Success

Transborder reality and processes like those above are also often buttressed by the promulgation of a second megascript: the quest for individual and familial success and material gain with its accompanying social, political, economic, and cultural perks, with sometimes melanin rationalizations thrown in as justifications. Such scripts are often beyond question so that populations easily can "normatively" and "naturally" agree to the general megascripts of scrapping labor and energy value from things and persons, including oneself.[10] Institutions of many sorts support such scripts and it is the case that judicial authorities of various sorts, including police and judicial agencies, protect the privilege of individual achievement and success. "Illegal" border crossers certainly are chastised for their attempts to follow the megascript of individual success, since this is restricted for those who are "citizens"—a privileged status often associated with melanin and/or cultural concerns especially in relation to language, familial dynamics, body shapes and sizes, and simple things like dress, proxemics, and sundry other cultural expressions. There may be something to the notion that if one has darker melanin, is elderly, a woman, Mexican, short, poor, and left-handed, then there is less probability of being, or of becoming, successful.

Transborder living gives us an unusually twisted manner in which to consider another dimension of this individualistic megascript. For many in southwest North America, transborder populations are double-helixed from both sides of the border. First, the immense demographic growth of Mexican-origin populations in southwest North America emerges from the integrated and asymmetrical structures of economy with its ups and downs. Upward mobility in Mexico is limited to the elite and the ever growing rich, while the professional classes increasingly work two or three jobs or migrate to Europe or Canada, where Mexican academics especially migrate for a more successful life. Certainly the U.S. academic enterprise has benefited from Mexican academic "white flight" regardless of the melanin of those academic migrants.[11] First, around six million undocumented Mexicans, mostly fleeing the lack of opportunity back home, work in the United States. Second, class divisions in Mexico are often articulated along melanin dimensions. Regardless of the public expressions of the wonder of Mesoamerican civilizations, "whiteness" is the expressed preference for elites and bleached blond upper class women, and male preference, regardless of melanin, tends toward dark consorts and light wives and children. Mexican class whiteness is accentuated in most mediums of expressions, and grandmothers often first ask about what color the newborn child is rather than about its health, with "como es?" ["And how is the baby?"]. There is a tacit agreement that a positive answer will provide its bearer with an easier fate.

The other half of the helix for Mexicans who have had the border cross them and who have crossed the border is the acquisition of a nonsuccessful definition, that of a "commodity," which implies that Mexican and cheap labor have become one and the same, and achievement is not included as part of this formula. There is a long history of how this has occurred, but without too much embellishment it can be said that Mexican-origin middle-class populations in border regions have tried desperately to ensure their difference from working-class persons and recent Mexican migrants, many therefore take on respectability with more accepted terms such as "Hispanic" or Latino and many other versions of those terms. Yet the only way for the first generation to escape commoditization is to work even harder as a commodity—working two jobs, both parents engaging in informal economies, and "slanting" by as best they can to ensure that their own children "do not have to suffer." Indeed many have achieved this state while many others have not, but in fact both groups hold on to the same basic megascript of achievement, mobility, and success—the means are different, some take shortcuts, others hang on to institutional dependency, and the children of some others do suffer. They work like mad in one way or the other to sheer themselves of commodity identities and gain other ones.

Coupled to this reality is that transborder living is a way of emotionally, cognitively, socially, economically, and, most importantly, culturally deciphering and living out the multitude of cultural scripts that transect daily existence because of border influences. Transborder living and remembrances touch all those living in the region and beyond it. Whether expressed in the latest anti-immigration T-shirt, intemperate ethnocentric remarks uttered by the ignorant in a clothing store, in the daily life of persons crossing our paths wearing Brooks Brother suits with brown faces and Aztec noses, the guys waiting patiently on the corner in the 110-degree weather for a hopeful ride to a low-paying backbreaking job, or the domestic worker making our bourgeoisie beds and caring and loving our children, the presence of the border and the necessity of transborder existences touch everyone within eyesight or earshot through the media and on the street, in our work places and schools, and in the multitudes of daily settings.[12] In a most contradictory manner, many transborder Mexicans have to live their lives by constantly changing and shifting identities, outlooks, positions, and selves to cope with the double helix of the quest for achievement and racialized transborder realities.

## Conclusions

I take a broad view of transnationalism and transborder phenomena that we discussed above, especially so given the special nature of the history of the region. Given the territorial conquest of parts of southwest North

America by the United States,[13] the Gadsden Purchase at the point of a gun,[14] the economic integration of the border region,[15] the continued linguistic and cultural exchange throughout southwest North America, the exchange of populations from south to north and north to south,[16] and the historical memory of individuals, groups, and networks as well as the mixed cohorts of citizens, residents, and undocumented members in the same household, then transborder and transnational behavior and culture cannot be confined to the frequency of interactions across the border or to the lineal acculturation model of language and cultural loss or simply to the great economic structures that are located on both sides of the border.

In fact, we all carry the border with us in one way or the other, including its dialectical dynamics that are expressed in even stronger contradictions, in which 25 billion dollars in commerce cross yearly along the Arizona-Sonora border and yet hundreds of persons cannot cross from south to north because of an artifact created in the original conflict and expressed as a contradiction that is termed legal "citizenship." It is in this region that great megascripts like those described are tended to and reinforced but also made questionable by their own internal contradictions, and which are carried over for new populations to negotiate in "slantwise" ways[17] and deal with the ramifications of double helixed ideologies of melanin and achievement.

These scripts fill the transborder spaces and places of the region and beyond and are buttressed by institutions of many sorts. When only the hundreds of institutions from museums to universities are considered, the population dynamics of travel and crisscrossing from Sonora, Chihuahua, Baja California, Coahuila, and Nuevo Leon to the reciprocal travel from Arizona, California, New Mexico, Texas, and Nevada, and to the literally hundreds of transborder spaces observed, such as the places where a Mexican flag waves next to a U.S. flag on joint flag poles, as in front of banks and state buildings, and businesses in Tucson, Albuquerque, and El Paso, then the notion of transnationalism cannot be considered narrow.[18] My view of contemporary transnationalism and transborder analysis is that it must connect all levels of social experience and all of their attending ideologies and contradictory scripts.[19]

This is especially so in the southwest North American region in that transborder and transnational phenomena are complex and multilayered and, as I have said, cannot be reduced to how many times a person interacts with an individual in Mexico or vice versa in the United States. There are myriad mediums by which transnational and transborder practices, ideas, feelings, emotions, materials, and values are articulated daily, frequently, and constantly in this southwest North American region and beyond. Yet, those two great megascripts are "distributed" and reinforced on a daily basis and mostly without the conscious awareness of its practitioners. Here lies the rub and the contradictions of adhering to scripts that in the long run may be deleterious to the sound social and cultural emergence of the population. These serve as the shining guideposts to success and the denial of cultural self in order to avoid the pain of being treated as a mere commodity. Yet somehow we not only survive but also excel, like Chon living out his multiple identities in the midst of a transnational world and transnational histories while dizzily being batted about by the megascripts that motivate and push these very worlds and histories.

## Notes

1. According to Cancian, the term *cargo* means burden, but its basis is the rotation of wealth through religious rituals/fiestas. Men, mostly, then generate prestige by expenditure. Through civil and religious offices, men must assume these duties or lose their rights even to common land usage. Migration to the United States pressures such systems, but as reported by Kearney (personal communication, 2004), arrangements by e-mail create adjustments made by groups like the Mixe. See Cancian's (1965) *Economics and Prestige in a Maya Community* and (1992) *The Decline of Community in Zinacantan*. See Taylor's "Cofradías and Cargos" (1985).
2. NAFTA is the North American Free Trade Agreement. See Portes (2006) *NAFTA and Mexican Immigration*, "Border Battles: The U.S. Immigration Debates."
3. Saldívar (2006) *The Borderlands of Culture*.
4. The Treaty of the Mesilla was signed in 1854, but Mexican troops did not give over control in Tucson until March 1856, and many stayed past 1857. The first "illegal aliens" in Arizona was the Mormon Battalion, which entered Tucson in the Fall of 1846.
5. The San Patricio were Catholic Irish soldiers who deserted from the U.S. Army to fight for the Mexican side.
6. I use "transcultural" as the consequence of "cultural bumping" between two or more peoples with different deep histories and in which localities on different sides of the political border have aspects of the other and in which following generations emerge already shaded by imperfect transmission of already hybridized cultural systems. See Vélez-Ibáñez's (1996) *Border Visions*.
7. For an excellent treatment of the political ecology of the colonias in the Hatch region, see Núñez-Mchiri's (2009) "The Political Ecology Of The Colonias."
8. This term is a U.S. federal designation for settlements within 100 miles of the Mexico-U.S. border characterized by lack of infrastructure and legal titles.
9. The former are characterized by isolated, nucleated households with little horizontal or vertical relations and the latter (fewer in number) are associated with the landlords who sold them the property in the first place.

10. See Vélez-Ibáñez et. al. (2002) *Transnational Latina/o Communities*. The notions of megascripts refer to ideologically driven naturalized rationalizations of power, dominance, and exploitation buttressed by local and regional scripts. These may be constituted as "values," beliefs, rituals, symbols, and other accepted "civil" discourses.
11. "Whiteness" is a megascripts tied to success, hard work, sacrifice, ingenuity, innovation, and generally superior intelligence. Physical work is not included but avoided by education, mobility, and success. It is congruent with a theory of profit gain, scrapping of labor value, and the conversion of energy from whatever source to accomplish some material gain. But this is not the central analysis in this work. There is a huge literature on "whiteness" studies, but the most important works include a black-white perspective: See Daniel's *The Birth of Whiteness* and his *Hollywood, Classic Whiteness*, also Hill's *After Whiteness*, McKinney's *Being White*, Jensen's *The Heart of Whiteness*, and Yancy's *What White Looks Like*. For other perspectives, see Delgado and Stefancic's *Critical White Studies*, Deloria's *Red Earth, White Lies* Rodríguez and Villaverde's *Dismantling White Privilege*, Arriola's *Difference, solidarity and law*, and others.
12. These examples are real. In order of discussion: (1) some sites sale, T-shirts and even thongs with the logo "My Mexican works for less than your Mexican," (2) in the language example, this refers to a short, dumpy, badly frizzle haired, bad blond-streaked matron at a major department store in Scottsdale, Arizona, who berated my niece because she was speaking Spanish to her Puerto Rican mother. The matron did not know that the rate of speech and the replacements of ls with ds came not from Mexican Spanish, (3) the Aztec reference is that of my friends, who sartorially garb themselves in blue Brooks Brothers' suits but look like Montezuma, and in actuality one of them is the chairman of his own law firm. The street corner reference and the domestic servant examples are numerous throughout the United States.
13. Conquered by the United States and acceding to the Treaty of Guadalupe-Hidalgo on February 2, 1848, Mexico had to negate its claim to Texas and to what is now New Mexico, Arizona, California, Colorado, Utah, and Nevada. This territory constituted about 200,000 square miles or two-fifths of its territory.
14. James Gadsden was a South Carolina railroad speculator who threatened Mexican negotiators with American armed force if they did not agree to the $10 million dollar purchase price of Mexican territory. See Vélez-Ibáñez (1996, 287; Endnote 53) for the actual ultimatum.
15. In 2005 California and Texas comprised 34 percent of the 44.3 million Hispanics in the United States. Hispanics comprised 15 percent of the total population. The number of Latinos has risen dramatically each decade since its 2.3 millions in 1950.
16. According to Morse (2007), the El Paso/Juárez metropolitan area included 2.6 million people and represented North America's fourth-largest manufacturing hub. In 2006, trade crossing its ports totaled $46.8 billion according

to the El Paso Regional Economic Development Corporation. Daily border crossings totaled 42,648 private vehicles, 2,122 commercial trucks, and 20,547 pedestrians.

17. See Campbell and Heyman's (2007) "Slantwise." Their approach is less economic than political; they are critical of the model used in discussions concerning the agency versus domination opposites along an axis. They emphasize acts that frustrate "the normal play of a given power relation by acting in ways that make sense in their own frameworks but are disconnected or oblivious to that power relationship's construction or assumptions" (2). I suggest that practices like rotating savings and credit associations, lending clubs, localized methods of exchange and lending function in similar ways in that they "take on" all normalized spheres of borrowing, lending, investing, and saving by creating their own spheres of slantwise action. The irony, however, as I discussed in my new work (*An Impossible Living in a Transborder World*) is that the formal economic sector has recognized the efficacy of these and have appropriated their forms and functions.

18. See Portes (2001), "The Debates and Significance of Immigrant Transnationalism"; and (2002) "Theoretical Convergencies and Empirical Evidence." His work restricts the transnational and transborder phenomena to those who constantly engage in transnational behavior. See also Cabral et al's (1999) "Mapping Dominican Transnationalism," which distinguished between narrow and broad transnationalism.

19. See those with a broader view like Kim (2005), "Wedding Citizenship and Culture," Levitt and Schiller's (2004) "Conceptualizing Simultaneity," Mahler and Pessar's (2006) *Gender Matters*, Smith's (2006) *Mexican New York*, and Morawska's "Immigrants, Transnationalism, and Ethnicization."

3

# Transnational Mexicano Cultural Production: *El Otro Lado* [The Other Side]

*Ellie D. Hernández*

When and how did the U.S.-Mexico border suddenly become transnational? Some critics and scholars would say that the U.S.-Mexico border characterizes the transnational process with its constant flow of people, goods, and services. This dynamic between border nations leads one to conclude that there is an inherent transnationalism taking place between such nations. But there is certainly much more to the transnational story than the common coincidental fact of two nations having a common border as its definitive entry into transnational capital. My intention is not to formalize an understanding of what constitutes the transnational border; however, it is important to note the social impact of recent advances in global capitalism and its effect on border life that necessitate a broader discussion, one I hope will lead to an in-depth understanding of culture. While border cultures deal primarily with spatial and economic terms, the geopolitics of the border also commands power dynamics that constantly inform gender, sexual, racial, and cultural differences.

Exploring what we mean by the transnational U.S.-Mexico border, this chapter looks at the exchange of ideas, social formations, and sensibilities important to framing the transnational U.S.-Mexico border. Most scholars would agree that this border is not a neutral demarcation of a line designating the natural delineation of national differences, but rather the U.S. cultural borderlands demarcate the cultural boundaries that people construct for themselves.

We have not always had the intensity or the drive of advanced capitalism forcing people from their homes and causing sudden displacement of people throughout Mexico in search of a better life along the border. We have not had such an intensive rise of maquiladoras, flow of commodities and consumer goods moving in and out with such ease and with increased force. At no other time has there been so much turmoil and frustration about immigration, the environment, human rights, and the war on drugs. This is truly a unique time and our current discussion about what constitutes transnationalism of the border should also include a discussion of the impact and effects of advanced levels of capitalism on the local communities. Too much has been touted about the benefits of developing the border economic infrastructure. As the economic zones of trade transform sleepy little towns, the frontier nature of the region loses its character and sensibilities to commercial interests. In most cases, tourism, the primary generator of income in border regions, no longer exists, because it's too dangerous to even cross over to the Mexican side to buy goods for everyday use. When we, the discussants and participants of the Lennox seminar, address here the transnationalism of border culture, we are also referring to the transformation of citizen-subject relations. As an example of this, I look to "No Country for Old Men," a highly acclaimed film by the director brothers Ethan and Joel Cohen that won the 2007 Academy Award for Best Film, which signals this very pattern of citizen-subject relations with a disturbing twist. The emphasis of the film is the recovery of a lost suitcase full of cash after a drug deal went bad.

Without necessarily getting into the entire plot of the film, the drive of the film is, of course, the recovery of the suitcase full of cash by different characters, thus depicting the semblance of a bad border subject in the quest for material opportunity. The point here is that this film is uncannily representative of the psychology and neurotic symptoms of advanced capitalism inhabiting this forgotten part of the United States. Like the old American genre of the Western films, the violence—no longer discreet or romanticized—spawns awe and amazement because the loss of human reflexes seems so easy to accept in the name of business. At no other time in my recollection has such violence along the border been so indiscriminate, as if daring to be normal.

Despite the critical distinction about always having been transnational, only recently have we seen the effects of transnational culture in the region; the U.S.-Mexico border in its present form still remains an enigmatic space because it often invites a provocative and yet demanding set of social relations. Almost every sector of the border life is influenced by the nuances of "third-space"—its otherworldliness and not belonging to either nation. Cultural scholarship often comments about the vibrancy of border life with its rich and varied semblances of aesthetic, its utter disorganization in many cases, and chaotic arrangement of the social order. Blending and sharing of customs and values are also common to the exchange between these two nations. The local character shapes the sharing of language, food, and home, and the sharing of other basic means of living is a common occurrence (I must've missed the episode on HGTV about the quaintness of border dwellings, but it's hard to find such representation of home and hearth through conventional means). Commerce, trade, and economic development of this region are also symptomatic of the daily exchange of goods and services, with trade being a strong contributor to the region's economy. But one also finds along the border the usual tensions of political struggle, with all types of transgressions in the act of crossing over.

Cultural critic Gloria Anzaldúa characterized this well in *Borderlands/ La Frontera: The New Mestiza* (1987), where she describes the ruptures of colonization across the sinuous border.

Gloria Anzaldúa's critically acclaimed collection of poetry and articles shed new light on life along the U.S.-Mexico border with its stark historiographical rewriting of the southwest Texas valley. This backdrop for Anzaldúa's borderlands also set a new standard for Chicana feminisms with its attention to queer culture. Anzaldúa's work certainly marks a departure from readings of nationalist subjects in their ethnic and feminist compositions by situating the border along with other marginal [subjects?] marked in the transient passages of nationalist discourses. Achieving this with its own language rubric for readings of gender, sexuality, and history, its influence as a major text would soon influence cultural studies across Latin America, United States, and Europe with its enigmatic prose style and global perspective. Remarkably, Anzaldúa's feminist criticism eludes its place among leading scholarly texts that illuminated the 1980s and 1990s. Despite the fact that Anzaldúa's main point of a nonnationalist subject draws heavily from feminist projects, the political treatise of *Borderlands* codifies the post-civil rights era with ideas about social and gender notions of liberation. One could also look at *Borderlands: The New Mestiza* as the unfinished business of *This Bridge Called My Back* (1981), where the writers had posed some elemental issues with respect to the collective voice of women of color. *Bridge*, as a critical anthology, follows the premise that writings by women of color lead to a model of radical subjectvity that reaches far beyond the limits of both Anglo-American feminism and paradigms produced by postcolonial or U.S. minority critics.

Moreover, Norma Alarcón's article on the subject of female inscription notes in "Anzaldúa's Frontera: Inscribing Gynetics" that Anzaldúa's use of a feminist model produces cultural studies criticism by noting that the female agent/subject needs to "repossess the land." In 'Borderlands,' Alarcón claims, "Anzaldúa's indigenous female (border) subject underwrites the basis of the female voice, [her] gynetics symbolizes the ruptures of the border figured as the female body" (Alarcón 2003). The border/frontera geopolitical region (gash, wound, vagina) refers to a virtual absence of female narrative production,

> The point of my analysis, however, is to call attention to the need to "repossess" the land, especially in cultural nationalist narratives, through scenarios of origins that emerge in the self-same territory—be it the literary, legendary, historical, ideological, critical, or theoretical level—producing in material and imaginary terms "authentic" and "inauthentic," legal and illegal subjects. (Alarcón 2003)

Anzaldúa's feminist work provides strong examples of the border as a counter-hegemonic discourse that occupies racial and gendered embodiments. The success, however, of Anzaldúa's *Borderlands* rarely occasions a feminist interpretation in many cultural studies offerings. Though in more celebrated terms of borderland terminology, "border crossing," "mestiza consciousness," and "third space" advance a feminist and queer encountered discourse as a gender-sex critique. By providing a lexicon for the new age of globalism that includes queer, global, and, of course, borderlands as its mode of resistance, a new site, simulation of third-world feminism, thus has been supplanted by the flat space cultural studies as a homogenous mapping of the global material borderlands. Elsewhere, Sonia Saldívar-Hull's "Feminism on the Borderlands" situates the practice of reading Chicanas within the borderlands of theory and conventional academic thought to be mired by all sorts of issues, Saldívar-Hull explains:

> In the same way we must break with traditional (hegemonic) concepts of genre to read Chicana feminist theory, working class women of color in other Third World countries also articulate their feminisms in nontraditional ways and forms. Chicana feminists acknowledge the vast historical, class, racial and ethnic differences among women living on the border. Further dividing them is the nature of hegemony practiced by the united powers of patriarchy, capitalism, imperialism and White supremacy, which promotes the illusion of an irreconcilable split between feminists confined within national borders. (Saldívar 2000)

Anzaldúa's project provides significant and intriguing outlets for the feminist voice, especially with the darker, less conciliatory dimensions of her work. References to female deities or goddesses represent the darker and intentionally grotesque vision of the female that has been formed. Some implications of the "border" identity consider feminist constructions of voice and figurative embodiment. Part of Anzaldúa's overall project to develop a theory of feminist practice that expresses relevance to a postmodern and cultural studies model, however, clearly offers the feminist a trajectory to follow. For example, Anzaldúa's notion of a liminal subject, drawing for postcolonial terminology, takes from a tradition that theorizes mestizaje (meaning racial, but also cultural, mixing) as a basis for thinking about marginalization. *Borderlands/La Frontera*, like the theories of mestizaje, alludes to the feminine principle and ultimately rests upon a nostalgic desire for wholeness, and it can easily slip into the centering of the subject in the Anglo-American hegemony and Western philosophy sense.

Anzaldua's feminist project begins with the concept of border culture and the luminal model of the subject's displacement of binary oppositions within the nation such as "center and periphery," or, in the case of the American Southwest, "Mexican and Anglo" (just as in some parts of the American South, social and cultural category confound the more common United States binarism of black and white). But the border identity is, nevertheless, informed by these oppositions. As such, it is subversive only in a context where the traditional binaries still hold sway. Once a notion of a binary falls apart, the configurations of power within the heterogeneous "border" space are dismantled. My brief discussion of the liminal/mestizaje tradition is intended to provide some concrete examples of these problems that present to nationalist constructions of the woman of color feminists. What border studies reveal is an attempt to work against the symbolically masculine nation with its defined terms and the unrepresented female subjectivity represented by the gash, or wound.

### Cultural Border and Cultural Boundary

Borders, by design, intend to designate a line that protects the resources belonging to a dominant group and separating the beneficial interests of the state or nation for its own self-interests. Borders are often less protected than most other parts of the nation, but at the same time it seems more regulated and policed than any other space. How is this so? Is not policing a form of protection? Not necessarily, because local interests are seldom protected, and protection would imply a service to the community that its serves, whereas the dominant interests are protected by police measures to secure trade and commerce, but rarely people and their well-being. Because borders are symbolic for their power to include and exclude, the more privileged dominant group will actively control the border to keep border crossers out, even if the former do not actually live in the area, region, or state. Since a border is a social construct that is geopolitical in origin, its definition changes according to the circumstances and across history. The cultural boundary rhetoric made available by CNN news, and in particular Lou Dobbs' now ignoble anti-immigration program "Broken Borders," operates from an essentialist view of culture. Dobb's show makes several assumptions regarding American culture and the delineation of the boundary that separates the United States and Mexico: (1) culture operates from a bounded hermetic system that is distinguishable from other nations according to history, race, sexuality, and language; (2) culture remains even and homogenous, even as it declares its own diversity celebrating its tolerance for others; (3) citizenship or belonging operates from a complex arbitrary system that requires stabilization by state and federal government as arbiters of the citizenship and culture; (4) globalization is seen as a policy that has promoted economic trends that have disenfranchised the American worker while increasing immigration as a cheap source of labor.

The cultural boundary is viewed as coterminous with a nation, a state, a tribe, a community, or an organization that is clearly defined by identifiable markers and often forms the physical borders. Franz Boas (1981), a pioneer German-American anthropologist, began to use "culture" to refer to the distinctive body of customs, beliefs, and social institutions that seemed to characterize each separate society (Stocking, cited in Goodenough, 48). The notion of one distinct culture for each separate society suggests that one culture represents a society and vice versa. This close match makes the conceptual interchange of culture and society acceptable. Henze and Vanett (1993) further explore this assumption of culture in the metaphor of "walking in two worlds" in their study of native Alaskan and native American students. One assumption of cultural homogeneity suggests that a homogeneous, patterned prototype of a culture can be abstracted. It implies that a "pure" form of a culture exists. Any variation from the pure form is treated as an exception, peripheral to "the culture." This assumption ignores the dynamic nature of culture, in which people of a society change at different rates for different reasons. The diffusionist view of culture argues against this notion of cultural homogeneity, for all cultures include elements borrowed from other cultures (Linton 1937; Wax 1993). Another assumption of the cultural border is that a culture is "shared" by members of a society. The extent of sharedness is debatable, yet sharedness is considered a trademark of culture. This assumption suggests that people within a cultural system share a set of traits unique to their group membership. Sharedness is considered a product of cultural transmission and acquisition that often take place through personal interactions among members with physical proximity. In other words, an Asian is expected to share with other Asians traits unique to Asian culture. When a group is small and specific, the extent of sharedness among members may be higher. However, if a group presents a large, cross-sectional or cross-national cultural identity, such as "female culture," "middle-class culture," and "Muslim culture," the sharedness of that particular culture is blurred by other cultural identities. Ewing (1998) examined how the cultural identity of Muslims shifts relative to national borders and the gender line. This territory-oriented rhetoric of culture, cultural border, and boundary faces a great challenge in a multicultural society because intense contacts between various cultural carriers blur the clarity of demarcation lines.

"Cultural borderland" versus cultural border is a term that originates from multicultural discourse to describe the dynamics that occur when two or more cultures and races occupy the same territory. According to Renato Rosaldo and James Clifford, the borderland generally refers to a psychological space at the conjuncture of two cultures. A cultural borderland is also a political space in which ethnic groups actively fuse and blend their culture with the mainstream culture (119). The borderland is viewed as a geographical space that also carries a psychological dimension to it and in which border crossers struggle with their bicultural or multicultural identities.

In this borderland, individuals decide within limits of power relation how much they want to identify with their cultures of origin or of adoption. Too much of either can be the subject of ridicule. Saenz (1997) compared two distinguished Mexican American writers who try to come to terms with their ethnic identities. He argued that Gloria Anzaldúa is "completely mortgaged to a nostalgia," a nostalgia to the Aztec origin of the Mexican culture (87). Richard Rodriguez, on the other hand, "is completely mortgaged to an ideology that privileges the category of individual" (87).

The borderland is also highly political. The borderland is never on center stage. It is often viewed as a marginal space for cultural hybrids—those who have adopted "foreign," distinctly different, cultural traits—who therefore do not fit the homogeneous prototypes of their original cultures (4). Some borderland rhetoric are still embedded in the essentialist view of culture. For example, Foley's notion of cultural borderlands creates an image of three separate zones: the "pure" Indian culture that is being guarded by "traditionalists" (Let's call it Culture A); the "pure" white culture that is distinguished from the Indian (Culture B); and the borderland between them, a space for border crossers (Culture C). Chang (1997) questions this essentialist presumption of culture by wondering "just where the Indian culture ends and the White culture begins for border crossers" (385).

## Transnationalism and Transborder

Not all transnational spaces occupy a border. In fact, the important qualification of most transnational discussions suggests overriding or supplanting altogether the governing rules of the nation. Our perspective here for the Lennox seminar is unique, because we have many qualifying factors to consider the broadly theorized transnationalism between the United States and Mexico and also to consider border culture as local theory for the global. For one, the proximity of Mexico to the United States offers the distinction of having a First World nation border a Third World nation.

Here the rules of exchange offer distinct power roles in that Mexico seems to always accommodate the U.S. economic power. Second, the neglect of the U.S.-Mexico border came about as a result of centralized federal and state governance. This left regions of the border from the nineteenth century up until the middle of the twentieth century unregulated and undisturbed. Scholars need to remind people that the immigration issues, the border surveillance, and drug wars were not big problems until the 1980s when efforts to create economic zones intensified capitalism as a way of life. Not only was capitalism being promoted along the border, but a very specific and aggressive type of capitalism was offering instructions to the local border communities about how to establish growth and prosperity.

Immigration and the exploitation of women also join the production portion of the transnational experience. Without some type of humanities-based critique, how are we to counter the dissonant effects of globalization? We need to valuate people back to respectable levels of living and place people, and not just capitalist interests, first. Carlos Vélez-Ibáñez illuminated our discussion with his lecture about the transborder culture. His discussion about growing up in Arizona animated our understanding of the way people navigate the corridors of reason and thought. Embedded in his anthropological work, he carefully details the personalized geopolitics of the transborder experience cleverly layered into the material concerns, such as dire living condition in the colonias, drug trafficking, migrations of various types (Irish, Italian, and Jewish), and the ever present chasm of contradictory formations that compose the border reality. In his own words,

> Whether a person is estranged and distant or crosses it daily to work on one side and live on the other, the Mexican U.S. border is like a permanent

dye marker on someone's clothes, no matter how many washings its presence may fade from the conscious cloth, in a thousand ways the color remains and becomes resurrected by economy and polity.

Adding to this reality of the transborder experience offered by Prof. Vélez-Ibáñez, I would like to also contrast the transborder logic with the dominant philosophy of European enlightenment. I would like to contrast both just to give you a sense of how distinct and oftentimes opposing these philosophies truly are. The Enlightened subject is (1) rational and privileges science and certainty, whereas the transborder is norteado, with no fixed set of terms or science to orient its purpose, (2) location, or sense of place, for Enlightened subject is situated as nationalized, whereas the transborder experiences offers displacement and migration, (3) freedom and entitlement for the Enlightenment subject is preserved in the citizen subject, whereas the transborder subject exists outside of the mainstream, creating citizens who exists outside of the national register, such as aliens, queers, transgenders, and feminists—not a bad place at all. These constituencies of the transborder experience, or should I really be saying el otro lado of the transborder experience, offer testimonies of perseverance and of progress. We inhabit both sides of these intellectual spaces. We have been living with a symbolic system that cannot register or recognize the border experience without some issuance of conflict.

What the U.S.–Mexico border culture also reveals is a semiotic system in distress, one side is confounded by the limits of its own national representation (its enlightenment) and the other side is offering alternative ways to conceive of culture. *El Otro Lado* has always been presented as a place to visit but not to inhabit on a permanent basis. These in-between geographies of national and transnational do not happen overnight, they have been brewing slowly over the past century. These spaces do produce odd circumstances, which defy conventional logics that register only to those who are familiar with border stuff.

I offer two recent examples. The first example took place during the 2008 Democratic contest between Barack Obama and Hillary Clinton. During the last Nevada Democratic primary race, Latinas helped propel presidential candidate Hillary Clinton to victory against her opponent Barack Obama. Though not even mentioned or discussed by the national press, many of the nameless and faceless Latina casino workers in the state of Nevada publicly, albeit quietly, sided on the side of Clinton; many of the women workers originating from places like Mexico and Central and South America banded together to formulate a constituency that pushed Hillary Clinton to her big win in Nevada. The Nevada exit polls revealed that 64 percent of the Hispanics voted for Hillary Clinton. Similar trends continued throughout the state of California, Texas, New Jersey, Arizona, and New Mexico where higher concentration of Latino voters could be tallied. According to CNN exit polls, California's Latina/o population voted overall 69 percent for Hillary Clinton, but the Latina women showed a larger 75 percent points. Similar trends continued in the state of Texas. There were no actual numbers that captured the intersection of gender and ethnicity, but the support of these women for Hillary registered in other ways through a few snippets of newspapers photo options and visibility in the media as they supported the first viable female candidate for president. Many of these women voted against their own labor union, in this case the Culinary Union 226 of Las Vegas workers. I mention this example from the recent political scenario because the chasms and assumptions about who actually is the transborder subject could be seen in their opposition to their own labor union, following a familiar theme in Chicana feminist discussions about activist organizations and their own political interests.

Another possible example of the transborder experience is the gay marriage tourist industry in Mexico. For example, La Villa Hidalgo Hotel in Cuernavaca, Mexico, is an exclusive adult Boutique Hotel. Its mission is to fulfill the needs of the alternative lifestyle community while maintaining the highest level of excellence and discretion. Among the guests you will find interracial, straight, and homosexual couples as well as singles from every walk of life. The philosophy of the Hotel Villa Hidalgo is "inclusiveness" and "camaraderie," which attracts many visitors from the United States, primarily folks in the entertainment industry and the arts and corporate worlds, who appreciate "the diversity of lifestyle choices." What makes this a unique issue is the way that capitalism advances and transforms sexuality as a form of human rights. The transborder experience uses the notion of rights as a means of appealing to marriage tourism. This is ironic because of the long-held assumption that Mexico follows Western human rights, whereas gay and lesbian tourism is illustrated here as a transborder experience that utilizes human rights under the terms of capitalism.

Transnational Mexican cultural production, as described in greater detail by Vélez-Ibáñez's "Fronterizo Transborder Existence," serves as a prime example of the large possibilities of transnationality between the United States and Mexico, because it addresses the exchange of people's ideas, thoughts, and ideologies, and not just goods and services. I also see transnational production as a dialogue with the global economy where cultural production begins with people and their sense of place, despite the uneven forms of economic development and adverse circumstances of crime and poverty.

Part II

# Voices and Literatures in *Las Fronteras* [The Borderlands]

# 4

# Dos Mundos [Two Worlds]: Two Celebrations in Laredo, Texas—*Los Matachines de la Santa Cruz* and The Pocahontas Pageant of the George Washington's Birthday Celebration

*Norma E. Cantú*

As a native of "Los Dos Laredos," as the twin border cities of Laredo, Texas, and Nuevo Laredo, Tamaulipas, are often referred to, I have witnessed and participated in the cultural production of the region for over 60 years. As a scholar, I have researched and theorized around border cultural production from my early work on children's folklore and the shepherd's play, La Pastorela, to my work on Quinceañeras, masculinity, and women's rites of passage. But one of my strongest sustained areas of research has been my long-range study of the two significant fiestas of the region, Los Matachines de la Santa Cruz and the George Washington's Birthday Celebration (GWBC). Although I have but a few published pieces on this ongoing study, I remain steadfast in researching and writing about the two—I see the two fiestas as intimately related, although they inhabit two different worlds, dos mundos, that sometimes collide but most often coexist as if in diachronic synergy. Not surprising in a community stratified along class lines, the celebrations and the performance of the community's identity occur on different scenarios and highlight different values, different codes, and coexist often without contact with one other but connected by a degree of separation, as it were. These two fiestas, the matachines and the GWBC, coexist in two very different worlds and serve different purposes as public celebrations and public displays of the community's identity; paradoxically, both signify and point to an indigenous past. My goal in this essay is to analyze these two cultural performances in an attempt to discern the complexity of the border as a site of confluence and of seemingly contradictory behaviors. But before I begin my analysis, I offer a brief description and historical overview of each celebration to situate them within the border paradigm that is Laredo; I then proceed to analyze each one—the Fiesta de Matachines and the part of the GWBC known as the Pocahontas Pageant—separately insofar as each functions as a site of the community's performance of its identity. Finally I draw conclusions and lay out a theoretical frame that I find useful in doing border cultural studies, a frame that albeit skeletal is much needed as we pursue to expand what Gloria Anzaldúa, Chela Sandoval, Daniel Arreola, and Emma Pérez have given us as first steps in the study of the area and its cultural production from a third space Anzaldúan theory.

## Laredo, a Brief History

In 1755 when the settlement that would become Laredo, Texas, was established by the Escandon expedition, Carrizo Indians roamed the area, drawn no doubt to the region by the river that the Spanish would soon name the Rio Grande or Rio Bravo because of its size and its treacherous waters. Aside from the Coahuiltecan groups, the various outside Native American groups like the Lipan Apache and the Comanche from the north and the Tlaxcalteca from the south also left their mark on the land and in the people. The bustling Spanish and then Mexican community soon developed into a commercial and cultural center, a crossroads for traffic of goods and people going north and south; the indigenous were killed off, driven off, segregated into reservations farther north, or assimilated through intermarriage along with other native peoples such as the Tlaxcaltecans who had been brought to the area by Spanish settlers. The religious fiestas that the Spanish brought with them mixed with the indigenous to form local calendrical and seasonal celebrations that occurred at key times during the year: during the liturgical celebrations such as Christmas, Easter, and Corpus Christi, and during the secular celebrations such as harvest time, and later during historical and political dates such as Mexico's Independence on September 16 and in February on George Washington's birthday. The resulting cultural mestizaje also included African American and other groups that found themselves in this part of northern Mexico and in this area of South Texas, in particular, during the nineteenth century, albeit to a smaller degree. According to Alwyn Barr, most of the African American population arrived with the U.S. military after 1849.

The history of the area is rife with violence. First was that of the Spanish as they clashed with the local indigenous groups, the effects of this genocide has not been fully studied. Later came the violence, which some say continues to this day in terms of the militarization of the border, that intensified as the Mexicano, or Tejano population, and the invading Anglo or northern forces, especially in the aftermath of the war ending with the Treaty of Guadalupe Hidalgo in 1848, arrived at an uneasy truce. The area becomes increasingly militarized and subject to all the activity and behavior common to areas where two nation-states meet. Evidence of the cultural tensions and of the violence inherent in a colonizer-colonized dichotomy exists in the ways that the fiestas coexist but remain as possible sites of resistance. In my analysis of the Matachines de la Santa Cruz, for example, I posit that the celebration is a folk religious performance functioning as resistance and affirmation to the hegemonic forces of both the United States and Mexico. But I go further into the analysis for my purposes here to show that the celebration is self-contained and identified within a specific site and for a particular group, and it functions to fulfill a need for the spiritual, faith-based belief system of the families whose legacy it is to dance matachines. Likewise, in my critical look at the GWBC, I find that the militarization and levels of celebration addresses a need in the community and a particular sector of the social structure of the city as it first becomes more anglicized and more recently displays the forces of power that govern the nation-state that the city is identified with by force since 1848.

## Los Matachines de la Santa Cruz de la Ladrillera[1]

Matachines dancing occurs all over South Texas and northern Mexico. In Laredo, the tradition goes back over 100 years, although it may have existed even earlier. I first experienced the fiesta de matachines as a child in northern Mexico. We were visiting my paternal grandparents in Anahuac, a small town in the state of Nuevo Leon, when, holding on to my older cousin's hand, at no more than five years of age, I first witnessed a matachines dance: the dancers gyrated and stomped to the beat of a lone drum that an older man beat rhythmically; the one thing I still remember is the fear. I was terrified that El Viejo, the dancer wearing a hideous and frightening mask, would single me out, as I saw he did other children, and poke me or force me to kiss the ugly doll he carried. I was also fascinated and curious. The brightly clad dancers' ghostly appearance in the yellow light of a few sparse light bulbs strung along the periphery, in front of the little church in Anahuac, elicited a deep sense of awe. I marveled at the way they danced and at the rhythmic sound of the drum and the sonajas they carried in their right hands. Throughout my childhood in Laredo too I encountered these dancers—but there was a twist, they danced to the music of the drum, accordion, and violin; they still carried the sonaja and also stomped and made a unique sound as the flattened bottlecaps strung on pieces of carrizo, or reed cane, along the naguilla or skirt swooshed with the intricate dance steps. In my childhood barrio, the matachines danced on the feast of the Holy Cross in May in front of Mother Cabrini Church. As a child, I would fall asleep on those spring nights with the sound of the Carrizo, the bottlecaps, the sonaja, the violin, the drum, and the accordion still playing in my head. It is no wonder then that after working on a dissertation on the pastorela, a traditional shepherds' play, often performed by the same matachin dancers, I would turn to the matachines as an object of study; they had after all haunted me for decades.

The Matachines de la Santa Cruz—a part of Folk Catholicism—exist in the United States as one of various folk religious dance traditions that includes the danza azteca, danza de concheros, and other "Indian" dances, or danzas de indios.[2] According to Brenda Romero, these dance traditions have existed in the Americas since about the fifteenth century. Various scholars have studied the tradition in New Mexico and generally defined it, as Sylvia Rodriguez does, as a religious folk dance with musical and dance elements of European and Indigenous cultures.

Because the matachines performances, as popular religious expressions, can be read as a text of resistance against the organized or formal church structures—and exist in contrast to organized sodalities or church-sponsored events—I ask a key question: how is the fiesta, the dance of the Matachines de la Santa Cruz, a text of resistance? Perhaps more importantly, why does the dance perdure in the faith belief system of the community so that they must dance year after year? While matachin groups exist in communities all over the Americas, as ethnomusicologist Brenda Romero has documented, little resemblance exists between the groups of the south and the groups of the north; the Laredo groups are most allied to the traditions of northern Mexico and south Texas. In Laredo, the group of about 50 families that gather every May 3 for the feast of the Holy Cross have their roots upriver in the area known as Las Minas, the mines; these coal mines have prospered there in the first half of the twentieth century and these families have danced there for over a century. Many of the workers in the mines came from the area in northern Mexico where the matachines tradition is steeped in the blend of Spanish and Coahuiltecan[3] rituals as it persists now—the area around Real de Catorce and down into Monclova. The Coahuiltecan type of matachin dancing, then, occurs in a wide geographical area that extends to the Gulf Coast on the east and into Arizona and New Mexico on the west (especially to communities of dancers in Guadalupe, Arizona or Tortugas, and New Mexico).[4] While in other communities the dance honors a patron saint, in Laredo, la fiesta, as the participants call it, consists of several days of dancing around the feast day of the Holy Cross, May 3. The dancers also celebrate December 12, the feast day of Our Lady of Guadalupe, and indeed matachin groups elsewhere in Greater Mexico and in Mexico also celebrate this feast day. The changes in the fiesta in the 30 years since I have been documenting and studying it are clearly tied to a cultural encroachment of U.S. popular culture. The most obvious changes have occurred in footwear (dancers would wear huaraches and now they wear tennis shoes or cowboy boots) and music (the music included guitar and violin and now it is just the accordion and the drum). But the materials used for constructing the traditional dress of the nagüilla, skirt, and the vest have also changed as have the dancers' beliefs about the devotion to the Holy Cross that resides in the "capillita" and which semiotically serves as a signifier for the faith and devotion of the people in the neighborhood. It is a loaded icon that stretches back to Christianity, for after all the cross is a strong Christian symbol, but as such it also exists in indigenous tradition, as the cross is "dressed" and functions as an icon of many referents. In the 1940s, women did not dance, but nowadays women too dance; indeed the majority of the dancers are female.

The changes in the tradition over time due to a number of factors signal the onslaught of hegemonic forces from both the United States and Mexico. Most recently, for example, due to homeland security policies the supply of cane reed, traditionally harvested from along the riverbank and used to decorate the nagüillas, has diminished due to defoliation of the area in an attempt to curb illegal drug trafficking. The area, being right on the border, is also a closely watched and monitored area. This policy has resulted in little access to the traditional carrizo or reed. Thus, many of the matachines substitute plastic drinking straws to decorate the nagüilla, stringing the jingle bell through it as they would traditionally string the six-inch lengths of carrizo. The consequences of immigration policies have had a detrimental effect on the tradition, whether the community realizes it or not. In fact, the dancers seem to be oblivious to the subtle changes wrought on the tradition over the past ten years or so, as the key tradition bearers, the Ortiz brothers, Pete and Florencio, have moved on and the political situation of the border has been shaping the emerging tradition. In addition to these factors, the tradition itself has been transformed, and yet it continues. The dancers include young participants, insuring its persistence, as the older siblings and parents teach the younger children the steps and inculcate the devotion to the Holy Cross. As most cultural practices, the matachines tradition continues to change even as it seeks continuity.

The matachines, a faith-based celebration outside of the auspices of the organized church hierarchy, becomes emblematic of how groups can defy existing structures of domination in a community, what Scott calls "hidden transcripts." The strong family-organized structure of the tradition and the fact that it has stayed on the same geographic space have insured the continued devotion of those who live in the area, descendants of the mestizo group that moved here from the mines area in the early part of the twentieth century. The miners and now the residents of the area hold diverse jobs in line with their educational achievement; one of the capitanes, for example, is a teacher, others work as stock clerks or cashiers at the local Sam's warehouse. So how do we explain the persistence of the fiesta outside of the formal domain of religious structures? The geopolitical border, as other liminal spaces, must allow the interplay of multiple and often conflicting cultural expressions, celebrations that often have a blatant colonizing agenda, such as the celebration of GWBC, or celebrations that reveal a subtle resistance to that same agenda, such as Kanto a la Tierra, a created pan-Indian celebration that was celebrated locally for about 20 years but has not been celebrated since 2006. I discuss the history of the GWBC and the Princess Pocahontas Pageant later in this chapter, and also discuss some of the specific ways that the matachines function as a resistance or as an oppositional narrative. For starters, both GWBC and the matachines exist outside of official celebrations: The GWBC, especially the Princess Pocahontas Pageant, outside any formal institutionalized celebration, and the matachines, outside of the Church liturgical calendar. While the feast of the Holy Cross with its origins in medieval Catholic Church folk tradition appears on the church calendar and is still celebrated in many locations in the Americas and in Spain (the Spanish village of Almagro, in La Mancha, for example, similarly celebrates with a procession and "dresses" a church that remains on display in the town square after the fiesta—but there is no dancing), the Day of the Holy Cross does not constitute an official liturgical feast day in the Church calendar. That is, it is not a Holy Day of obligation observed by the Church the way Easter or Christmas, or even the Feast of Corpus Christi are celebrated liturgically. Curiously enough, the processions for Corpus Christi, a continuing liturgical feast day, have all but disappeared in the Laredo area. Additionally, the group finds in the Holy Cross celebration a unifying and cohesive momentum that brings together the various sectors of the subcommunity that the barrio de la Ladrillera constitutes. An analysis of the various matachin groups elucidates a discernible power structure that, unlike the political and social power structure in the community, defies classification. Functioning as a loose collective, the group's allegiance to the fiesta, above and beyond allegiances to family or formal structures, reveals a protocol for performing a belief system that includes rituals of prayers of thanksgiving, a system of gifting, and informal kinship system akin to compadrazgo.[5] Some of the dance and music elements are no doubt remnants of an earlier tradition made up of various indigenous and Spanish festive elements. The elements of resistance embedded in the celebration encompass both religious and social scripts that perforce demand a resistance to the established church dogma in so far as the dancing happens outside of the church liturgical structure. It may be a stretch to liken the matachines as an act of resistance to the assimilationist project of the GWBC, but there are elements, such as the barrio-based communal and familial ties that bind the group, that could be interpreted as establishing solidarity against an assimilationist agenda. At times the church has been antagonistic to and at other times accommodating of the matachines dance rituals. In all instances, it is a folk Catholic tradition, and whether aligned with the official church calendar or not, it sustains the folk belief system that serves to fulfill a private and limited communal purpose that is purely faith-based and which provides the group a sense of identity and reveals a strong allegiance to the place and to the group.

While a religious celebration, albeit a folk Catholic one, the matachines still rests within religious ritual. The GWBC, on the other hand, a purely secular celebration, exists to fulfill a different and significant public purpose. The folk religious celebration of Los Matachines and the purely secular GWBC along with other fiestas, such as the semi-secular quinceañeras,[6] all function within the Laredo community on various levels and allow for the complex performance of class and ethnic identity, at times offering spaces for the performance of dissociative texts.

I now turn my attention to the GWBC and how it explodes many of the myths about the "sleepy border town" associated with Laredo; although the current focus on border violence have disturbed this myth somewhat, the area remains exoticized and othered by the media and by scholars who tend to see the border as a homogenous zone. This brief analysis seeks to present aspects of the celebration that can easily be framed within the sociopolitical secular celebration as constituting a hybrid colonizing practice that encompasses elements of a number of hegemonic traditions from Mexico and the United States and resists and accommodates a larger hegemonic force that is land-based on the border between these two governmental powers. In my analysis of the GWBC, we find that the border space where the celebration happens offers a complex system of kinship, governmental and familial power dynamics that may offer an explanation for the sustained repressive society that has reigned for over 100 years. The site of confluence and contradiction yields ample room for questioning of what the border offers in terms of significant information that helps in the theorizing project that scholars like Américo Paredes and Gloria Anzaldúa began in "With His Pistol in his Hand: A Border Hero" and *Borderlands/La Frontera*, respectively. Both scholars and others further developed border theory in subsequent articles and book projects. In terms of the GWBC, I ask a key question: how is the GWBC's Americanizing project faring in its attempt at assimilating the population? More importantly, why does the GWBC, and more specifically how does the Princess Pocahontas Council and the Pocahontas Pageant, sustain the GWBC and resist its assimilationist project? A brief history of the GWBC and the Princess Pocahontas will help elucidate the relevance and the contrapuntal nature of these in regard to the matachines.

## The Princess Pocahontas Council and Pageant

Princess Pocahontas has been part of the GWBC since its beginning in the late 1800s, when the daughter of one of the local ranchers would be selected to portray the character of Pocahontas, yet, the Princess Pocahontas Council did not officially take charge of this part of the GWBC until the early 1980s. Its principal charge is to select the young women who will participate in the Pocahontas Pageant presentation, including the one chosen to perform the title role of Pocahontas at the annual pageant and dramatization. The young woman, who must fulfill certain criteria, including outstanding horsemanship skills, leads the "Native American delegation" and receives the keys to the city during the International Parade. During a reenactment of the first mock battle of Indians attacking and finally living in peace with the Europeans, she and her "court" display their finery escorted by young men who also wear elaborately beaded costumes.[7] The celebration itself is an ostentatious display of wealth, or of the desire for wealth, by the upper middle classes. The true elites belong to the facetiously called "Marthas" members of the GWBCA Society. The Pocahontas Council members are playfully dubbed the "Pokies" by everyone. In both cases, the element of class is tantamount and only those who can afford the dress and to participate in the numerous social functions can participate. Nevertheless, the Pokies offer those who could never dream of participating at the level of the Marthas an opportunity to engage in the celebration in a significant fashion and in some ways resist, albeit while reinforcing it, the hegemonic narrative of colonization that is historically anachronistic and in many ways off-putting to the local population. While an extensive discussion of the GWBC is not in the purview of this brief essay, I must focus on some key points to draw out the contrast between this celebration and the matachines and establish a common link insofar as both are reflections of a sector of the community's inhabitants who are united and yet different.

### Performing What Has Been Suppressed

For a few years in the 1980s and even through the 1990s, a created spring festival was held in Laredo by a group of Chicanas/os and Native Americans. The Kanto a la Tierra was the brainchild of Raymundo "Tigre" Pérez, a high school classmate of mine who had moved back to Laredo and wanted to bring to the border a celebration to heal the borderlands, especially the land near the river. After serving in Vietnam, Tigre had joined the Chicano movement, especially those who sought to reclaim the indigenous identity that had all but disappeared from our cultural practices. He along with others, such as Luis Diaz de León and his family, an English professor at the local community college, Carlos Flores, and numerous others, created Kanto to remind us that Laredo and the border had been indigenous before the Spanish settled there in the mid eighteenth century. After Tigre died, the celebration went on for a few more years and was subsequently stopped. It remains one of the few attempts at Indianizing or reclaiming the indigenous practices of the region. Other traditions like conchero dancing still persist but on a smaller scale, and while the groups have ties to other such Chicano groups in San Antonio or Austin, it is sporadic and almost always aligned with a group outside of Laredo. On the other hand, the Princess Pocahontas celebration, a curious stylized celebration of indigeneity, has survived as part of the George Washington's Birthday festivities for over 100 years; and since the 1980s, the more formalized Princess Pocahontas Council and Pageant celebrates an imagined indigenous past for the community of Laredo. While the matachines reach back to a tradition whose roots are firmly established in a real indigenous past, the created or mimicked, to use Said's term, past of the Pokies points to a desire to recall an indigenous identity but also a desire to disassociate with that true indigenous past that may be too problematic insofar as it is too close to a real class and racial difference that the mestizo community is reluctant to claim. For instance, we can deduce that it is easier, or perhaps better, to imagine belonging to the Algonquin or Navajo nations from the United States than to the Coahuiltecan or Tlaxcaltecan from Mexico, especially since the organizers insist that the participants do research on the nations they represent.

Like the matachines, the Pokies perform a ritual, albeit as a performance and not a religious ritual. Unlike the matachines, the Pokies do not adhere to a faith-belief and instead perform the reenactment as a secular and perhaps a political ritual. The conciliatory gesture of offering Princess Pocahontas the key to the city functions as a normalizing event in the ritualized conflict that no doubt reflects the very real and violent conflict that occurred between the Spanish and the inhabitants of the area. Curiously, it is displaced and disidentified characters from the northeast, that is, Princess Pocahontas, who are involved instead of foundational mythic characters from Mexico. Yet, the purposes of the two in terms of unifying the community may function in similar ways. While a true indigeneity might be too much for this sector of Laredo society to admit, an imagined, fabricated, and distanced reality is more palatable.

## Pocahontas: Performing an Imagined Indigenous Identity

As far as the performance aspect of the GWBC goes, one can say that it is a true disidentification with the real life of the community. For one, going back to eighteenth-century northeastern culture to celebrate George Washington's birthday is anachronistic and disassociative, as anyone can note from the signifying elements of the celebration. Often the script is situated in imagined time and collapses various epochs of the era so that the script for the birthday party may include characters who came before or after Washington; or it may add elements that would be foreign to an eighteenth-century celebration in the northeast. Anachronism aside, the disassociative nature of many of the elements of the celebration, like the Jalapeño Fest with its Jalapeño-eating contest or the abrazo ceremony where the dignitaries of Mexico and the United States meet on the bridge between the two countries for a traditional abrazo [hug], signifying friendship and good will, can be interpreted as armature that sustains the impossible premise of an eighteenth-century celebration occurring in Laredo in such a fashion.

No doubt, in the 1700s the newly founded settlement of San Agustin de Laredo held celebrations around its liturgical feast days as well as secular feasts at harvest time. What was farthest from the newly founded community with its tiny church and a handful of families was the northeast and the British colonies with their revolution against England. What was immediate were the indigenous who peopled the area and who either resisted or assimilated the Spanish onslaught. This settlement of Laredo was one of many established with just one purpose: to make Spain's presence in the area visible and viable. To the north San Antonio and its five missions and to the south Monterrey with its obispado were already burgeoning locations with an imposing Spanish presence at the level of religious and military institutions and the Jewish converses that Carbajal brought to the area. But what must have been a violent and brutal battle to survive must have allowed for celebrations since the earliest days. Slightly over a hundred years since it was established and now under U.S. rule, Laredo began the annual celebration of George Washington's birthday, the celebration that survives to this day as an amalgam of U.S. and Mexican elements and includes one particular performance of what is ostensibly indigenous, the Princess Pocahontas pageant. Choosing the enigmatic indigenous female figure of Pocahontas versus the indigenous female and perhaps more known figure of Malinche (there's even a street named Malinche in Laredo), for example, underscores a contextual colonial condition that the GWBC epitomizes. Just like the early GWBC planners sought to "Americanize" the locals, almost 100 years later the Pocahontas Pageant planners sought to highlight and elevate the minor indigenous element in the celebration by instituting the mechanisms for a performance of indigeneity, but one that was palatable. After all, Malinche was the traitor, the betrayer, the concubine who putatively becomes the mother of all mestizos and mestizas. Could it be that the true indigenous reality of the local population, the Coahuiltecan tribal origins of many of them, was just too close to home? Not prestigious enough? Or maybe it was just convenient since the Pocahontas character was already inscribed into the GWBC events since the outset. Whatever the reason, the fact remains that Pocahontas is the indigenous representation chosen to be the focus of the celebration.

### Conclusions

In studying the cultural production of the area, I have often asked why certain practices survive. For example, the practice of protecting a baby from "mal de ojo" uses elements of both native and European traditions. Pinned on the child's clothing around her wrist you will find an "ojo de venado" (a seed that resembles a deer eye) and a bit of coral, often found in

Spain as an amulet of protection. The former is the native practice and the latter is European. The quinceañeras have changed with the times, but they are still an integral part of the community coming-of-age celebrations for young women. Thus it is with the celebrations of the matachines and the GWBC that indigenous and European elements function within the community's image of itself as having had indigenous and European origins and having assimilated both to such an extent that they celebrate both. Of course, the level of celebration is different and the basis for each is also quite distinct. For the matachines, it is a matter of faith and spirituality, for the GWBC, it is a matter of politics and money. But for both it is a matter of group identity.

As I draw this chapter to a close, I signal four main points: first, I contend that the indigenous past that has been erased or at least put in the background is gaining favor and is being recuperated, for it was never truly lost, only just transformed; the sense that the indigenous is at the root of the cultural production of the community has never truly died, it had just gone into the practices of the community that were not at the center of the colonizing project. Hence, even in the GWBC the Pocahontas aspect was kept at a minimum and functioned in a paradoxical fashion until the Pageant foregrounded the indigenous, and although the group sought the indigenous in all but the local roots, the desire is there. Similarly, the matachines celebration reminds the participants of their indigenous origins while it has remained ostracized, outside of the community's realm, and not a part of the larger group: knowledge of their existence has remained limited to the local priest and to the barrio where they dance. Second, the matachines and the princess Pocahontas are relics of an earlier time, but they function to cement the community's sense of self; the celebrations allow for the group to come together and for the individual to feel as part of the group. The matachines ingroup solidarity is such that it extends far beyond the geographical site to wherever members of the community have moved. A case in point is the celebrations in Sugarland and in Dallas, Texas, where matachin dancers from the group in Laredo have moved to and started their own dance groups.

A third conclusion revolves around the ways that the border collapses the hegemonic influences of both Mexico and the United States. In the matachines dance tradition, whether in Mexico or the United States, the dancers conform to a third space aesthetic and inhabit that third space at least during the fiesta as adherents to a faith belief that extends to the vows or promesas, the chief reason for the tradition's survival. The Pocahontas pageant recreates a nonexistent event, thus it is anaspatial as well as anachronistic.

The fact that it occurs in Laredo, Texas, along the U.S.–Mexico border further supports claims that the border is at once a cultural region, as scholars such as cultural geographer Daniel Arreola claims, and a place of confluence and contradictions, as Gloria Anzaldúa claimed: "the border es una herida abierta (is an open wound) where the third world grates against the first and bleeds" (25).

Finally, an analysis of these cultural expressions yields insight into the practices of the communities within the larger group of Laredo and present a model for analyzing other cultural manifestations at various levels from the local to the national and to the transnational. The matachines exist as a working-class barrio phenomenon and the Pocahontas pageant exists within the larger GWBC event at a community-wide level. Yet, they function, in hidden fashion, as resistance to the perceived and often very real onslaught of assimilationist forces. Any study of the cultural expressions of the border must consider how the border draws upon the cultural and national narratives of both nation-states, the United States and Mexico. The transnational movement of the fiesta de matachines stands as proof of the permeability of the border insofar as cultural expressions are concerned. In terms of the GWBC, it is the transnational aspects of the celebration that gauge how the border is indeed one despite the many barriers or walls that seek to separate the people and structures of the first- and third worlds that meet there.

In this brief analysis I am merely pointing to an examination of the cultural practices in this land and space where the indigenous has been all but erased. Because it is on the border, in a liminal third space, I find it useful to reference the work of Gloria Anzaldúa, who writes that "the border es una herida abierta where the third world grates against the first and bleeds" (ídem). The bleeding that has been constant since 1848 when this contested area of Mexico finally ceded to the United States remains and cries out for healing. The wounding occurred even earlier with the first incursions by Europeans to the area and the Spanish colonization project. The matachines and the GWBC Princess Pocahontas may be the ways that the community has learned to survive the bleeding. As the drug wars of this century intensify and as the area becomes increasingly militarized, the GWBC and the matachines must adapt to the conditions. For the GWBC Pocahontas, there is little impact, but for the matachines dancers, the impact is significant. This situation is evidence that the two are indeed worlds apart, and yet both share the link to the indigenous traditions of their forbears. As the traditional life along the border transforms itself according to the push and pull of hegemonic forces, these two will survive and accommodate the changes as they have for over a hundred years. It is my expectation that the next hundred years will bring transformations and change, but that both will continue to exist as long as the community's need for an identity distinct and apart from the larger mainstream forces exists.

## Notes

1. The group's name derives from the object of veneration, the Holy Cross, and the location in the Laredo, Texas neighborhood or barrio of La Ladrillera. More recently the group has dropped "de La Ladrillera" and retains "de la Santa Cruz," also the name of the local small chapel. While scholars have found various etymologies for the word "matachin" from the Spanish *matachin* and Italian *matto*, to the Arabic, *mutawajjihim*, and even the Nahuatl—*matlachin*, I believe that the way it is used in northern Mexico for the folk Catholic dance tradition it is more likely derived from the Spanish, since the character of the dancer as a matachin originates in the court dramas of Spain's Golden Age in the sixteenth century. See Rodríguez (1996), and Cantú (1995).
2. See Elisa Huerta's discussion of these various dance traditions and how they exist in Chicana/o communities.
3. Carrizo Indians belong to the Coahuiltecan people of northern Mexico. Among the myriad groups that the Spanish encountered were the Bobolo.
4. A fuller discussion on matachines can be found in Brenda Romero's article in *Dancing Across Borders* and in a number of works by Peter García and in my own work.
5. Compadrazgo is discussed in my article on quinceañeras in *Chicana Traditions*.
6. See my chapter in *Chicana Traditions: Continuity and Change* and Julia Alvarez's *Once Upon a Quinceañera* for a discussion of the tradition in Latino communities.
7. For a description and analysis of the celebration, see Green and Barrera.

# 5

# Transnational Narratives, Cultural Production, and Representations: Blurred Subjects in Juárez, México[1]

María Socorro Tabuenca Córdoba

This public struggle over the social identities of the victims [of femicide[2] in Juárez] and the meaning of their deaths raises broader issues of cultural representation and its role in our effort to construct a meaningful narrative.

–Rosalinda Fregoso (2003)

**Transnational Narratives**

In June 1993 Ciudad Juárez woke up to terrible news. Something inexplicable and unbelievable had happened: nine young female bodies[3] were found in the city's outskirts. All nine deaths were apparently perpetrated by an alleged serial killer. The most stunning part of the discovery at that time was that there was no indication in modern Mexico's crime history of any other act of similar nature and magnitude except for Goyo Cárdenas, a serial killer in the 1950s, "Las Poquianchis" in the 1960s in México City, and Adolfo de Jesús Constanzo and his followers called *"los narcosatánicos"* in Matamoros, Tamaulipas, at the end of the 1980s. The Juárez society was shocked with the findings. We have never felt so threatened with an act as such. Maybe because in our minds those types of criminals were far from us in some distant place in the United States or in other parts of Mexico, but never in our hometown, never so close to our border.

By 1999, femicide in Juárez transcended local and national news and became a global phenomenon due to its international exposure, mainly because of the failure of the state to provide murdered women—and their families—rights and justice, and by promoting reprisals to different groups claiming the rights and justice they lacked in Mexico, "Access to international exposure, funding and expertise has expanded the spaces of opposition for members of the grassroots protest movement. International ties currently represent the most crucial source of support for women's incipient claims to group autonomy apart from the nation-state" (Schmidt Camacho 260).

During the first years of the murders, journalists, filmmakers, academics, and writers examined the relationship of the impacts of the maquiladora industry and the sexual killings of Juárez women. Scholars such as Alicia Camacho Schmidt (2006), Rosalinda Fregoso (2003), Alicia Gaspar de Alba (2003), and Melissa W. Wright (2006), amongst others, have concurred that for transnational companies these women are disposable objects/subjects who can be exploited and replaced, without the companies having any involvement or scruples if their workers are kidnapped, raped, tortured, and killed. "[T]he managerial discourses of non-involvement in the serial murders of young female employees are indeed linked to the materialization of turnover as a culturally driven and waste-ridden phenomenon attached to Mexican femininity" (Wright 74). These disposable women can also be interpreted as "blurred subjects" (Sassen 2003, "Citizenship Destabilized"), given that a blurred subject is a "citizen who is authorized yet unrecognized due to discrimination and racialization" (6). As a result, Mexican border women, murdered women, poor women, dark women,—women who are kidnapped, tortured, mutilated, raped, or who disappear and are disposable—have become blurred subjects. Subsequently, it is not important if these women are recognized and authorized as citizens because the institutions in charge of that recognition and authorization are the same that have been unsuccessful in providing them the basis of citizenship: "access to goods and services, justice, security, and political representation" (Schmidt Camacho, 260).

The state and hegemonic groups in Mexico have devoted their efforts to stereotype and stigmatize murdered women. In addition, media accounts of the killings, documentaries, films, plays, and so on have helped in the construction of the slaughtered victims as maquiladora workers. But as Monárrez (2002) has mentioned: "the use of stereotypes makes society disregard the required seriousness and importance of male violence against women" (88–89). In other words, focusing on depicting the victims of femicide as purely maquiladora workers allows the erasure of other women who have also been brutalized and murdered. In this sense,

Monárrez and I have concurred that we also need to study the problem from within our own transnational patriarchal culture. Not only do we need to analyze why such crimes are committed but also why the state has assumed a position as an accomplice by not solving the crimes, avoiding its responsibility, and diminishing the problem.[4] Fregoso's words shed light on our question: "Femicide in Juárez makes evident the reality of overlapping power relations on gendered and racialized bodies as much as it clarifies the degree to which violence against women has been naturalized as a method of social control" (2). Schmidt Camacho's ideas also complement our argument: "central to current contests over the governance and governability of the border region is the problem of how neoliberal policy permitted (or necessitated) the conversion of poor migrants into a population with little purchase on rights or representation within the nation-state or new global polities" (258).

This article examines transnational narratives as a core reflection on the femicides in Juárez, since nearly one-third of the murdered women were maquiladora workers. The maquiladora industry is a fundamental expression of transnational economy, and femicide in Juárez is related to questions of transnational migration, drug, and human trade, theories of snuff videos, organ trafficking, and transborder serial killer(s). I examine how femicide in Juárez has been depicted in U.S. films, like *The Virgin of Juárez* (2005), *Bordertown* (2006), and *Juárez: Stages of Fear* (2005), because transnational cultural productions and representations represent global capital. Because they reach broader audiences, I am concerned about how fiction and reality get intertwined and the types of narratives constructed regarding the victims, their families, the Mexican authorities, the perpetrators, and the city as a transnational space.

## Cultural Productions

The international exposure of the femicide in Juárez led to different types of manifestations. Perhaps the most notorious has been the V-Day Demonstration in Ciudad Juárez on February 14, 2003. There were 7500 people from 20 countries on that particular day, and amongst the victims' families and Mexican NGOs' representatives there were also Eve Ensler, Congresswomen Jan Schakowsky (IL) and Hilda Solis (CA), actors Jane Fonda, Sally Field, and Christine Lahti, Lifetime Television CEO Carole Black, PBS CEO Pat Mitchell, and Lifetime EVP of Public Affairs Meredith Wagner. The purpose of the demonstration was to raise awareness regarding the crimes and to end the violence against women. However, in Mexican patriarchal society it seems that women's voices, no matter how high in the social, racial, economic, or international hierarchy, are not enough to end this femicide, because the crimes continue.

Another important manifestation to Juárez's femicide has been the artistic/cultural response. There have been groups of artists from the United States, Spain, the Netherlands, England, and Germany—amongst other countries—who are committed to spreading the word on what has happened in Juárez. People have mobilized due to the lack of interest and responses from the federal, state, and municipal administrations in preventing and solving the crimes. These efforts have brought worldwide attention and the UN Human Rights Commission has offered several recommendations to the Mexican government. Yet, in order to achieve justice for the murdered women, more aggressive actions are needed; an example of this is the law suit against the Mexican State by three victims' families at the Human Rights Inter American Court.[5]

Aside from the films studied, there are some video-documentaries such as: *Performing the Border* (1999), *Maquila: A Tale of Two Mexicos* (2000), *Señorita Extraviada. Missing Young Woman* (2001), *On the Edge* (2004), and *Border Echoes-Ecos de unaFrontera* (2006). Internet access, like YouTube, has allowed authors to show their work electronically. Various titles available on the site include: *City of Dead Girls, From Pomona to Juárez, The City of Dead Women, Juárez: Unsettled Dust, Women of Juárez, Amnesty International-Mujeres de Juárez, Ciudad Juárez, Mexico, The Big Borderland*, and *420 Women Killed in Juárez*.

There are also various publications on the matter, such as academic and newspaper articles and essays, academic books, testimonials, novels, poetry, and plays.[6] The most famous piece is the one incorporated in Eve Ensler's Vagina Monologues. Other artistic manifestations include the collective Binational Art Exhibit Mujeres de Juárez: Art against Crime, promoted by the group VIEJASKANDALOSAS at the Nevada State Museum in 2004; the group exhibit Lines of Sight: Views of the U.S.-Mexican Border presented at UC Riverside in 2002; and the exhibit by Lise Bjørne Linnert: Frontera 450+, at the Station Museum of Contemporary Art in Houston, in 2006.

The works mentioned are only a fraction of the production created in the United States, and as I stated, there are many artists in other countries who have devoted their work to this cause.[7] However, as a border dweller, as an inhabitant of the Juárez-El Paso area, I have noticed, in numerous works I have examined, that in most cases they portray the cultural binary that has characterized U.S. hegemonic culture when referring to the U.S.-Mexico border. The director, producer, screenwriter, playwright, journalist, or writer develop only one or two hypothesis of the crimes and only one possible victim: the maquiladora worker. They also present the main character—an American male or female-journalist, scholar, or detective—as the sole person truly committed to solving the crimes. In many of them, local efforts are obliterated from their stories and the city is depicted as an inhospitable place.[8] Most of their reflections evolve on the concept of police corruption and the connections between a sole policeman, the maquila managers, or other members of the police force. In some instances it is the American journalist, scholar, or detective who discovers one or more of the criminals, sometimes helped by one or two locals. But in a transnational reflection one has to be aware that binary oppositions are deployed by power, hegemony, inter-intra ethnic and patriarchal ideologies, and can eventually cause cultural damage.

## Cultural Representations

Since the beginning of silent cinema, the U.S.-Mexico border has been a topic of numerous films. In Garcia Riera's chapter, "*una cantina fronteriza*" or a "border saloon" (13) is the site of the U.S. film *The Fight of Freedom: A Story of the Arid Southwest*. For Leobardo Sarabia "[i]n this genre, border cities are [...] spaces of vice and moral collapse. Tijuana and Ciudad Juárez, the main cities—real or simulated—are, by a sort of identity symbiosis, the only image of the border: that is to say, the scenarios of licentiousness and permissiveness, a world of delinquency and easy business" (in Iglesias I, 12; my translation). Adding to Sarabia's sites, the Arizona desert, the Texas Valley, and the area from Reynosa to Matamoros are the places where the Almada brothers[9] fight fiercely as drug dealers, coyotes, gamblers, or smugglers. In both the U.S. and Mexican cultural imaginary, the border is a no-man's-land and its inhabitants are prostitutes, pimps, exotic dancers, coyotes, drug lords, smugglers, gamblers, and, lately, killers of women and hired assassins.

Unfortunately, as mentioned above, femicide in Juárez is a devastating reality that in the United States has drawn the attention of filmmakers (such as Dobson, Alejandro, and Nava) who have devoted their efforts to produce feature films on the topic. Consequently, Juárez's femicides are inserted within a transnational market, responding to an international community whose cultural imaginary is already influenced by U.S. hegemonic discourse. Nonetheless, there are certain facts depicted in these films regarding transnational corporations, of which the U.S. general audience (common people) is not aware. Those representations are an eye-opener regarding the colonization practices of these corporations in Third World countries. All three directors present different perspectives on the topic but all concur that the slaughtered women are maquiladora workers, that the police is either involved in the killings or is not professional enough to solve or prevent them, and finally that the women's massacre will continue, and it still persists.

*The Virgin of Juárez* narrates the story of Karina Danes (Minnie Driver), a Los Angeles-based reporter, and Mariela (Ana Claudia Talancón), a survivor of a vicious attack. Karina goes to Juárez during the V-Day demonstration and continues investigating the murders. She meets Father Herrera (Esaí Morales), a priest who is following the cases, activist Patrick Nunzio, from the Workers' Rights, Norman Unger, the PR for a consortium of U.S. factories, the prosecutor for the Crimes against Women, detective Gabriel Lauro, Mariela the survivor, and Isidro,[10] a janitor from the hospital where Mariela was taken after the attack. During the first twenty minutes the film follows the "true events" on which the film supposedly based its story. However, after Mariela survives the attack, she starts having visions of the Virgin Mary and begins experiencing the phenomenon of stigmata, all of which results in demerits to the actual events, the victims, and, finally, the film. Mariela is taken to Los Angeles where she is under the custody of a dangerous gang. In L.A. she continues to deliver sermons through a radio station, and her speeches encourage people to take action. By the end of the film, she discovers, confronts, and forgives her perpetrator while visualizing and remembering her attack. He is killed by a gang member and the gang members are killed by the police. Mariela enters a room on fire while Karina tries to save her, but it looks as if she dies in a blast.

The film begins projecting newspaper clippings reporting the Juárez murders and also scenes from the V-Day demonstration while narrating the events: "Since 1993 murder has claimed the lives of over 300 women. Scores of other women are missing; their fates unknown. Over and over without end, girls go missing and other girls are found murdered, raped, mutilated, dumped; bodies discarded in the desert like refuse." In that scene we can observe the transnational activism that Fregoso examines (20–24).

*The Virgin of Juárez* points out the idea that the maquiladora industry is responsible for the crimes. According to activist Patrick Nunzio, if you "step across the border the laws that govern us no longer apply. It is time that the companies that profit from these conditions are held to account for perpetuating them." The film illustrates both faces of the maquila industry through Nunzio's discourse and through Norman Unger, the PR representative, who argues that the maquiladora industry provides housing, transportation, and other benefits to its workers who go to Juárez (and other border cities) to "benefit from the economy they come for and they find a better life." Evidently, that is the life Mariela is searching for.

However, the benefits the industry provides are inappropriate, because one of the perpetrators is a bus driver from the corporations.[11]

While conducting her investigation, Karina meets detective Lauro and the Special Prosecutor for Crimes against Women. Different to other films I have studied, where policemen are either implicated or careless about the crimes, this film gives the police the benefit of the doubt. When questioned by Karina about the murders that have not been solved, the prosecutor avoids full responsibility by stating, "We are a small police force with a massive task. We are not the FBI." These were the kinds of responses the real authorities gave during the first years of the killings, and later they become more cynical, as we will see in *Bordertown* and *Juárez: Stages of fear.*

The depiction of the other is also worthy of note in this film regarding Juárez as an urban space, the police, the conspiracy theories, the transnational relations, and the colonizer[12] who believes he is the only person concerned with solving the problem. All of these issues are treated in detective Lauro's discourse:

> Do you think that because you are here everything will stop? There were a couple of men selling alcohol, tobacco, hookers and now, now is hundreds of millions of dollars in drugs and human trade. Machine guns, airplanes, and the drugs fuck everybody up. But the American dollars keep pouring in. So if there wasn't a demand for cheap Mexican labor and drugs, maybe Juárez would not be a playground for killers; supply and demand.

Historical coherence is established as Lauro traces the events in Juárez and finds U.S. capitalistic society responsible for the damage caused not only regarding industrial growth but also concerning drug and human traffic. The empire uses different strategies to achieve control without suffering any political damage. In this case, subaltern states are the ones that bear the consequences. The significant aspect is that a policeman who, in the eyes of the audience, is not trustworthy posits this. Nonetheless, complicity is established between Lauro (the good cop) and Karina (the journalist).

It is revealed that Karina's interest in the story of the Juárez murders is related to other transnational phenomena of supply and demand she was covering: human sex trade. Karina was informed about a ship container full of young Chinese women but she fails to inform the police on time because she wanted to wait until she had the news crew and the police together, and as the latter arrived late, 36 women die. She felt guilty but was not held responsible, because her reporting was interesting and finding the culprit will ameliorate her guilt. Again, the language and the story of the colonizer were worth more than 36 poor racialized subjects. Karina also investigates sex trade in Los Angeles and she brings up a brothel that was discovered there "full of young girls from Juárez." These actions reflect "[t]he informal economies of human smuggling, drug traffic, and pornography service and expand the formal economies in Mexican women's labor in the United States" (Schmidt Camacho, 279).

After recovering from the attack, Mariela is able to cross the border. Yet, in her case, the idea of migrating is what makes her a "hybrid subject" and not the migration itself (Sassen 2003, "The Reposition of Citizenship"). Before leaving her home she begins to study English in order to be ready for her "new life" in the States. Thus the language of the hegemonic country is depicted in this film as a means for ascending socially. Mariela suffers a transformation when she crosses the border: prior to her attack she is portrayed as being a shy, "decent" dressed, rural woman from a low-income family. In the United States she becomes outspoken; she is then a transnational migrant who has exchanged her sweater and dress for a tank top and tight jeans. She is also fair skinned and has green eyes. It seems that by crossing several borders from rural to urban spaces, from death to life, from dark to white, from Mexico to the United States, she has become autonomous. Nevertheless, she is not able achieve full autonomy because Mexican and Chicano patriarchy are overwhelming: she is protected first by father Herrera, later by Isidro the janitor, and at the end by the Chicano gang.

While Karina claims that the women of Juárez have no spokesperson, Mariela is granted a voice that reaches audiences from L.A. to Juárez, but her message is misinterpreted. In Juárez she was experiencing the phenomenon of stigmata, and poor people there believed she was some sort of a saint. During her sermons she demands peace, love, and justice, but images of crimes and vengeance are in the background. Here, language, religious fanaticism, and race get connected, resulting in lawless acts against possibly innocent people. Therefore, Juárez is portrayed as an inhospitable city not only because of the murders but also because of the common people who live there. Juarenses—mostly poor people—are portrayed as having dark skin and being uncivilized, lawless, fanatics who are driven to commit vengeful acts against those who are suspects of the murders, regardless of the verdicts.[13] Juarenses follow the "an eye for an eye" rule in the Old Testament, even though Mariela is delivering a message of love and understanding, as Jesus Christ did in the New Testament. Due to the killings perpetrated by her "followers" in Juárez, the authorities on both sides of the border persecute Mariela.

Dobson's depiction of Juárez is mainly through its inhabitants, and even "good people" there cannot be trusted because they are capable of being driven by their passion due to religious radicalism. The director also indicates the hypocrisy of society through Patrick Nunzio's persona. Throughout the film, Nunzio blames the maquiladora industry for not respecting Mexico's rules and regulations and he fights for the workers' right to better salaries and working conditions. Yet, he is presented as Mariela's perpetrator. Even when it is not clear whether or not he raped Mariela, his physical and psychological violence against her is evident. In Nunzio's case, the figure of the white male, aside from being a metaphor of his power over blurred subjects, also reflects the immorality of Anglos when they are in a lawless city as Juárez. He is presented as a human rights advocate and a perpetrator who attempts to kill Mariela. However, when he goes back to the United States he is punished and killed after confessing his crime and asking for forgiveness, as if this could not be accomplished in Mexico.

*The Virgin of Juárez*'s ending is ambiguous regarding Mariela's life; her apparent sacrifice as she enters a room in flames can be interpreted as if she is healed by the fire[14] or as if she takes advantage of the blast to escape the police. Both readings concur with Karina's last words when talking to Lauro on the phone: "It's over...*ella está viva*...*ella está viva.*" Mariela's "being alive" means that she actually escaped from the flames or that her message of peace, love, and justice will be achieved sometime. In spite of this apparent hopeful ending, Karina's last words are contested by the final scene: it shows a young woman arriving in Juárez, the same way Mariela did. There is also a closing written message on the screen: "There are hundreds of missing women unaccounted for in Juárez. They continued to be abducted, brutalized, and murdered."[15] Consequently, the message sent by the film is that the crimes will continue and little hope is left for the city of slaughtered women.

Regrettably *The Virgin of Juárez* depicts a hegemonic discourse in which events and people are distorted. By exaggerating and twisting Mariela's story into a religious parody and transforming her from "brown" to "white," the film loses credibility and power. The message Dobson tries to get across by constructing Juárez as the eerie space where transnational realities are produced by U.S. colonialism is diminished by his representation of national cultural and religious beliefs. However, the concluding remarks of the film represent one of the most distressing realities for the people of Juárez and others around the world who care about these women and their families.

The construction of Juárez as the uncanny place[16] where transnational realities are produced by U.S. colonialism is extensively developed in *Bordertown*. Gregory Nava delves on the concept that NAFTA has caused tremendous damage to Mexico, but specifically to poor, racialized women in Juárez due to the exploitation and discrimination they suffer inside and outside the factories. This is the most famous film on the topic (it features Jennifer López and Antonio Banderas), but it was not widely distributed in either country because, according to the director,[17] it holds both the U.S. and Mexican governments with their Free Trade policies responsible for the crimes.

Similar to the beginning of *The Virgin of Juárez*, where Karina the journalist narrates the events, *Bordertown* presents the situation in writing in order to capture the audience's attention. This narrative refers to NAFTA, the advantages of cheap labor, no tariffs, the number of maquilas in Juárez, and statistics about production in the maquiladoras. It also explains, as Melissa Wright has done (86), that young women are hired because they are more docile and willing to work more hours for less money. And it concludes stating: "Most maquiladoras operate 24 hours a day. Many women are attacked while traveling to and from work in the late night or early morning. The companies provide no security for the workers. The following is inspired by true events." As observed in *The Virgin of Juárez*, where there is a reporter who goes to investigate the murders of women in Juárez, in *Bordertown* Lauren Adrian (Jennifer López) is an ambitious newspaper reporter who was sent to Juárez by George Morgan (Martin Sheen), her editor, to investigate what has happened to these women and how the police and authorities have been covering up the atrocious rapes and murders. Lauren looks for Alfonso Díaz (Antonio Banderas), her former collaborator who is running the local paper *El Sol de Juárez*.

Díaz is reluctant to help her since he knows that she is in Juárez not because of the murdered women but because of her ambition to have an exclusive story. In the process of negotiating, they come across one of the hottest stories when they stumble on the only identified survivor (Maya Zapata) of a brutal attack. Eva, the victim, seeks Diaz's protection because she knows he is an honest journalist, truly interested in the cases, but Lauren intervenes by promising to help her find her attacker. While working on the investigation, she discovers that the perpetrator is a very powerful man who uses a maquila bus driver as his accomplice. She tells Díaz and convinces Eva to testify, but after a series of ordeals Díaz is killed in a drive-by shooting, Eva testifies and Lauren returns to Juárez to become the editor of *El Sol de Juárez* after the *Chicago Sentinel* refuses to publish her story.

*Bordertown* elaborates on a number of topics already studied in *The Virgin of Juárez* and in other films not included in this chapter.[18] These topics are: the victims being poor and racialized subjects, the maquiladora management as an accomplice with the police, the bus drivers' involvement in the murders, the U.S. reporter/detective in charge of their own investigations due to corrupt Mexican authorities, the death of the criminal by the victim's friend or by the victim herself, the serial killer being a psycho, and the police solving the crimes.

However, Nava's film presents the larger scale of transnationalism involved in the crimes because in *Bordertown* the cover-up of the murders comes from U.S. senators, the head of the syndicate operations of the *Chicago Sentinel* where Lauren works, and even from George Morgan, the editor who, according to Lauren, had never before put corporate responsibility above the truth, until up to that moment when she unveiled Eva's story. The film exposes hegemonic power relations in Mexico and the United States and their work in at a global scale. We observe these relations—aside from the politicians and the union leaders—through Marco Salamanca (Juan Diego Botton) and Aris Rodríguez (René Rivera), two wealthy men whom Diana Washington calls "los juniors," slang for children of wealthy families (3). Aris happens to be Eva's, and later Lauren's, perpetrator, and Marco is Aris' close friend who becomes Lauren's lover.

"Aris Rodríguez [belongs to a] family [who] is involved with NAFTA factories, a very old [juarense] family too" (*Bordertown*). Therefore, the juniors are protected by both countries' authorities, as we see in Marco Salamanca's argument when Lauren confronts him when she discovers that Aris is the perpetrator and that Marco knew it all along: "Who am I going to tell? The people I could tell they already know. They know more than me. Besides if they arrest Aris nothing will change." In the same conversation Diego Salamanca concludes that industrial growth and political power go together: "there are two sets of laws in any country: the laws for people with money and influence and the laws for everybody else. And don't think that is different in the United States, because I buy politicians on both sides of the border all the time. What do you think built this?" (pointing to the factory they're in). But even when Lauren replies, "I wish people like you didn't exist," and Marco seems embarrassed, the reality is that we live in a globalized world where, as Marco said, the colonizer's laws are the ones that prevail. In this film, as we can see, the construction of whiteness is similar to the one we saw in *The Virgin of Juárez*, but here the treatment of the problem is more open and presents a direct critique to both hypocritical governments.

In *The Virgin of Juárez* we saw a transformation in Mariela, the victim; but in *Bordertown* the transformation is in Lauren the journalist. At first we observe an ambitious reporter who goes to Juárez with the idea of being a foreign correspondent, but as she encounters Eva, the police corruption, the difficulties Díaz faces to keep his alternative newspaper alive, and, most important, when she gets in touch with her past and acknowledges her diasporic self, she "becomes more human," as George, her editor, comments. For many years Lauren has rejected her Mexican roots. Still, Eva's tribulations and her own as a child,[19] as well as her disappointment with the *Chicago Sentinel* and the politics involved with her story, Diaz's assassination, and the maquilas' corruption are what make her return to Juárez. It is her circular migration, her return to the motherland, that makes her settle in Juárez (of all possible places).

Migration, transborder commute, and multiple identities and nationalities are also part of the border life and citizenship in a transnational city (Sassen 2003, "Citizenship Destabilized"). In *Bordertown* we observe these elements in characters such as Eva and her family, or in Marco Salamanca, who confesses to being a "gringo," born in the States, raised in Mexico, and educated in the States, a very common phenomenon in U.S.-Mexico border cities. There are, of course, the protagonists Alfonso Díaz, who has worked in the United States and is back in Mexico, and Lauren herself who after a long stay in the United States is back in her native country.[20] Regarding those elements and Sasen's definition of a transnational city, we can also include the cast that includes actors from the Americas and Spain.

Ethnicity tied to migration and blurred subjectivities are other issues *Bordertown* deals with. "The dead women frequently have been displaced migrants from central and southern Mexico and potential transnational migrants" (Schmidt Camacho 275). In this film Eva has migrated from Oaxaca because her family has lost their land to the government. In the process of migration she has learned not only to master Spanish, as a means of survival in a nation-state that has imposed Spanish as a "national language," but also English, in order to survive in the borderlands, because, as her mother says, they "work in El Paso."

An interesting issue that is developed in the film is the way Mexicans perceive indigenous culture. When Eva claims she was attacked by the driver and by *"el Diablo"* (the Devil), Teresa Casillas (Sonia Braga), a wealthy woman from Juárez, and Díaz dismiss the story of the Devil (Aris). Teresa insists that her second perpetrator does not exist. She mentions that the psychologist who is treating Eva is convinced that she believes it to be true because of her indigenous culture. They explain that natives sometimes have trouble distinguishing reality and fantasy. Consequently, every time Eva sees Aris or feels his presence, Teresa dismisses it. Díaz associates the story of *el Diablo* with an urban legend. He says that people insists that the killer sometimes "appears as the Devil, [some] nights he is a dandy... he appears, kills the women and takes them to hell."[21] The only one who believes Eva's complete story is Lauren, who has created a female bond with her.

In *Bordertown* the policemen are depicted as elusive, arrogant, and vicious. During the first scenes we can observe them confiscating an issue of Diaz's newspaper because he was publishing "the truth" about the cases. When Lauren confronts the District Attorney about a recent femicide, he answers that the mastermind is in prison and that his name is Al-Awar; when questioned about other murders, he responds that most of them are due to domestic violence.[22] The inspector and his assistant are looking for Eva mostly to silence her because, as Teresa suggests, Eva is in more danger with the police. In the film it is unclear if the police killed Diaz or if it was a group of hired assassins.[23] What is very clear is that the police will not investigate the case. Their mission is to keep the phenomenon of femicide in Juárez silent because, as mentioned before, the political forces are pushing for obliterating the truth—whatever it might involve and whatever the cost.

*Bordertown* differs from *The Virgin of Juárez* concerning the blurred subjects' agency. In Mariela's case, she vanishes before being questioned by Mexican and American police and before her message of love reaches the people. Yet, in *Bordertown* Eva is successful in her attempt for justice. From the beginning of the film she has the idea of finding the men who attacked her and with Lauren's support she succeeds. The police capture the bus driver (Aris' accomplice) and he is under arrest awaiting Eva's deposition. Aris dies in a fire trying to kill Lauren. After these events Eva is ready to testify. When she arrives at the DA's office a crowd is waiting to give her support. In this sense Eva achieves a degree of citizenship and agency that was missing at the beginning of the film. Although justice is achieved in her case, Lauren denounces publicly the impunity regarding the murders.

A topic that remains connected to impunity in *Bordertown* is the approval in the U.S. Congress of CAFTA (Central America Free Trade Agreement), and the lack of provisions protecting the workers. There is also the connection between politics and trade, police and hegemony. *Bordertown* raises awareness regarding the femicides in Juárez. However, the voice that prevails is not a voice from within the community. It is the voice of the other, a hegemonic other. *Bordertown* gives Eva the opportunity to testify, but only because Lauren was there to support and protect her. It is difficult to distinguish in the film which story is more important: Lauren's or Eva's. Juárez dwellers are erased from the scene and Díaz also mediates Eva's mother's voice. Not even Teresa is able to fully understand Eva and take her to the police; she has to trust Lauren and Díaz. It took a Mexican American reporter to go to Juárez and "do the job," as if the Juarense activists were passive and needed an outsider to arrive in the city to solve the problem, and as if we were not doing anything or have not done enough.

As mentioned before, Juárez as an urban space is depicted as a place where "even the Devil is afraid of living" (Bowden 44). The city is deterritorialized since it portrays a landscape that is not its own.[24] It is divested of its own geography and peoples and it is depicted as dirty, poor, and underdeveloped; even if it has wealthy residences and a few restaurants, the image that prevails is that of a poor, inhospitable city. One can understand that the director wanted to make a point between the topic of the picture, the message it wants to carry out, and the scenery; however, I believe there is a problem of representation. Yes, it is true that "[sic] high order criminals also operate in the city and they appear to have a free rein [but] Juárez is not a dusty border town. It is Mexico's largest border city with nearly two million souls and about 300 assembly plants, almost all of them owned by fortune 500 companies. People work and carry out their normal activities of life" (Washington-Valdez 3).

The problems of representation in *Bordertown* and *The Virgin of Juárez* are that they follow one genre and one story (detective/thriller/drama) and give the message that transnational markets allow illegal activities such as organ and human trafficking, sex trade, influence trade, free trade, and a criminal Mexican police, all of which allow the continuation of femicides. The films devote their time to focus on one character and one issue: detective/reporter investigates, finds a lead, and solves the problem. Their narrative, because of the genre, presents only one side of the story, and, unfortunately, the result is that of one hegemonic voice and not a polyphonic one.

I consider *Juárez: Stages of Fear* (2005) a more complex film that captures the problem thoroughly and manages to problematize the current situation. Although Alejandro, the director, uses the image of a maquiladora worker as the murdered women, as the other films do, he also deals with another category: the sex worker. It presents three important problems in Mexico and particularly in Juárez: the femicide, express kidnappings,[25] and police corruption. As a result the narrative is not linear and has various stories, and for each story there is a different voice, or silence. It also presents several written texts regarding these topics, and they are intertwined with each other.

The film starts by giving dictionary definitions of "boundary, fear, frontier, kidnap, murder, rape, neglect, stages of grief, and stages of fear," and after one reads the definitions it is implicit that the author himself has been kidnapped. Contrary to *Bordertown* and *The Virgin of Juárez*, *Juárez: Stages of Fear* never mentions that it is "based on true events," yet it is easy to infer this because most written texts deal with statistics and relevant information regarding the femicides and kidnappings. Among all the information it also includes the idea that "[a]ccording to the FBI profiling unit, a serial killer (most likely American) is responsible for at least one-third of the victims.[26] But due to excessive violence in the area, some other predators (kidnappers and drug lords) have turned into copycats." This information suggest the collaboration between Mexican and American police forces, as well as the possibility of a transborder murder, which agrees with Alicia Gaspar de Alba's findings regarding half-way homes for sexual predators in El Paso, three blocks away from the El Paso del Norte International Bridge (2001).

*Juárez: Stages of Fear* introduces another idea of colonization, not only by economic means (as the other films deal with regarding maquiladora industries) but also by cultural means: by sexual serial killing.[27] The film examines police corruption, and this matter has been well documented by human rights organizations; they have found "a pattern of police manipulation of crime scenes, intimidation of witnesses, and use of torture to procure confessions (...) in these circumstances it is easy to believe that the police are either perpetrators or complicit in the crimes..." (Schmidt Camacho 268). Different from the way *The Virgin of Juárez* presents the police, embodied in Lauro, a helpful and committed detective, or in *Bordertown*, which characterizes the police as neglectful and arrogant, here we observe a truly vicious top member of the federal police—Chuck (César Alejandro), who is the head of the kidnappers' gang. The cops delude and use sex workers as baits to kidnap American businessmen, and after they get their prey, Chuck and his gang rape the prostitutes, kill them, and dispose of them. As for the kidnapped men—John (Chris Penn) and Raúl (José Solano)—they are subjected to physical and psychological violence before being set free.

Parallel to the story of the sex workers' murders[28] and the sequence of kidnappings, there is the story of a single serial killer who follows and kills a prostitute first and later a maquiladora worker. The significant issue on the representation of the victim is the absence of explicit violence in these scenes. Alejandro is very cautious about not including any visual effects regarding the violence inflicted on the women. In the scenes of the single sexual killer (we never see his face, only his car with Texas plates, and a UTEP parking permit), he is in his car, he invites the women to get in the car; they chat with him, and we only hear a moan and a car door closing. That's the sign we identify that the woman has been slain. However, in the case of the sex workers' killings, when the women are raped and murdered, everything happens behind closed doors, which creates more anxiety and impotence on the kidnapped, as well as on the audience.

Throughout the film the viewer is also subjected to several stages of fear due to the implied violence inflicted on the women and the psychological and physical violence imposed on the men. The message of these problems is delivered differently than in *Bordertown* and *The Virgin of Juárez*, where both reporters were pushing their editors for their stories to be told. Here the director narrates the stories by placing the audience in the characters' shoes and, as such, we feel as threatened as John does, for example, when he thinks "this is something I read in the papers, something that happens to somebody else."[29] Thus, we are warned that what we are looking at is something real that can really happen to us. It is not something that occurs only in a distant place but can occur very close to home.

Significantly, the director manages to complicate the stories and achieves a different type of cultural representation by avoiding simple binaries. Therefore, not all colonizer subjects are white and not all victims are dark and Mexican. Not all the killers are men and Mexican, even though the majority are; not all police officers are corrupt, and not all are Mexican—Chuck has a contact in the FBI—and not all Anglo businessmen are honest or evil. John's thoughts are a good example of this: "I am the only one responsible. We think that Mexico is a toilet. We do things here we wouldn't do at home, and we expect to be treated like gentleman. I want to pay the price." His words go beyond a binary opposition, and by assuming his responsibility John begins to disarticulate the hegemonic discourse of otherness.

We see the same reaction in Raúl (kidnap victim) when he is willing to cross again into Juárez and denounce Chuck to an honest state police officer, knowing that he can be killed, and ultimately he is. But he overcomes his fear because he is willing to stop the femicides, as well as the kidnappings. Both Raúl and John can appreciate the sex workers as human beings and try to do something about their victimization. Raúl is killed by a corrupt FBI agent while John is rescued and returns home to his wife. In the end, transnational connections on illegal police activities show that impunity will prevail because power and money are interconnected in the borderlands.

This film confirms the same message as in the other two films: murderers will continue because there are many other problems that need to be solved. In this film there are no heroes or heroines, like in *Bordertown* or *The Virgin of Juárez*, there are only voices that are heard and silenced at the same time because of the stages of fear, the lack of governance, and the type of citizenship that global cities or denationalized metropolitan spaces involve. Cesar Alejandro as the director, writer, and actor achieves in his film what the other films did not:[30] he respected the victims by not showing their deaths and the violence inflicted on them; he presented diverse stories connected by one or two characters and/or acts of violence; he did not elaborate on one subject or give all "the glory" to one character but instead documented the facts in such a way that the message got through without falling into stereotypes.

I am aware that making a film on current events is not an easy task; especially when the topic refers to inexcusable acts of violence against women and men that have not been solved, have been ignored, covered up, or diminished by the state. Hence there is always a problem of representation, and perhaps it is more so when the events have occurred in a foreign country. Filmmakers from any country who depict the Juárez femicides must be extremely cautious about the way they depict not only the events and the place but also the people they try to speak of. This is especially so when those films deal with a transnational topic such as this. These three films are projected and distributed in different countries around the world, they use international means of advertising, include actors and crew members from at least three different countries, use English, Spanish, and an indigenous language (in *Bordertown*) as well as subtitles in Spanish or English, and have access to a multicultural/multinational audience. By depicting a one-sided perspective and excluding other local cultural productions, efforts, and voices, we will continue building walls—real or symbolic—between the peoples of the United States and Mexico while we continue to produce the same discourses and stereotypes developed since 1848 toward the U.S.-Mexico border and its dwellers.

## Notes

1. This article was written before the violence in Ciudad Juárez escalated; it is now known as "the most violent city in the world." From January 2008 to September 2010 there have been 6939 people killed (Molly Molloy's electronic news bulletin from NMSU). Unfortunately, after January 2008, drug cartels and other common criminals have taken advantage of the state of impunity that has reigned since the femicide started. Today there's a generalized sense of insecurity and the city's infrastructure looks decayed. Consequently, several observations regarding the city's landscape are not now valid, it is because three years ago Ciudad Juárez was still a "livable" and secure city for most people.
2. In "Serial Sexual Femicide in Ciudad Juárez: 1993–2001," Monárrez cites different theories to analyze sexual killings through gender.
3. The data presented here is from Monárrez's, unless otherwise specified.
4. I am referring here to the sexual serial crimes or systemic sexual femicide, since the State claims that most of the murders have been solved.
5. In November 2009 the Court held the Mexican State responsible for the deaths of Esmeralda Herrera Monreal, Claudia Ivette González, and Laura Berenice Ramos Monárrez, in a case known as "Campo Algodonero," where

eight women's bodies were found in November 2001. The families had to appeal to an international court and waited nine years to receive justice. Today the case of María Sagrario Flores Bonilla is still in progress.

6. Amongst the ones published in the United States, which stays within the context of this study, there are: *Juárez:*, Bowden (1998) and *Desert Blood*, Gaspar de Alba (2003), among others.
7. Perhaps the most renowned is the novel *2666* by Chilean author Roberto Bolaño, who was raised in Mexico.
8. It is interesting to note that when we talk about perceptions it is hard to agree on one definite conclusion. On the one hand, we have facts that show that more than 2,000 people have been killed since January to mid-September of 2010, and the mayor of Juárez (José Reyes Ferriz) decided to cancel the ceremony of the *Grito de Independencia* on September 15, arguing the lack of security in the city. On the other hand, on September 17 there was a public concert with international singers Lila Downs, Silvio Rodríguez, and Willy Colón, which gathered more than 3,000, and no acts of violence were reported. No extra security was needed for this event and people attended regardless of the insecurity that has been prevailing since 2008.
9. Mario and Fernando Almada are well known for their B films on border cinema genre. At times they are drug dealers or detectives.
10. Isidro's wife has also been killed and her perpetrator was a bus driver from the maquiladora where she worked.
11. In the actual events there have been seven bus drivers arrested and charged for the murders, but only one has been fully identified by his victims. The rest are fabricated scapegoats.
12. I use the word "colonizer" to refer to U.S. hegemonic discourses regarding the U.S.-Mexico Border and its dwellers. There is a substantial amount of literature on this topic.
13. According to Norma Klahn, Anglo Americans have invented and constructed the image of Mexicans with the trope of difference, as the other.
14. During the Inquisition and the witch hunt, people were burned alive to redeem their sins. In Mariela's context, she either gets burned to heal herself from the suffering of being abused, or she is punished for being responsible for the vengeance over innocent people.
15. According to Monárrez's database "Base de datos Feminicidio" (1998) [archivo particular de investigación], Ciudad Juárez, which is updated daily, the number of women killed were 904, and 122 of those could be considered as sexual serial femicides (May 2010).
16. Remember, before 2008 Juárez was still a safe place for most of its inhabitants.
17. Information included in the DVD's special features.
18. The films are *Juárez, México*, mentioned above, and also Mexican films such as *Espejo retrovisor*, and *16 en la Lista*, among others.
19. Lauren sees her parents, who were Mexican immigrant workers, being killed when she was only a little girl.

20. For a Mexican audience, Díaz or Lauren cannot be taken as Mexicans due to Jennifer López's heavy Puerto Rican accent when speaking in Spanish and Banderas' unconvincing Mexican accent.
21. Díaz here makes reference to an old urban Juárez legend that refers to a young woman who went dancing to "El Carrusel" without her mother's permission. She was dancing with a very handsome man and at midnight the lights went off and there was a terrible odor. The moral of this story is that women should not disobey their parents to go out dancing, otherwise they will be punished. It may also be a legend from other Mexican border cities well known for their nightlife. In "El diablo también baila en el Aloha," Tijuana's writer Regina Swain recounts a similar legend (*Señorita Supermán y otras danzas*, 1993).
22. There is a clear reference to Abdel Omar Latiff Sharif, the first scapegoat presented by Barrio's administration. Sharif died in prison in 2006. The police could never prove he had murdered anyone. In my article "Baile de fantasmas en Ciudad Juárez al final y al principio del milenio" (2003), I elaborate on how Mexican authorities used Sharif as the "uncanny other" to prove that Mexicans could not commit such heinous crimes. In the character's response there is also an allusion of the declarations made by DA Jesús Antonio Piñón Gutiérrez, from Patricio Martínez's administration. Piñón Gutiérrez minimized the crimes, denied there were sexual serial murderers, and even declared that most of those deaths were either by a car accident or in the bathtub.
23. The scene is hard to believe because they shoot Díaz from a running car while he is seated at the desk in his office. The office is in the second floor and he gets shot in the stomach.
24. I take the concept from Deleuze and Guattari (2009) as they relate to people who "live in a language that is not their own" (59).
25. In a "secuestro express" they kidnap people and take them to different ATM machines to collect money from their bank accounts or to drop money from their credit cards. After the kidnappers collect certain amounts of money, they release them. Another form of this express kidnapping is to call the family and ask for a not very considerable amount of money, and try to collect the money in 24 to 48 hours, sometimes in less than a day.
26. This statement is based on the affirmations of former FBI agent and serial killer profiler Robert Resler when he arrived in Juárez to help municipal and state police to profile the assassin.
27. Mexico doesn't have a long history of serial killers.
28. This information concurs with the statistics of 1993–1998 in Monarrez's "Feminicidio sexual sistémico."
29. Since the violence started escalating in Juárez, many people who have been affected by different acts of violence (kidnappings, killings, extortion, etc.) have stated the same thing.
30. Alejandro was born/raised in Chihuahua City and has lived in El Paso for more than 20 years. He has businesses in both countries and knows the

problem personally. He has taken several courses about the border at the University of Texas, El Paso. He was also a victim of an express kidnapping in Mexico City. I don't suggest that only longtime residents of the area can have a better understanding of it. But Alejandro has problematized the femicides and connected them to other violent crimes.

Part III

# Performing Borders: *De Aquí y de Allá* [from Here and from There]

6

# Performing Borders: *De Aquí y de Allá* (Preliminary Notes on Mexican and Chicana/o Transnational Performance Art)

Laura G. Gutiérrez

This chapter was first rehearsed (as a presentation) during the Lennox Seminar at Trinity University in 2008. In an effort to offer a panoramic glimpse, in the truest sense of the word, I performed a *recorrido* (or run-through) that attempted to highlight, but in no way exhaust, artistic performances from the two sides of the U.S.-Mexico border of the last 40 years or so. This chapter picks up that *recorrido* and replays it here by discussing two video performances, collective performance art groups from the 1970s and 1980s, and two U.S.-Mexico border/performance art organizations. However, before rewinding and replaying, but never entirely replicating the *recorrido* or journey in the form of an article, I feel obliged to say a few words regarding the chapter's title, particularly the second part, which may in fact offer an opening to discuss theoretically ephemeral transnational performance art practices and production.

### From *Ni de aquí, ni de allá* to a Transnational Double-Belonging, *De aquí y de allá*

The "de aquí y de allá" part of the title performs a double-insertedness, or what I want to emphasize as a shift that takes us from a "double unbelonging" signified by the *ni de aquí, ni de allá* ("neither from here nor from there"), which is often used to describe the sentiment of uprootedness and "un-belonging" that nomads, migrants, and diasporic subjects in general feel in regard to both their place of origin and their new "home," to a "double belonging" signified by the *de aquí y de allá* ("from here and there"), which may convey a certain level of comfortability, either in one's home of origin or in the adopted one. This shift can best be illustrated anecdotally.

At first hearing the second title of what was to be my presentation at Trinity University, "de aquí y de allá," my mind's eye immediately read the title in the often-heard double negative, "ni de aquí ni de allá" and its variations in the form of film and song titles. Within film production *Ni de aquí, ni de allá* (1988) is directed, produced, cowritten by, and starring María Elena Velasco (aka La India María). The film uses stereotypical characterizations all the while attempting to speak for and to the lower classes of Mexico, particularly the landless, rural peasants and (im)migrants. This film uncovers the harsh labor conditions endured by undocumented workers in the United States and ultimately denounces the ways in which they are neither accepted in the receiving country nor in their homeland.

The double negative sentiment of "uprooted-ness" and "un-belonging" is also present in various songs and song genres, perhaps the most well regarded being "No soy de aquí, ni soy de allá" ("I am neither from here nor from there") written by the Argentine singer/songwriter Facundo Cabral.[1] Various singers, including Alberto Cortez and Joan Manuel Serrat, have covered this song, but here I would like to channel the song through the voice of Chavela Vargas who recorded the song in the 1970s, which is now being used as a sort of anthem for minoritarian subjects, racial and/or sexual.[2] It is perhaps because Vargas's rendition of "No soy de aquí, ni soy de allá" is unsettling beyond the song's lyrics that the Chicana filmmaker Rita González uses this queer interpretation at the end of her experimental documentary on the (in)famous B-Movie "Mexican Spitfire" Lupe Vélez in *The Assumption of Lupe Vélez* (2000). Vélez was a Mexican actress who, after working on the popular theater stages of Mexico, traveled to the United States to work in the early Hollywood machinery until she committed suicide, a death that has been immortalized in camp fashion by Kenneth Anger and Andy Warhol.[3] In her documentary, González sets out to reclaim Vélez for Chicanos, but because it is an experimental queer reclamation she never wholly resolves the Vélez narrative. Vargas's song serves to situate her and, in turn, the spectators in this place of "un-belonging."

This more ambiguous use of the "ni de aquí, ni de allá" trope, however paradoxically it may seem, works better with the sense of double belonging than the second part of my title that I am trying to sketch out here. That is, I would like to propose that the shift from "ni de aquí ni de allá" to "de aquí y de allá" be more descriptive of a transnational sense of belonging (for either people or cultural production, whether it be material or ephemeral), albeit, one which carries with itself a certain sense of "dis-comfort."[4] Beyond offering thanks to the Lennox Seminar organizers, particularly Rosana Blanco-Cano, who perhaps has unwittingly given me the opportunity to turn these "negations" of belonging to symbolically represent a double-presence, there is a need for a more adequate representation of what it means to not only practice transnational culture but to study multi-situated performances. Stated differently, this shift reasserts or reaffirms the necessity of having a double vision of sorts when it comes to examining a cultural production that crosses borders, particularly if the cultural work is ephemeral.

So, what does this transnational performance circuit look like? From the perspective of a scholar that is multi-situated, bicultural, and bilingual, artistic performance practices by Mexican and Chicana/o artists straddle the U.S.-Mexico border and are seldom situated comfortably in any specific locale. Additionally, when studying culture and cultural producers that straddle different borders, in this case, specifically those that are cultural and national, I suggest that we, as cultural critics, politicize this sense of un-belonging. It is within this very same gesture that I aim to rethink the un-belonging in productive ways that could potentially transform it into a double-belonging, one that, however, is never entirely fixed and is more in-line with the concept that I have developed elsewhere, "unsettling comforts." In the introduction of *Performing Mexicanidad: Vendidas y Cabareteras on the Transnational Stage* (2010), I propose that "unsettled comfort" or discomfort—just as the concept that I am trying to tease out here, the not belonging (to one particular locale)—should be rethought to be productive categories of analysis, where a certain level of comfort or belonging is paradoxically achieved, particularly in regard to the formation of counterpublics, however transitory or ephemeral these may be.[5] The work of contemporary Chicana and Mexican artists, again, particularly those that straddle national boundaries, can be better discerned if we reread tropes such as "ni de aquí, ni de allá" and resignify the sense of not-belonging to acquire a sense of belonging that is multilocated. These ideas are highlighted by two video performances—one by Nao Bustamante and the other by Ximena Cuevas—examined in the following section.

## Transnational (Mis-)Encounters:
### The Chain South and the Back North Again

In 1996, Chicana performance/conceptual artist Nao Bustamante baptized herself as the vagabond Ronaldo McDonaldo, packed her bags—including a fake 1950s contract that entitled Ronaldo, according to Mayor

McCheese, to a free meal—and, along with Mexican visual artist Miguel Calderón, embarked on a road trip that took them from San Francisco to Mexico City. As they traveled, they were to stop in as many McDonald's restaurants as possible in their route. At each stop—whenever Ronaldo got a Big Mac attack—Bustamante, in a yellow suit, big red shoes, red wig, and made-up face, walked in to demand her Big Mac, Calderón, with camera in hand, videotaped Ronaldo's "misencounters" with managers of the transnational franchise, who often told him to turn off the camera as he was in violation of "company policy." In spite of the initial resistance by the restaurant's on-site supervisors, Bustamante as Ronaldo McDonaldo always received "free meals,"[6] talked to customers inside the restaurant, mostly racial minorities, both kids and adults, and was only jokingly harassed or harassed people standing or walking by the restaurant. The footage recorded by Calderón was edited into a short video, or "performance document," entitled *The Chain South* (1998), which highlights moments on the trip on the U.S. side of the border. The last two scenes of *The Chain South* are particularly indicative of the point that the two artists are trying to drive "home." That is, as Bustamante prepares to cross the border into Mexico, still dressed as Ronaldo McDonaldo, she makes one last stop at a McDonald's restaurant, possibly her "last chance to get American food," according to a worker of that particular McDonald's. This assumption is, of course, readily undermined in the subsequent scene, which is eerie in that it is framed by the ironic deployment of a pop song. After receiving directions from a Border Patrol agent at the U.S.-Mexico border-crossing station, Bustamante as Ronaldo McDonaldo is seen driving and singing along to the 1980s pop disco song "Maniac" by Michael Sembello, which was popularized through the movie *Flashdance* (Adrian Lyne 1983). Before the credits start to roll, we see one of the most powerful symbols of transnational capital literally cross the border, bound south. My detailed description of this performative intervention and the video that was created about this "cross-border" road trip aims to not only highlight the political commentary, through aesthetic innovation, of the artists, but to also pinpoint the idea of *dis-*comfort that I have been threading into the "de aquí y de allá" trope. As Bustamante and Calderón made their point, *The Chain South* illustrates the ways in which "capital" travels across national borders and, more specifically, the ways that the United States and Mexico are bound historically and economically: a chain, allegorized here by the McDonald's restaurant, binds the two countries. Thus the transnational franchise, its spokesperson, and the double-arch McDonald's sign are all part of the chain of significations and function as stand-ins for Empire and transnational domination, something that was later sampled by another artist situated south of the border.[7]

Five years later, Mexican video/conceptual artist Ximena Cuevas adds a few links to Bustamante and Calderón's "Chain South." For my purposes here, I propose a reading of a fragment of Cuevas's video montage *Cinépolis* as the continuation of the McDonald's trip or "Chain South" discussed above. *Cinépolis* is a lyrical, visual meditation on multiple forms of invasions (military, economic, political, and cultural), but what received the press's attention is one scene that Cuevas recorded herself during a McDonald's commercial shoot in Mexico City.[8] The commercial was subcontracted by a television commercial company for the Spanish-language network Univisión and featured the popular culture icon and now famous *ranchera* singer Pedro Fernández. What ostensibly drove Cuevas to pull out her personal camera and clandestinely record what was transpiring behind the scenes during the commercial shoot was the way in which excessive "makeup" (i.e., paint) was being applied to the burger to create the illusion of an aesthetically appropriate and highly desirable consumable product.[9] What Cuevas managed to capture with her camera points to the jarring difference that exists between what happens off camera and in the postproduction phase of the making of these types of commercials. More specifically, the sort of language that the director in this particular instance uses: the offscreen stage directions that feminize and sexualize the burger so that it be more enticing to the actor in order to elicit a feel-good gesture of oral contentment and pleasure. The success of this commercial, which is ultimately distributed and repeated between Univisión's programming, depends more on what is edited out than what is left in. At the end of the segment recorded by Cuevas that is part of *Cinépolis* (and part of the video's critique), we see Fernández spit out the toxic burger, appropriately so, into a McDonald's bag.

In this sequence of *Cinépolis*, Cuevas juxtaposes the machinery of transnational capitalism with Mexican national(ist) constructions of masculinity. And, after *Cinépolis* begins to be screened at festivals and exhibited in museums and galleries, and is reviewed in some alternative art magazines, the corporate-minded individuals in the Miami-based advertisement production company begin to spin her infiltration as a threat. *Cinépolis* represents a threat to the career of this favored pop icon, and one the company's executives begin to accuse Cuevas of being a "terrorist" and an "anti-imperialist."[10] Because of the multiple accusations and (lawsuit) threats, the video artist has to pull the video from festival screenings in the United States. What is ironic, and perhaps superfluous to say at this point, is the fact that Cuevas's major critique in *Cinépolis* is "imperialism," the very same critique that Nao Bustamante and Miguel Calderón enact with *The Chain South*. In Cuevas's case, a reading that counters the executive's can be produced here: the figure of Pedro Fernández, dressed as the epitome of the Mexican macho, the *charro*, in the act of spitting out the McDonald's burger has the potential of becoming a national and even nationalist hero, and it goes without saying that this hero has cross-border and transnational appeal. Let me explain this further: while two cameras have seemingly recorded the same footage, in the editing process two different, and directly opposing, products are produced. One product is for a transnational corporation that has jumped on the "Hispanic" bandwagon by figuring out that it can mobilize national and cultural-specific identities to target and make consumers out of the fastest growing market in the United States.[11] And this is the purpose of the McDonald's commercial, while the other product produced out of this footage serves to contest capitalist domination by, ironically enough, using the same nationalist symbols—the *charro* and the *ranchera*. In other words, what the television commercial production company executive is concerned with is not the tainted image that the actor-singer Pedro Fernández may garner because of this "negative" exposure, but the complex web of signification that they are trying to link in one single moving image: McDonald's product consumption and *mexicanidad* (or even *latinidad*, let's remember the commercial was for the U.S.-based Univisión) are intimately linked, again, as *The Chain South* suggests. This is a point that Cuevas "drives" home (as we saw in *The Chain South*) when, in the sequence prior to the commercial in *Cinépolis*, she goes through the McDonald's drive-thru demanding various Mexicanized McDonald's products in order to highlight the ridiculous and excessive way in which these have different (and at times opposing) signifiers.[12] To disassociate the product from the cultural-specific nationalist image would signal a marketing failure, that of not being able to interpolate specific cultural and identitarian formations into the McDonald's "family." And this is precisely what Cuevas succeeds in doing: she dislodges transnational capital from national identity. Far from suggesting that she is rescuing nationalist symbols and myths, what she is intent on doing is to place an obstacle, however temporary, in neoliberalism's fast-paced tracks.

The use of McDonald's in both these video performances to link the two countries historically and economically—particularly in the historical present through the expansion of U.S.-based transnational companies into Mexico (and into the rest of the world)—unwittingly proposes that we, academics who often celebrate transnational cultural production, do not forget the other meanings of transnationalism, particularly the one that free-market capitalism begets. Additionally, *The Chain South* and *Cinépolis* are documented performative interventions that can help illustrate some of the characteristics of what performance art is, particular the more experimental kind. For the purposes of this chapter, which aims to think through Mexican and Chicana performance art practices through a transnational lens and in addition to the video performances by Nao Bustamante and Ximena Cuevas discussed above, I have selected what I perceive to be two areas, both in geographical and temporal terms, where performance art has flourished in the context of Mexican and Chicana/o cultural production, and I have selected a number of examples from each: art collectives from the 1970s and 1980s that were considered avant-garde and art that takes place along the U.S.-Mexico border.

### Collective Challenges: Performance Art Groups Across the U.S.-Mexico Divide

In the early seventies, in the middle of a turbulent era epitomized by the Vietnam War, a group of Chicano high school students from East Los Angeles, not necessarily thinking themselves as artists but as student activists, founded the art collective Asco (1971–1987).[13] The four founding members, Harry Gamboa Jr., Gronk, Willie Herrón, and Patsi Valdez, used art, rather than using real weapons, as a way to give vent to anger and frustration. Working within the context of youth urban culture, the strategies that *Asco* developed were different from those used a decade earlier by Chicano traveling theater troupe Teatro Campesino, as well as those that were being engaged by most muralists, writers, and cinematographers during the Chicano Civil Rights Movement. Asco began doing collaborative work that expanded notions of what was being defined as Chicano art during this particular period, later dubbed the Chicano Renaissance. But Asco was also going beyond conceptions of what avant-garde art was at that time. Rather than simply transgressing the limits of art in order to shock their audiences, Asco was invested in creating political art that also expressed some sort of resistance to hegemonic forms of oppression, whether these came from the outside or were intra-ethnically circumscribed. Asco's explorations within conceptual art straddled avant-garde expressions often associated with bourgeois artists and the nationalistic symbols that were being used by most Chicano artists in a process of self-affirmation during the Movement. And because of the internal critique of both paradigms, Asco has been, until recently, marginalized from Chicano and (mainstream) art history.[14]

Asco's public performance art pieces ranged from the conceptually charged *No-Movies* to the antiwar and anti-Chicano nationalist *walking murals*. Both were street performances; however, whereas the *No-Movies* were pieces that were staged and photographed (not filmed) and distributed as propaganda for *real* movies, the *walking murals* were simply performed for the various pedestrians in East LA's Whittier Boulevard. The *walking murals* critiqued the privileged yet fixed murals of the (*authentic* and *committed*) Chicano artists, the *No-Movies*, as Chavoya states, "were conceptual performances created specifically for a still camera. The *No-Movies* typically appropriated two models of presentation: the Latin American *fotonovela* and the Hollywood film still" (3). The *No-Movies* were also those interventionist performance pieces that many times engaged the mass media, given that Asco wanted to reach the highest number of spectators as possible in the Los Angeles area. As Harry Gamboa Jr. himself has written, the "multi-media works were intended to galvanize a response from the community" (67). So, for example, the *No-Movie* performance piece *Decoy Gang War Victim* (1978)—which aimed to avert gang violence in the "barrio" through performance and media intervention—was photographed and sent out to various newspapers and television stations. This piece posed as a *real* event; another East Los Angeles gang member had been shot. After closing down a city block and lighting up flares, Gamboa took a photograph that featured Gronk lying down in the middle of the street with ketchup all over him. Gamboa has explained: "We would go around and whenever we heard of where there might be potential violence, we would set up these decoys so they would think someone had already been killed" (quoted in "Pseudographic Cinema" 6). This process might have backfired once this performance had passed as *real*, further incrementing the already damaging stereotype of Chicanos as gang members. But perhaps the performance piece did serve to temporarily restore peace in East Los Angeles, and it definitely, as Chavoya states, "exposed the possibility of media manipulation to [the] artists" (6).

While the *walking murals* that Asco created had a different function, they were considerably less interventionist in degree, since they operated on a more symbolic level while still remaining critical. The first walking mural that the conceptual art group performed, *Stations of the Cross* (1971), was a public performance protesting the Vietnam War and the high number of Chicano casualties in it. On Christmas Eve of 1971 and along the main street that crosses East Los Angeles' Whittier Boulevard, three members of Asco performed a procession dressed in campy "religious" garb as last-minute shoppers and police officers looked on with awe.[15] As Herrón carried the cross, Gamboa and Gronk followed silently down the boulevard until they deposited the cross at the final station, a U.S. Marine Recruiting Station. *Stations of the Cross* was "an alternative ritual of resistance to belief systems that glorified useless deaths" (Gamboa, 76-77). This sort of heterotopias, to use Foucault's terminology—created by Asco's *walking murals*—are not simply heterogeneous spaces of sites and relationships (as in a cemetery, church, theatre, and garden).[16] The artists and subjects, who (temporarily) reclaim these social and public spaces, historically have been denied access to them by societal and spatial mechanisms of control.[17] However, with this performance piece Asco was going beyond the reclamation of space and critiquing the complicitous relationship that existed between the church and the government in the deaths of Chicanos and other people/men of color. Asco's *walking murals* were also contesting the static nature of the overvalued Chicano murals that began to proliferate in the walls of East Los Angeles.

The majority of the muralism that began to flourish during the sixties and the seventies was reduced to the incorporation of pre-Columbian motifs, dichotomized female figures (*La Virgen de Guadalupe* or the sexy *cholas*), emasculated urban youth (*pachucos, cholos*, or *vatos locos*) and other gang symbols, and politically didactic imagery (farmworkers, Ernesto "Che" Guevara, César Chávez). This form of an ethnic-specific aesthetics "began to bring positive publicity to a community that until then had only been maligned or neglected by the mass media" (Gamboa, 77). However, for these four young Chicano artists, the limitations of what defined Chicano art were too constricting; they wanted to go beyond those same parameters that sought to contain them. Humor, or camp humor to be more precise, seems to be an alternative for these artists.[18] I align myself with García who develops the notion of a "Chicano camp style that ironizes, parodies and satirizes the very cultural forms that marginalize and exclude" (1). It is precisely at this *impasse* and with the deployment of this discursive strategy that Asco *walks* into (as it were) dominant Chicano discourse in order to disrupt and multiply it. I agree with Chavoya who states that the group's "work critically satirized and challenged the conventions of modernist 'high' art as well as those of 'ethnic' or community-based art" (1). Through the deployment of camp strategies, Asco was able to parody and thus challenge conventions from the center as well as those that were ethnic-specific. Asco was not interested in creating "art for art's sake," as modernist paradigms encouraged, at the same time that it challenged the lack of self-criticism and essentializing gestures of the Chicano cultural nationalist framework. In the process, during the decade of the seventies, Asco was also redefining (or pluralizing) the avant-garde. Their political art was not transgressive; rather, it was resistant and contestatory.

The type of street actions, or time-based performative interventions, during the 1970s and 1980s were not exclusive to Asco or other U.S.-based conceptual art collectives. "Acciones"—as they were being dubbed in cities across Latin America—were taking place also throughout the Americas, including cities such as São Paulo, Santiago, Buenos Aires, and Mexico

City.[19] As Mexican artist Felipe Ehrenberg, who himself was part of two different performance art groups in the 1970s, *Proceso Pentágono* and *Peyote y la Compañía*, recalls, in Mexico City the conceptual art groups were simply called *grupos* and the term that they employed to describe their public performance art interventions was "Arte Acción."[20] In addition to being politically motivated and oriented, one of the characteristics that helped to define and unify these artists in the different *grupos* was the need to challenge the notion that art was static and permanent (as in literature and the plastic arts), in other words, the bulk of artistic and cultural production from the postrevolutionary period. I am referring to the need to challenge the social realism aesthetics that have helped to construct the nation and had also congealed notions of *mexicanidad*. Thus, a sort of parallel movement can be discerned between Asco and the *grupos* in Mexico in regard to the aesthetic challenges that the conceptual art collectives on both sides of the U.S.-Mexico border were engaging: on both sides, conceptual and artistic performative activities were tapped for their potential to challenge rigid conceptions of what socially conscious and politically oriented art could be.[21]

In perhaps the best account of the *grupo* movement, art critic, scholar, and performance artist Maris Bustamante gives a historical description of the *grupos* that existed (and some which still exist) in Mexico's capital city.[22] An important element, in Bustamante's assessment, is the context in which the *grupos* flourished and the role that Alejandro Jorodowsky played in this milieu. This Chilean artist belonged to the *generación de ruptura* (1952–1965), which preceded the generation of the *grupos* and worked on happenings and street actions (Bustamante, 227).[23] In the 1950s and early 1960s Jorodowsky was collaborating with other "Rupture" generation Mexican artists (José Luis Cuevas, Manuel Felguérez, and Arnaldo Cohen), but Bustamante credits him for the first theoretical approximation for an "aesthetics of performance art in Mexico" (Bustamante, 230). Bustamante describes Jorodowsky's contributions to the reconceptualization of art in this particular context when she asserts that Jorodowsky's theoretical article "Hacia el efímero pánico O ¡Sacar el teatro del teatro!" (1963) "proposes to take painting out of painting, the theater out of the theater, to mix them, then see what happens" (230). This proposition was further supplemented with "the concept of the ephemera, making it intersect with the notion of party and the 'party spectacle'" (Bustamante, 230). Thus, the idea of art as ephemeral and nonobjectual (mixed with the notion of the spectacle), in addition to the fraught post-1968 political moment that these artists were living in, are the primary reasons that may explain what gave rise to the *grupo* movement in the seventies in Mexico City.[24] However, while the *grupos* did not term their mode "performance art," just as the LA-based Asco, they were insisting on process over product (i.e., nonobjectual art), the disruption of a passive audience, the redefinition of the museum and/or gallery, and the reclamation of the public space.[25]

In addition to this reclamation of the public sphere, it is particularly noteworthy to mention the role that feminist theory and discourse played in the work of some of these *grupo* artists, particularly female artists such as the aforementioned Maris Bustamante. Influenced by her male counterparts from her own generation or the generation that preceded her, the feminist art being produced in the United States, particularly in the Women's Building in Los Angeles, and Mexico's own popular performance traditions of the early twentieth century, the "acciones" executed by Bustamante were hybrid in nature. However, in spite of the different *grupos*'s more "democratic" nature as they included a large number of female participants, and while gender critique was interwoven into the larger discussions and critiques of Mexican society, it was Bustamante's work and her collaboration with other artists, particularly Mónica Mayer, that pushed the boundaries of art and feminist expression.[26]

In the late 1970s Bustamante constituted her *grupo*, her self-mocking "No-Grupo," and began to create what she described as nonobjectual art, which is particularly interested in art as a process as opposed to the creation of objects as material for consumption and collection. This performance art group, which had used black humor in most of its "acciones," sardonically staged its own death; their last performance piece was appropriately called *La muerte del performance* (*The Death of Performance*), and it took place during the Primer Coloquio de Arte No Objetual in 1983 (Bustamante, 235). After her "No-Grupo" experience, Bustamante decided to form another *grupo* in 1983, "Polvo de GallinaNegra," with visual artist Mónica Mayer, who, according to Bustamante, "had a family history of women struggling for women's rights" (235). Thus, collaborating with Mayer allowed Bustamante to integrate larger doses of gender critique into her artistic expressions since, in her own words, the aim of "Polvo de GallinaNegra" was to "modify the image of women in the mass media through performances on radio, television, and the print media" (236). Therefore "Polvo de GallinaNegra," with its explicit feminist agenda, was interested in challenging the fact that art and its multiple mediums are male-dominated (i.e., "the evil eye").[27] In the nineties and since "Polvo de GallinaNegra" disbanded (1991), Bustamente's performance art shifted from particularly collaborative work to mainly solo performances.

One of the things that I have tried to do with the above examples is to eradicate the idea that avant-garde performance art is a so-called first-world phenomenon, a notion that is widely held. In doing this, I also align myself with Coco Fusco, whose critical work has consistently challenged this dominant idea. This cultural critic and performance artist has been consistent in her critique of what appeared to be a phenomenon in the 1980s and, most definitely, the 1990s when multicultural or intercultural performances where in vogue among U.S.-based art critics. Fusco's criticism has pushed us to reconsider not only what intercultural performance is but also what its roots are. According to Fusco, we must rethink these concepts beyond the historical present; they are rooted in an ignominious past that is not only characterized by conquest and colonization but by the process of "Othering" non-Western people through their exhibition.[28] Following Fusco, the majority of the studies that have been produced seldom make the association with other artistic performance traditions of early twentieth-century Mexico (*teatro de carpa*) or with the avant-garde movements of the Americas, like the Mexico City *grupos* or Asco's street interventions, to name just two. And, of course, the "genealogies of performance" pace Joseph Roach—and as they pertain to performance practices of Greater Mexico—have to be redrawn (or are currently being redrawn by some scholars such as Coco Fusco). However, I also want to emphasize that we have to keep in mind that taking historical and geographical contexts into account would mean that artistic movements are not simply duplicated and transplanted, but that they perform a different task if we situate them, say, at the U.S.-Mexico border and, additionally and importantly, in the context of the emergence of neoliberal economic policies, which I examine in the following section.[29]

## Border/Performance Art Since the 1980s: From Site-Specific to Metaphor (to Site-Specific?)

The Border Art Workshop/Taller de Arte Fronterizo (BAW/TAF) has been of great importance in the elaboration of San Diego and Tijuana as a "laboratory" for border culture. As the other collectives discussed thus far, the aim of the BAW/TAF, specifically during the mid-1980s to early 1990s, was the incorporation of time to the plastic arts in order to create site-specific and ephemeral performances along the San Diego-Tijuana border. Stylistically, as Fusco has stated, the BAW/TAF "performances, early exhibits, and multiples resembled the work of Mexico City conceptualist *grupos* and the LA-based collective Asco" (*Corpus Delecti* 265). However, the cultural work of the BAW/TAF has taken place in the growing volatile atmosphere of the U.S.-Mexico border that has experienced a series of transformations due to the restructuring of the economy (what I refer above as neoliberal economic policies), the subsequent increase in the movement of peoples, and further racial and class stratification.

Engaging mostly site-specific strategies, the BAW/TAF performance art pieces began to take place in 1984 when the group was formed. In an attempt to specify the importance of the San Diego-Tijuana border for this collective, David Avalos, one of the members, has stated: "There's something that's specific to our particular place; and we are trying to affect the attitudes of this place" (196). This statement clarifies the manner in which the art produced by this group (whose original members, with the exception of one, have left) has worked and continues to work on issues related to the always volatile and transforming relations between the two bordering countries. But since the BAW/TAF is working within this particular geopolitical border, the actual U.S.-Mexico border is always signified. Removing the site-specific agenda from this collective will render the border a mere working metaphor for all other existing borders (geopolitical or otherwise), for better or for worse, as has occurred in the work of an ex-member of this collective, Guillermo Gómez-Peña.[30] Performing the same pieces in other regions within the United States or other countries, if one is not careful, would be to merely export the so-called border experience (Avalos, 196). The spectators situated beyond the specific geopolitical border (between the United States and Mexico) also lack the concrete referent. Thus, meaning is being constantly deferred, potentially rendering the intervention a mere poststructuralist linguistic and visual diversion. In addition to this, in order to be able to work within this specific context, the BAW/TAF had to be composed of artists working with different national, cultural, and gendered experiences. As Avalos points out: "We wanted to form a group that included Mexican citizens, U.S. citizens, Chicanos and non-Chicanos, because the border is a place and an issue that affects us all. The border is people, the people that occupy the particular space of the border. But the border was initially peopled by expendables, those who can be lost" (194). While Avalos does not mention gender differences, the female members (Elizabeth Sisco in particular) played a crucial role in the inclusion of a gender critique within the overall framework of the BAW/TAF.[31] It is precisely from this intersection of experiences that the members of BAW/TAF want to speak. Their ultimate aim is to shift the dominant notion of the border as peripheral to the production of culture *and* history. In this sense they are claiming that the inhabitants of the border region are agents of culture *and* history.

It is from this cross-cultural and site-specific experiences that Gómez-Peña chose to depart and begin doing "solo" performances. His departure in 1989, according to the artist, was due to the manner in which the so-called Anglo art world was appropriating border art produced by this group. But this is paradoxical given that Gómez-Peña has received prizes and honors by major (governmental or not) organizations and his art has been promoted and sponsored by national and international institutions.[32] This might seem ironic, but according to Johannes Birringer, Gómez-Peña's move contested the "myth that artists of color are only meant to speak for, or from within, their own 'ethnic communities'" ("Border Media" 62). In order to back up his argument, Birringer explains Gómez-Peña's redefinition of artist as activist in this so-called postmodern world; he states:

> [I]n his travelling solo performances, pirate radio projects and collaborative productions he has donned the role of the trickster by promulgating a new international activism ex-centris, acting as a cross-cultural "diplomat," nomadic "chronicler" or "coyote" (smuggler of ideas) promoting the so-called "free art agreement" (el tratado de librecultura)...which focuses strongly on cross-contextual alliances and inter-community projects. ("Border Media" 62)

As Birringer himself warns, Gómez-Peña's trickster diplomacy is not an option to the "Latino youth in Chicago's barrios" ("Border Media" 63). But I believe that there is still another problem in the strategies that Gómez-Peña has been deploying during the decade of the nineties, which is his notion of plural or multiple identities. As Ramón García points out: "Gómez-Peña's free-floating bordered identities end up universalized *as* the new condition of living in the postmodern world, to the extent that the material specificity of any geographic border becomes secondary" (9; García's emphasis). However, I will distance myself somewhat from García's remarks since Gómez-Peña's postmodern strategies do serve to deconstruct essentialist notions of identity. Moreover, once Gómez-Peña exits the BAW/TAF's doors, it would be a false assertion to call his performance artwork entirely a solo endeavor, as one of the things that has helped to define him and his work are his collaborations with other artists, including James Luna, Roberto Sifuentes, and Michèle Ceballos. These artistic connections were formalized with the creation of La Pocha Nostra, which later acquired the status of a nonprofit organization. As a loose-knit group of artists, La Pocha Nostra provides a forum for other artists to come together in order to, as their manifesto reads, "cross and erase dangerous borders between art and politics, practice and theory, artist and spectator" (n. p.).³³ This philosophy is evidenced by their nomadic workshops, particularly their International Summer Institute, where, in addition to "teaching" the ins and outs of artistic performance, there are important avenues and venues for international, cross-border, and cultural artistic collaboration as well as sites to theorize these very same collaborations.

In this sense, it is important to distinguish the external markers of specific ethnic and/or cultural identities that Gómez-Peña employs in his performance pieces, from *Border Brujo* (1988, 1990) to *New World Border* (1997), and in his writings, which discuss these same ideas. In his repeatedly reedited articles, Gómez-Peña seldom deploys ironic distance to critique *essentialisms* and *truisms*, rather than being deconstructed, it seems that they are merely transformed and then reified. Yet, in his performance art, Gómez-Peña *is* highlighting the constructedness of these same performed identities, whether they are American, Mexican, or Chicano. However, what I find particularly problematic are his utopic assertions of border identities and subjectivities and, by extension, of border cultures and the privileged role that artists such as he play in this multicultural landscape.³⁴ For Gómez-Peña, as he affirms in his article "The Multicultural Paradigm," "[t]oday, if there is a dominant culture, it is a border culture," since all of its inhabitants are, or have the potential of becoming, "border-crossers" (46–47). This Mexican performance artist (in the process of Chicanization), a "border-crosser" himself, does not take into account that the border-crossings that are enacted throughout the Americas, more often than not, are on the terms that the ruling classes and the hegemonic and institutionalized systems determine.³⁵ A decade after the BAW/TAF began to create site-specific border performances, the binational arts organization located in San Diego, California, and Tijuana, Baja California Norte, InSite, set out to further challenge, through public art interventions, concepts such as "public," "urban," and "border."³⁶

At various points, InSite has intersected with the BAW/TAF while converging at other moments. For example, site-specificity has also been a preoccupation of InSite, and the example that perhaps best highlights this philosophy is the installation for InSite97 by Mexican and border-inhabitant artist Marcos Ramírez ERRE, who designed, constructed, and positioned a large-scale, wooden horse at the border crossing station in Tijuana, Mexico, purported to be the busiest crossing point between the two countries. Entitled *Toy An Horse*, the installation referenced the famed Trojan Horse as depicted in classic Greek literature, but this one was featured with two heads, one facing south and the other north, thus calling into question the mechanisms that control the flow of humans and goods between the countries. In other words, the large wooden structure was strategically positioned along the border line for all to see, so that they can deduce the complicity of the two countries' governments that, through their transnational political and economical accords, on the one hand, bring about immigration, but, on the other, control it.

Ten years or so after ERRE's public art intervention, as well as the implementation of NAFTA (the North American Free Trade Agreement) that *Toy An Horse* was critiquing "head-on," Argentine-born, Brooklyn-based artist Judi Werthein produced an intervention for InSite05 that complicated the notion of what border art was, particularly site-specific art that had been so prevalent in art circles along the San Diego-Tijuana corridor.[37] The 2005 installment of InSite was conceived in the spirit of 1970s avant-garde performances by focusing on process over product through its instituted artistic residencies, which took place over a two-year period. Some of these residencies did result in products, as was the case with Werthein, who launched a new sneaker line with the trademark name *Brinco* (or "Jump" in Spanish) that was, much like the site-specific *Toy An Horse*, a critique of global economy and neoliberal policies that propel people to move, yet state authorities institute control measures to inhibit these flows. After an extended residency along the border, Werthein began to conceptualize her utilitarian art object when she began to focus her "public intervention" on what she thought to be the most pressing issue in the region, illegal immigration. After numerous conversations with would-be border crossers, most of whom had been deported at least once, immigrant activists, and *coyotes* (or human smugglers), she designed the shoes to include a small flashlight-compass combination gadget, a map of the U.S.-Mexico border imprinted in the pullout insole of the shoe, and a pocket on the shoe's tongue to hide aspirins or money, in addition to culturally and nationally specific references from both sides of the U.S.-Mexico divide. The shoes where designed and manufactured with the colors of the Mexican flag, but it also featured the U.S. eagle on its toes, as it appears on the 25-cent coin and which gestures the direction of the migrants and reason for the movement north, economical. What is visible on the sides of the shoes is the Aztec eagle that is used as a trademark to signify "Hecho en México" (or "Made in Mexico"), signaling the point of origin of the migrants. And, lastly, on the backside of the ankle was a small picture of the patron saint of migrants in Mexico, Father Toribio Romo, who, according to popular folk legends, has helped countless migrants in the route to the United States since the 1970s.

The manufacturing of these shoes, a limited number of only 1000, occurred offshore, in a factory in China. In doing so, the artist wanted to make a point regarding the complex contradictions and obvious tensions around free trade, international labor policies, and corporate globalization. Moreover, it should be noted that Werthein was also commenting on the fact that in recent years numerous *maquiladora* plants, or assembly-line factories that have dotted the northern Mexican border region since neoliberal economic policies have been in rigor (i.e., the 1970s) and which have provided low-wage jobs to people in Mexico for decades, have begun to move further offshore, particularly to China, because of the much lower wages there, which translates into more profits for companies. To highlight this link in the commodity chain, Werthein included a note inside the shoe, which read: "This product was manufactured by workers in China who were paid a minimum wage of $42 per month and worked 12 hours a day." Half of the manufactured shoes were available for sale in a shoe boutique in downtown San Diego (for $215.00) while the other half were donated to three migrant shelters in Tijuana, Mexico, including La Casa del Migrante. This public art intervention caused much polemical debate, particularly when the mainstream media—from Univisión to CNN and from Fox News to MSNBC—picked up the project and made it into a "story" of not only the creation of a pair of specially designed sneakers that would make "border crossing" easier, but that they were getting them for free and not as a public art intervention. That is, Werthein's shoes generated a performance of national anxiety regarding the immigration of Mexicans into this country, but it should be noted that it also succeeded in intervening in one of most pressing issues in contemporary politics and society, "illegal immigration."

### Mexican and Chicana/o Performance Studies: Possibilities for the Future

In this chapter I selected a number of artistic interventions in order to illustrate some of the concerns that propel these artists to create, as well as some of the strategies that they deploy in their politically oriented artistic interventions. I set out to offer a sort of *recorrido* of what I consider to be important politically and aesthetically innovative artistic interventions. But, in doing so, I have also suggested some possible avenues for future research and critical scholarship into all aspect of artistic performance in the Mexican and Chicana/o contexts. In particular, I emphasize the importance of thinking of artistic and political projects (transhistorically and trans-geographically) as scholars engaged with the methodologies that transnational studies provides, as genealogies. In examining and critically engaging with alternative genealogies (of performance practices in this case), we will begin to unearth different locales important in the production of knowledge (and to, of course, value them). This will aid us in our own scholarship as transnational studies scholars, creating a "de aquí y de allá" methodology, if you will. This chapter has tried to demonstrate that the study of artistic performance, housed within a larger project of Performance Studies, is intimately bound to other areas of study that concerns us in this volume: Border Studies, Latin American Studies, Mexican Studies, Chicana/o Studies, and Literary Studies. Taken as a whole and in conversation with one another, these chapters are not only indicative of the political themes present in the work of cultural workers from the Mexican and Chicana/o contexts, but they are also testament to the need for future cross-disciplinary and collaborative work among scholars in the above-mentioned disciplines.

## Notes

1. Two musical productions that recast the "neither here nor there" trope are the *norteño* group Los Tigres del Norte in their CD *Jefe de jefes* (Fonovisa 1997) and Chicano rapper Jae-P in his CD entitled *Ni de aquí, ni de allá* (Univision Records, 2003).
2. Chavela Vargas is a Costa Rican-born and nationalized Mexican singer regarded especially for her *ranchera* songs. She is considered a transnational queer icon.
3. See Anger's "Chop-Suicide" in *Hollywood Babylon* (1975) and Warhol's film *Lupe* (1966). For two critical examinations of Vélez's, Anger's, and Warhol's work, see Fregoso's *MeXicana Encounters*, Nericcio's *Tex[t]-Mex*.
4. As Danielson notes, "de aquí y de allá" ("from here and there"), in its very own language, connotes a level of inequality. The enunciating subject speaks from one side and can never be doubly situated. I thank her for her comments.
5. My book *Performing Mexicanidad* proposes that "unsettling" in "unsettling comforts" functions as an adjective and a verb because the work of queer artists can unsettle homonormative culture; comfort is also unsettled at the level of spectatorial practices. The next section is an abbreviated analysis of the work I discuss in *Performing Mexicanidad*.
6. It doesn't look good that Ronald McDonald cannot go into his "house," doesn't get a Big Mac, and the managers or police harass him.
7. More on Bustamante's work can be found on www.naobustamante.com. The video is also available via the Hemispheric Institute of Performance and Politics's library: http://hidvl.nyu.edu/video/000509596.html.
8. Cuevas' video art is not lucrative as she mostly lectures on her work in U.S. universities. *Cinépolis* is a short video conceived around 2003 during the Iraq invasion.
9. Personal interview with the artist, August 2003.
10. Ibid.

11. See Dávila's *Latinos, Inc.* "Over eighty Hispanic advertising agencies and branches of transnational advertising conglomerates...now sell consumer products by shaping and projecting images of and for Latinos" (2).
12. In my book, *Performing Mexicanidad*, I devote a chapter to Cuevas's performative interventions.
13. The group had collaborated for a year before adopting the name Asco in 1973. The name identifies the roots of their unconventional aesthetics and refers to the nausea, disgust, and/or repulsion from the spectators they would scream "¡qué asco!"
14. Many critics such as Noriega have written Asco into Chicano art history and avant-garde art by writing critical articles and editing anthologies. See Noriega's work on Gamboa, *Urban Exile*. Rita González included Asco's work in *Phantom Sightings*; see the exhibit's catalog.
15. In his article "In the City of Angels, Chameleons, and Phantoms," Gamboa writes: "Herrón was the representation of Christ/Death, dressed in a white robe that bore a brightly colored Sacred Heart, which he painted in acrylic. His face had been transformed by makeup into a stylized calavera. Gronk personified Pontius Pilate (aka Popcorn): he wore a green bowler hat, flaunted an excessively large beige fur purse, and carried a bag of unbuttered popcorn. Gamboa assumed the role of a zombie altar boy and wore an animal skull headpiece to ward off unsolicited communion" (*Urban Exile* 76).
16. In "Of Other Spaces" Foucault discusses how space, public in particular, functions as a structure of power.
17. East Los Angeles and other Mexican neighborhoods were transformed and controlled spatially throughout the twentieth century to contain working-class Mexicans/Chicanos. The building of highways and sports arenas was a common strategy to displace, marginalize, and contain them to/within those areas. During the late 1960s–1970s, East LA was an active site for student walkouts, demonstrations, and riots, thus the police became more visible then. See Gamboa's *Urban Exile* for his account of the political climate. See also García's "Against *Rasquache*" and Chavoya's "Orphans of Modernism" for a discussion on Asco's work.
18. The political art during the Chicano Renaissance took itself too seriously to incorporate humor. In the 1980s–1990s, Chicana/o performers started to change this and by cloaking their political-ness and/or resistance with humor they were able to achieve greater results.
19. See Fusco's *Corpus Delecti*.
20. Personal interview with Ehrenberg, 1998.
21. In "Navigating the Labyrinth of Silence," McCaughan writes: "The 1968 student movement in Mexico City was a watershed event and continues to be an important point of reference for social movements and their loosely affiliated artists today" (44). See also his discussion regarding the *grupos* and feminist art post-1968.
22. Aside from McCaughan's work there is little critical work on the *grupos*. Blanco-Cano's *Cuerpos disidentes del México imaginado* analyses how the feminist art collective Polvo de Gallina Negra (Maris Bustamante

and Mónica Mayer) challenged static notions of motherhood. There's also Bustamante's article "Non-Objective Art in Mexico 1963–1983," regarding the *grupo* movement in Mexico City.
23. Jorodowsky is known for his films: *El topo* (1970), *The Holy Mountain* (1973), and the controversial *Santa Sangre* (1989).
24. Bustamante's article "Non-Objective Art" translates "no-objetual" as "nonobjective," but I prefer "non-objectual."
25. See Bustamante's article for the events these *grupos* staged, especially her own: "No-Grupo" and "Polvo de GallinaNegra."
26. According to González and Lerner, these performance and conceptual art collectives were "more democratic [in] shape" (91). Sáenz's article, "Ocaso de la escuela Mexicana," discusses the *grupos* formed throughout the country from 1973 to 1976 and states that a number of them continue their work. Sáenz lists numerous women as members. Bustamante is also a research scholar and the coordinator of "El Primer Inventario de las Formas PIAS (Performance Instalación Ambientación)," her forthcoming book is on Mexico's history of performance (1922–1992).
27. Bustamante explains: "the [*grupo*'s] name... [is] based on the powders that are sold in small bags at traditional herb markets. They purport to offer a perfect protection against 'evil eye,'" 237.
28. See Fusco's article "The Other History of Intercultural Performance," and her video *The Couple in the Cage*, on her collaboration with Gómez-Peña as undiscovered Amerindians.
29. For example, Gómez-Peña is the darling of Mexicano/Chicano performance, but within a larger history of performance in the Americas, what would these genealogies look like if we state his "mentors" are Ehrenberg and Bustamante and that he belonged to one these *grupos* in the 1970s before relocating to the U.S.-Mexico border?
30. I cannot discuss Gómez-Peña's solo work here, but for a critique of his erasure of the U.S.-Mexico border and its metaphorization, see Fox's *The Fence and the River*, especially "Mass Media, Site-Specificity, and Representation..."
31. Yet another multinational/cultural/ethnic visual art performance within the San Diego/Tijuana border is the all-female and (once) anonymous group *Las Comadres* (1988–1992). A member stated: "Fundamentally, we were committed to perceiving the border experience as a bridge rather than a barrier to dialogue, a foundation on which to build a discussion of art making and activism" (Mancillas 107). Their famous performance piece is *Border Boda (Border Wedding)*.
32. In his article "A Binational Performance Pilgrimage," Gómez-Peña describes the *ambience* of the BAW/TAF in the late 80s. The group gained national attention and was commissioned to perform throughout the country, but internal divisions caused tension that led most artists to abandon it, 28–29.
33. The manifesto is available at, http://www.pochanostra.com.

34. Another problematic aspect in Gómez-Peña's work is the representation of female (particularly Latina) subjectivities. For a critique of his approaches to gender, see Chávez-Silverman's "Tropicolada" in *Tropicalizations*.
35. I might be missing the performed irony in this essay.
36. There have been five instantiations of InSite since 1992. See www.insite05.org, especially its "history" section, for the conceptualization of each installment.
37. For an analysis of Werthein's performative intervention, see my article "Sneaking into the Media: Judi Werthein's *Brinco* Shoes..."

# 7

# *Aquí y Allá* [Here and There]: Distance and Difference in Monica Palacios's *Transfronteriza* [Transborder] Chicana Performance

Marivel T. Danielson

Ay, ay, ay, soy mexicana de este lado.

—Gloria Anzaldúa[1]

As a mexicana de estelado,[2] Gloria Anzaldúa's discourse performs a uniquely transfronteriza identity—one that confounds and conflates simple divisions between cultures and nations. Her flesh itself becomes her line drawn in the dirt. The cries with which she punctuates her admission lend a performativity to her theorization. Whether wails of lament, loss, or melodic musing, Anzaldúa's "ay" voices both the passion and pain of her borderlands experience. Blurring the line of separation between United States and Mexico, the author repositions seemingly mutually exclusive sides of national and ethnic identity as fluid spaces of being. Anzaldúa extends her analysis of sides within her poem "To live in the Borderlands means you," as she details being "caught in the crossfire between camps/while carrying all five races on your back / not knowing which side to turn to, run from" (216). Here, rather than sites of origin, Anzaldúa experiences sides as embattled opponents in a disorienting war. Though she identifies with all sides—this time not two nations but the five races she lists as "hispana India negra española" and "gabacha"—she finds no easy refuge or enemy among any single group. The crossfire she describes between the warring sides stands as an important visual translation of the violence and intersectionality inherent to the interstitial borderlands spaces Anzaldúa maps. At the close of the poem she reiterates the necessity for borderlands inhabitants to embody the many points of intersection represented by race, ethnicity, gender, nation, and culture, "To survive the Borderlands/you must live *sin fronteras*/be a crossroads" (217). In the transition from crossfire to crossroads, Anzaldúa shifts her vision of borderlands intersectionality from alienation to inclusion, as the speeding bullets become roads, paths of multidirectional movement that connect rather than separate communities and individuals. Whether violent threats or survival strategies, these interstitial crossings form the foundation for a discussion of transnational, transborder, transcultural, and transfronteriza/o experience.[3]

Anzaldúa's unique analytical style, with her poetic narrative, corporeal emphasis, and genre-blending approach to scholarship, lends itself to discussions of the staged Chicana body in contemporary theater and performance. In her solo performance work, Los Angeles-based Chicana artist Monica Palacios stages the spatiality of the theoretical metaphors of transfronteriza experience explored within Anzaldúa's work. Through my analysis of Palacios's performative development in general and her 2007 production "Greetings From a Queer Señorita" in particular, I will argue that transfronteriza performance grounds itself in a constant renegotiation of the distance and desire between aquí y allá. Releasing the border from the limits of a two-dimensional map or binary equation, Anzaldúa's work on the borderlands insists on the primacy of gender and sexuality for borderlands inhabitants. For writer and performer Palacios, this mode of borderlands being lives and breathes most freely on the stage, through voice and movement, language and song. Anzaldúa's theoretical negotiation of sides and crossings helps to map Palacios's position astride borders of nation, language, gender, sexuality and culture, but also exceeds the limits of creative form, popular representation, reception, and academic scholarship. I propose to interpret Palacios's performative text "through the lens of space" as Mary Pat Brady suggests, tracing authors and artists abilities to "see and feel space as performative and participatory" (6). An emphasis on the politics of space—whether physical or representational—offers unique insight into the resistance, reconfiguration, and reclamation of agency and voice. Through the staging of spatial reclamation, the treatment of citizenship, the centering of the queer Chicana body, and transformative border crossings, Palacios's transfronteriza performance work negotiates myriad personal and professional expectations, strategically staging her own body and borders as artfully crafted affronts to a divided world.

## Multisided Selves: Anzaldúa's Transfronteriza Legacy

As academic institutions increasingly move toward transborder and transnational paradigms as tools for conceptualizing human experience on a global level, it is crucial to theorize how the performative work of queer U.S.-based Chicanas and Latinas—along with other multiply marginalized minority communities—fit within these "trans" critical movements. In particular, how do queer, gendered, and racialized subjects translate the paradigms of "trans" in order to define autochthonous or homemade strategies of resistance by acknowledging the relevance of a global perspective without effacing the specificity of the local.

Gloria Anzaldúa's transformational text, *Borderlands: The New Mestiza*, provides invaluable insight into the negotiations of aquí and allá, since her work offers a theoretical framework of queer Chicana transborder subjectivity that challenges the notion of rigidly defined categories of identity or scholarly production. Just as she envisions mestiza identity straddling across the U.S.-Mexico border, Gloria Anzaldúa's scholarship bridges opposite banks of academic and creative production, as both passionate poetry and engaged critical theory. In Spanish and English, in verse and testimonio, in discourse and self-reflective meta-discourse, Anzaldúa's own words speak the silences between "aquí" y "allá."

While beginning con los dos lados—México and the United States—este lado o aquél, Anzaldúa's vision moves immediately into a dialectic of "sidelessness"—más allá de los dos lados, where bodies betray, belie, and become the borders of simultaneous separation and union. Although Anzaldúa builds her conceptualizations of borderlands and "the new mestiza" around the U.S.-Mexico border, she clarifies the broad scope of her theory beyond geopolitical boundaries and nation-states:

> the Borderlands are physically present wherever two or more cultures edge each other, where people of different races occupy the same territory, where under, lower, middle and upper classes touch, where the space between two individuals shrinks with intimacy. (19)

Here Anzaldúa moves más allá de las fronteras—beyond national divides—to address the fluid nature of transnational and transborder subjectivity. She is careful to define these spiritual, sexual, and psychological "borderlands of being" as having a physical presence equal to that of any wall, fence, or line in the dirt, yet these borders are marked in the flesh.

Performance scholar Laura Guitérrez further shapes the notion of here and there, the sides of transcultural narratives, with her reinscription of the popular refrain "ni de aquí ni de allá."[4] Reversing the traditional double negative, from neither here nor there, Gutiérrez offers the doubly affirming reinscription, "de aquí y de allá," building upon Anzaldúa's discourse of multiplicity and intersectionality.[5] Rejecting the notion of abject alienation, Gutiérrez situates home within what she terms the transborder "double consciousness"[6] of "multi-situated" performing subjects. Yet while both Anzaldúa and Gutiérrez's theorizations of transfronteriza Chicana identity speak the double allegiances of here and there, the discourse of sides and sidelessness remains embedded within the concepts of distance and difference.

The phrase "ni de aquí, ni de allá" voices an identity born of deferral: an individual whose origin cannot be located on this or that side of the border. Yet spatiality marks even this negation of both sides, since the refrain suggests the subject's positioning in the "here" and distancing from the "there." Though the speaker claims to belong to neither, the language reveals an intimacy or proximity with one of the sides, "aquí." While an alternate version of the saying, "ni de México, ni de los Estados Unidos" would express an equal sidelessness[7] without positionality, "ni de aquí, ni de allá" discloses the unavoidable politics of position and proximity—the Chicana subject who adopts this phrasing is situated in the United States with a cultural and familial legacy in Mexico. Though her discourse and experiences do not belong to either country or culture exclusively, the different distances that define her connection to, or disconnection with, Mexico and the United States reveal a perpetual renegotiation or balancing of sides as they come together within her.

María Lugones emphasizes this perpetual negotiation in her discussion of mestiza subjectivity. Invoking the culinary metaphor of mayonnaise, Lugones suggest that while the "sides" of oil and egg may come together to produce a uniform emulsification, timing can quickly derail delicate balance of ingredients, leaving a curdled mass no longer distinguishable as oil, egg, or mayonnaise (458–459). This state of curdled multiplicity—many things, yet none purely—represents a powerful position of unruliness for Lugones: "Mestizaje defies control through simultaneously asserting the impure, curdled multiple state and rejecting the fragmentation into pure parts. In this play of assertion and rejection, the mestiza is unclassifiable, unmanageable. She has no pure parts to be 'had' controlled" (460). Much like Anzaldúa's borderlands, Lugones posits this in-between space as a site of agency and resistance for Chicana subjects. Transfronteriza experience is rarely a static or symmetrical state. Though a subject may identify with both sides of a border—as do Anzaldúa, Gutiérrez and Lugones—the usage of "aquí" and "allá," of this or that side, positions the transfronteriza subject as a perpetually readjusting fulcrum, shifting to negotiate the languages of distance and proximity that intertwine to create discourses expansive enough to stretch from side to side, and even más allá, beyond the paradigms of sides, borders, lines, and limits.

## Monica Palacios: Pathways to Performance

For performer Monica Palacios, the metaphor of sides also extends far beyond national or ethnic communities and into discussions of artistic production and popular reception. Born in San Jose, California, Palacios grew up with a musical and comedic family who inspired her creative talents from an early age. She began her professional career in the early 1980s, doing stand-up comedy in mainstream clubs in San Francisco, where she encountered the ignorant and hateful attitudes of club owners, fellow comics, and audiences alike:

> mainstream clubs were tough—
> did I say tough?—I meant
> homophobic, racist, sexist.
> They didn't want me.
> They wanted to fuck with me. (283)

Initially Palacios attempts to move forward in this mainstream comedy world, silencing her queer, Chicana, and female sides in an attempt to blend in with the successful comics that surrounded her. Yet such an erasure proves as impossible as a reversal of Lugones's curdled state. Palacios's performance persona, Monica,[8] relates her professional difficulties in her 2007 performance of "Greetings From a Queer Señorita" at Arizona State University: "I tried my darndest to act like a generic comic: straight, white, male—always on, cruising chicks—talking fast, always networking—always. But it just wasn't me. And every time I'd tell male comics I got my start San Francisco, they would respond with a stupid homophobic comment. I wanted to smack them in their abdomens with an oar! Instead, I walked away angry, confused, my tummy ached. So you can imagine how I felt on stage."[9] In an introduction to her 2000 published performance script of "Greetings," Palacios also characterizes the venue of mainstream comedy as a wholly hostile and uninspiring space: "I hated the club scene: dealing with hecklers, drunks, smoke, getting stuck on stage at two in the morning. And if that wasn't bad enough, I had to put up with homophobia, racism, sexism—not an ideal creative environment. Experiencing the harsh comedy scene truly made me realize that I needed to create the space where I could feel safe and be in control of my subject matter" (Monica Palacios, "Greetings from a Queer Señorita," 367). Caught in the crossfire of antagonistic audiences and club managers, Palacios identifies her role in the crossing over and forging of new spaces where her narratives of intersectionality and multiplicity will be embraced. Seeking out safer creative sites, Palacios turns to cabarets catering to gay and lesbian audiences and artists. In queer-friendly spaces like the Valencia Rose Cafe, Josie's Juice Joint, Artemis Cafe, and Fanny's Cabaret, Palacios helps establish a thriving community for gay and lesbian comics in San Francisco.[10]

In addition to her solo comedy performances, Palacios also worked alongside Marga Gómez, a Puerto Rican and Cuban-American solo comedian and performer, as the self-proclaimed "Only Latin Comedy Duo in the Universe!" In 1985 Palacios and Gomez joined Richard Montoya, Herbert Sigüenza, Ricardo Salinas, and José Antonio Burciaga to form the first incarnation of the nationally recognized performance collective Culture Clash.[11] After less than two years of strained collaboration, both Palacios and Gomez found their creative voices stifled by the other group members' artistic vision. Consequently, they each elected to shift focus back toward their solo careers away from traditional stand-up comedy.

Following a move to southern California, Palacios once again ventured into mainstream comedy venues for experiences that were similarly marred by the oppressive sexism and homophobia that sent her reeling from comedy clubs in San Francisco years earlier. Not unlike her experiences in mainstream comedy clubs, Palacios's venture into the entertainment industry proved equally unreceptive: "But hey, life wasn't that gloomy! Because the commercial world of comedy led me to TV auditions. For Consuelo *the maid*! Maria *the maid*! Anita *the maid*! Believe me folks, I did not want to go, but I figured this was how every great Latino actor got their start—a foot in the back door."[12] In Los Angeles, however, Palacios also discovered the venues of theater and performance, which proved to be the perfect match for her politically charged and unapologetically queer and Chicana voice. In this instance, a change in genre, rather than venue, provided Palacios with the appropriate space to voice her multi-situated self. With an increased emphasis on oral traditions, like storytelling and musicality—rather than punch lines and commercial appeal—performative genres allowed Palacios to share her own experiences and create art from an empowered state of love and acceptance, unlike anything she had felt in the mainstream entertainment industry in San Francisco or Los Angeles. Over the past two decades, Palacios's plays and performances have been recognized by academic institutions and community organizations. She is a widely respected university educator, journalist, filmmaker, and dramaturg, transforming the arenas of creative production, critical performance studies, and education.

## Performative Possibilities

Performative genres/forms of expression allow not only for an additional element of corporeality so important to many postcolonial and neocolonial subjects and discourses, but these genres also emphasize the performative nature of the representational process. By breaking free from the constraints of the page and the written word, artists embody their texts, circumventing, at least in part, the limitations of language, both as an issue of genre, and power. In the world of performance we no longer read words. We read the performer, her orality, her expression, her gestures, and her silence. Language is a tool for the communication of ideas, but it ceases to be the sole or principle communicative instrument. The dethroning of language is essential to understanding the freedom that performativity affords artists and its boundless potential for transforming identity politics for those subjects whose voices have been silenced or deferred within dominant historical and cultural domains.

Due to the limitations presented by comedy clubs and television production during the 1980s, both Gomez and Palacios turned to alternative venues where they performed for audiences more receptive to their nonconformist work. Palacios explains her professional epiphany in another excerpt from *Greetings From a Queer Señorita*,

> Fuck this shit man! I have to be what I'm about!...I stopped going to all these clubs and those stupid auditions! I couldn't put my Latin lesbo comic self into those Hollywood molds. I figured it out, I now only did shows and got involved with projects that had to do with me: gays and lesbians, Chicanos, Latinos, women, politics—bikini contests![13]

Yet, ultimately the venue seems of less importance than the genre of creative production itself. Of her transition from stand-up comedy to theater, Palacios explains, "I am a story writer and a storyteller, so it was destiny for me to end up doing theatre and performance. As a standup comic I was telling stories, but I didn't appreciate that I had to stick in a joke every twenty seconds" (Monica Palacios, "Greetings from a Queer Señorita," 367). For Palacios, because of this more flexible, less formulaic structure, as well as issues of authorial control, this new performative genre represented a freedom not available in more traditional comedic avenues, "Theatre has truly allowed me to explore my story writing and storytelling. I believe theatre and performance go hand in hand. I love the fact that present day theatre and performance have no limits" (Monica Palacios, "Greetings from a Queer Señorita," 367).

In addition to the more inclusive and supportive atmosphere that performance as an expressive genre affords its artists, one of the most significant characteristics of theatrical production is the literal embodiment of its textual presence. In the case of solo performers such as Palacios, performance represents the "staging" of bodies, subjectivities, and histories previously ignored by dominant audiences. The centrality of the solo performer's body is an undeniable power, as David Román states, "In solo performance the body of the performer emerges as the primary site of representation, interpretation, and, consequentially, possible intervention" (117). Alicia Arrizón also notes that the works of Monica Palacios "literally embody cultural resistance," and when these staged bodies are marked by sexual as well as ethnic or racial alterity and accompanied by a voice in overt opposition to the institutions of heteronormative patriarchy, the performance's transgressive potential is amplified (163). José Esteban Muñoz expands this possibility with a conceptualization of "queer worldmaking" where performers move beyond the staging of one single subject and instead transport spectator and artist alike to a world where the transgression of hegemonic worldviews is possible,

> The concept of "worldmaking" delineates the ways in which performances—both theatrical and everyday rituals—have the ability to establish alternate views of the world. These alternative vistas are more than simply views or perspectives; they are the oppositional ideologies that function as critiques of oppressive regimes of "truth" that subjugate minoritarian people. Oppositional counterpublics are enabled by visions, "worldviews," that reshape as they deconstruct reality. (196–197)

Jill Dolan also suggests the potential for performative reinscriptions of disappointing realities. Dolan theorizes a "utopian performative" that, much like Muñoz's queer worldmaking, poses new ways to see one's surroundings. Dolan and Muñoz both identify the power of performance to claim alternative spaces, constructed outside the limitations of institutionalized oppressions and bounded only by the confines of the performers' and audiences' imagination. Through her staging of both body and voice across boundaries of ethnicity, gender, nation, and sexuality, Palacios's transfronterizo performative production challenges traditionally homogenous worldviews and creates a space for a multiplicity of experiences and perspectives within minority and majority groups. The power of performance lies in its ability to stage both voice and corporeality for subjects for whom representation has never been taken for granted.

## Borderlands Girl, Borderlands World

On November 2, 2007, Palacios presented her one-woman show, "Greetings From a Queer Señorita," as part of the yearlong Performance in the Borderlands series at Arizona State University in Tempe, Arizona. It was billed by the artist as "an evening of wholesome lesbo raunch [with] righteous rants of nationality, sexuality and middle age flab."[14] For many theater scholars, the corporeality of live performance does not stop with the staged body, but extends to the dramatic form itself. David Román affirms, "A performance... is not the same as a production. A performance stands in and of itself as an event; it is part of the process of production. A performance is not an entity that exists atemporally for the spectator; rather, the spectator intersects in a trajectory of continuous production" (xvii). For Palacios, this is certainly a relevant methodological approach to her creative production, since she has performed "Greetings" throughout the United States, in academic and independent theater settings, from its debut in 1995 in Tucson, AZ, to her latest revision, in Santa Ana, CA, in the summer of 2008. While many of the structural elements remain unchanged, including the organization and dialogue of particular scenes, other edits result in dramatically different performances from one setting and one historical context to another.

For example, Palacios's 2007 performance of "*Greetings*" in Arizona included significant additions that focused on the matters of borderlands, immigration, and Latina/o representation, largely because of the show's inclusion in this particularly themed series. In a four-week run of "Greetings" six months later in Santa Ana, CA, Palacios stripped much of her critique of Latino and immigrant misrepresentation in popular media, and instead she shaped the performance around the issue of same-sex marriage—its legalization by the California Supreme Court in May 2008 and subsequent dissolution by California voters in the general election in November 2008.

For Palacios the recirculation of material is a nod to the quality and universality of the material: it stands the test of time and space. She likens herself to jazz and popular vocalist and musical icon Tony Bennett, imploring, "there are certain songs he has to sing every time."[15] And while a show like "Greetings" contains a great deal of "oldies but goodies," I believe Palacios is additionally engaging in a politics of representation that merges Dolan's "utopian performative" and Muñoz's "queer worldmaking." Within the context of Latina theater, Alberto Sandoval-Sánchez and Nancy Saporta Sternbach define a politics of representation as "the double-pronged conscious process whereby playwrights dismantle and undo dominant stereotypical representations at the same time that they revise and rearticulate new ways of seeing" (4). Again, the notion of broken binaries and new perspectives lays a foundation for performative agency. Just as Anzaldúa voices and embodies the productive spaces between sides, Sandoval-Sánchez and Saporta Sternbach posit theater and performativity as revolutionary modes capable of negotiating seemingly dissonant representations. Dolan, Muñoz, Sandoval-Sánchez, and Saporta Sternbach's theories map the reconfiguration of oppositional sides and the forging of new sites of inclusive multiplicity. Sandwiched between California's historical Supreme Court ruling and the looming vote threatening to strip gays and lesbians of basic rights to the institution of marriage, Palacios used the familiar performative framework of *"Greetings,"* alongside newer material, to interrupt pervasive narratives of homophobia. In a scene in the Santa Ana production, Palacios staged an innocent and loving marriage ceremony between two lesbian brides alongside the three-ring circus atmosphere many media outlets expected to report. In the face of a homophobic reality, Palacios staged both the excessive overreaction by local and national media as well as the quiet reality of same-sex unions themselves. In Palacios's performative world, lesbians can marry,[16] audiences will cheer, and the utopian vision offers a glimpse of myriad revolutionary possibilities afforded by socially and politically engaged art.[17]

Although Palacios's Santa Ana performances emphasized the topical issue of same-sex marriage, her use of the familiar framework of *"Greetings"* provides a solid foundation in matters of Chicana/o and Mexican heritage, queer Latina desire, and politically conscious dialogue. Palacios's continuous adaptations of *"Greetings"* provide the "trajectory of continuous production" Román stresses in his scholarship. Like the artist herself, the performances span decades of social transformation, shift with the geographical settings and political climate, and evolve to encompass the worlds Palacios envisions and her audiences are willing to see.

### Are You Scared?

In addition to the evolution of the performance, Román's definition of production as a constantly evolving process reaches beyond the walls of the theater to include acts of performance and production surrounding the dramatic text. Echoing Janet Wolff's work on the sociology of art,[18] Román challenges performance scholars to extend a critical eye beyond the stage and page and toward power structures at play leading up to, and following, any given performance. As with funding sources, promotional and preproduction materials shape the type of audiences and potential reception of a particular event. Much of the promotional material for Palacios's Arizona State performance emphasized what Laura Gutiérrez would term "multi-situatedness" at the limits of language, identity, gender, and sexuality. For some, however, the limits of decency were of far greater concern. The university-sponsored website for the series contained a special note warning theatergoers about the content of Palacios's upcoming show. Upon learning of the disclaimer, Palacios chose to address the cautionary tone of the promotional materials in her performance by feigning enthusiasm:

> I was especially excited to find out on the website, my performance was promoted with a special note that read: *Note: This performance contains adult themes and may not be suitable for all ages*...are you guys scared? I'M FORBIDDEN. I'M DANGEROUS. I'M AN OUTLAW. I'M A BORDERLANDS GIRL!
> I'M GONNA TAKE YOUR JOBS...YOUR HEALTH CARE...AND YOUR PARKING!! YOU BETTER BE SCARED!

In defiantly claiming the scandalous label, Palacios pokes fun at the boundaries she exceeds through her artistic production and ethnic/cultural categorization. Rather than outright rejection of the criminalized stereotyping, Monica—in her performance persona—relishes in the illicit categorization of her material as "adult" and "unsuitable" for particular age-groups. Further, she extends the monstrous metaphor to include popular representations of Latina/os as invading, imposing, and unlawfully acquiring economic and social resources meant for U.S. citizens. Yet her desire to be feared is clearly anxious, as she repeatedly inquires about the audiences' state of mind: "are you guys scared?" and a few seconds later, "YOU BETTER BE SCARED!" In order to perpetuate the stereotype, the audience must accept the performer's innocuous threats as viable and perilous possibilities.

Palacios stages her own borderlands body as a physical manifestation of monstrous hyperbole of menace and greed. Upon delivering the above lines, the staging shifts from general wash lighting to a dark stage, lit only by a single tempestuous, thunder and lightening-filled spot narrow enough to contain only the performer's body. The spotlight positioned at Palacios's feet casts her shadow, massive and distorted, against the back curtain of the stage. At the first sound cue, a sharp crack of lightening, Palacios thrusts her right arm toward the ceiling, her hand transformed into a gnarled claw. She slumps into a deep lunge, dragging a useless left leg and foot behind her as she plods slowly to her right. This corporeal shift, from amiable performer to mutant Frankenstein, mocks representation of Chicana/os and Latina/os as invading threats to the values and resources of the United States and its citizens. Simultaneously, it connects to an identical staging of the monstrous figure following a reference to lesbian sexuality earlier in the performance. The trajectory of Monica's argument, from the advisory note to her exaggeratedly menacing borderlands subject, merges her political, cultural, and sexual platforms to suggest that not only oppressions but also resistance to those oppressions are linked. The fact that Palacios is a queer artist dealing with issues of gender and sexuality outside the heterosexual norm is not at all unrelated to her hybrid experience as a Mexican-origin woman born and raised in northern California, or her politically charged Chicana consciousness. Because the promotional materials do not specify which portions of Palacios's material have been deemed inappropriate for audiences, she invokes the vagueness of the warning to mock the hysteria surrounding any art and identities that emerge in excess, somewhere outside the lines of what is perceived as appropriate and unthreatening.

## My Parents Crossed the Border

As she paints a portrait of her transfronteriza identity, Palacios grounds herself in the music, food, and language of her Mexican heritage. Lola Beltrán's "Si tú también te vas" soars over the theater's sound system as Monica begins to sing and offer gritos of Mexican regional pride to her audience: "Eso es Chihuahua! Ay, ay, ay, Jalisco! Sinaloa! Tempe!" In this series of call-outs, Monica negotiates her aquí and her allá from in between the notes of a familiar ranchera melody. With a deep booming voice punctuated by piercing gritos, she announces three Mexican states, Chihuahua, Jalisco, and Sinaloa, starkly contrasted with her high-pitched and cartoonesque pronunciation of "Tempe," the Arizona town where the evening's performance takes place. Placing the small college town at the end of a sequence that begins with three prominent Mexican states, Monica interrupts her own narrative of Mexican pride with a squeaky reminder of the site where the narrative of Mexican origin comes to life, on this Arizona stage. Ultimately Monica illustrates the transfronteriza performance strategy of situating discourse about one side ("allá") within the space of another side ("aquí"), merging the two sides into a dialogue of negotiated distance and proximity.

Monica shares her parents' immigrant narrative with the audience, noting the hardships and ingenuity that marked their struggle to establish a life on "this side" of the border:

> They traveled from Chihuahua all the way to San Jose IN A CANOE with only the clothes on their backs made from tamale husks.
> And they built themselves a 2 story hut out of toothpicks and churros!

Building upon a stereotypical mainstream version of the immigrant dialogue, Monica paints her parents' tale in exaggeratedly absurd strokes, from the canoe trip to northern California, to the clothes made from cornhusks, and the beautiful home constructed of little more than splinters of wood and sugared street snacks. Her incredulous claims establish a tenuous trust relationship between the audience and performer. Even Palacios's delivery proclaims the inauthenticity of her claims. Her voice frequently cracks with emotion as she describes the trying circumstances under which her parents established their new home in California. The performer even stumbles slightly, as though shaken, both emotional and physically, by this account of their harried journey. When she describes her mother and father's organic attire, she extends the final three consonants of the word "husks," slithering through the now awkward-sounding word with delight. With each hyperbolic claim and exaggerated delivery, Palacios challenges her audience to accept her truths or question their own expectations of the performer, a queer Chicana subject and a dramatic persona. Certainly, the desire to share in the pleasure of Palacios's humor takes precedence over the need for a believable immigrant narrative.

### Our Beloved Quartito

Tracing the lives and experiences of herself and her family, Monica covers the span of a lifetime of transborder experience. In her one-woman show "*Greetings*," she addresses both her parents' generation and their physical journey across the U.S.-Mexico border, as well as her own movement along boundaries and limits defining culture, ethnicity, gender, and sexuality in her home in the United States. In the scene that immediately follows her discussion of her parents' physical border crossing, Monica offers insight into the domestic phenomenon of the "quartito," which she describes as: "a requirement for all Mexicano families." Spatially, the performer establishes the quartito—or little room—as an important but displaced site of ethnic identity. The space is partially defined by its distance from the main dwelling and centers of family activity: "We had a beautiful front yard, a back yard, and way, way in the back, we had our beloved quartito." She informs audience members of the quartito's definition and primary functions: "For those of you who are unfamiliar with this structure.... A QUARTITO is a toolshed and guesthouse.... For those relatives on a budget or hiding from the law." Continuing her riff on Mexican ingenuity, Palacios demonstrates yet another strategy for creating something out of little or nothing. A no-frills storage shed is transformed into a guesthouse—a freestanding structure found on the grounds of affluent homeowners. While the toolshed provides a space for equipment necessary for performing manual labor jobs, the guesthouse offers respite for visitors fortunate enough to travel and enjoy leisure time away from home.

Palacios's "quartito" suggests a merging of the two concepts, with the structure housing both frugal and fugitive family members. Here, working-class ideals and the collectivity of Mexican-origin family combine to span the gamut of Chicana/o stereotypes. Representing the criminalized Chicano, Palacios portrays Tío Chuy, one of the beneficiaries of the quartito's safe haven. Pure Chicano caricature, Palacios, as Tío Chuy, slides into a pachuco and lean with one leg extending forward and a hand thoughtfully at her chin as she agrees with the relatives' pleas to stay out of sight: "Simón...I will stay low to live in the QUARTITO." Tío Chuy speaks in a raspy low voice punctuated by Spanish utterances ("simón"), and a smooth unmarked pronunciation of both Spanish and English position him as a fluid borderlands inhabitant. Embodying the criminalized version of Chicano subjectivity, Palacios simultaneously subverts the stereotype by shifting focus from the criminal act to the family bonds that define Chicano family tradition. The guests in Monica's family's quartito do not enjoy relaxing in luxurious accommodations, but they do relish the support of a family network and the anonymity of a remote space, where, if they "stay low," they may avoid the gaze and apprehension of authorities.

Language adds another layer of transfronterizo experience to Palacios's characterization of the quartito. Spelled with a "qu" rather than the standard "cu," the phonetic spelling in the scripted version of the performance suggests a stronger oral, rather than written, connection to the Spanish language. Vibrant and removed from the written page, Palacios's vision of the quartito speaks the realities of many Chicana/o subjects' linguistic experience in the United States. Born, raised, and surrounded by both English and Spanish, Palacios's fluency in either language is shaded by her proximity and emotional connection to the other. Certain constructs and concepts indelibly linked to her Mexican family and traditions, such as the quartito, cannot be verbalized without Spanish, while her written and sometimes oral production of Spanish bears witness to her physical presence and history in the United States.

Finally, as she closes her study of the quartito phenomenon, Palacios opens the forum to her audience inquiring, "Are there any white people here who have a QUARTITO? It's possible. It's the Southwest. It's the Borderlands." Citing her and her audience's geographic positioning in the southwestern state of Arizona, the performer claims a collectivity that reaches beyond an ethnic or national categorization. From the beginning of the scene, when Palacios deems the quartito as "a requirement of all

Mexican families," we intuit that her invocation of the term "Mexican" serves as a synonym for "Chicano," since her own U.S.-based immediate family is the source of her memories of the quartito. Thus, "Mexican" suggests "Mexican-origin" and later "quartito" pushes at the limits of Chicana/o experience, being a requirement for Mexicans and a possibility for Anglo dwellers of the southwestern United States.

### Tía Cuca and the Transborder Menu

According to Palacios's performance, quartitos are not the only concept shared by residents of the southwestern United States. As an integral element in almost all of Palacios's performative work, food stands as the ultimate transfronteriza experience. In her Arizona State University performance of "Greetings," Palacios offers two mergings of Mexican and U.S. epicurean experience. The first transforms the icon of Americana, baseball, and Independence Day—the hot dog—into a borderlands delight: "It's the Southwest. It's the Borderlands. You can't help but have a hot dog in a tortilla. That's what we would do. In my family, we would get a weenie, roll it up in a corn tortilla, fry it up a bit, make it crunchy...Mexican Hot Dog, Ghetto Gourmet." The addition of the corn tortilla and its crunchy preparation elevates the backyard standard to working-class "gourmet" status for Palacios, who prompts cheers of identification and enthusiasm from audience members upon hearing this description of a familiar favorite.

Palacios informs her audience that the "Mexican hotdog" is actually a dish inspired by her Tía Cuca. Following her earlier lead of utilizing very specifically Mexican-identified items—such as the quartito—to embrace collectivity with a nonethnicity-specific southwestern U.S. community, Palacios declares: "We all have a Tía Cuca...even the white people." Here Palacios utilizes the performative strategy of repetition, as she again extends a specific reference to Mexican/Chicana/o culture—a relative named "Cuca" in this instance—to include Anglo subjects. Monica's pairing of stereotypically Mexican names, cultural practices, or food items with the stereotypically vague community of "white people" serves to explode both ends of the representational equation. By expanding the purported universal of "Tía Cuca," Palacios simultaneously shrinks the representational distance of othered Latino subjectivity from centralized or unmarked discourses.

This particular tía is significant for having been the inspiration for yet another Mexican penetration of an even more iconographic emblem of United States culture, the fast-food restaurant, McDonald's. According to the performer's account, her aunt's order at the local fast-food establishment spawned the "Transborder Menu," which includes a hybrid assortment of Mexican and U.S. fast-food selections such as "a Big Mac with papitas and tacos de lengua." Here the "tacos de lengua" stand in where Tía Cuca and the quartito stood before, exemplifying the difference and distance of a Mexican and Chicana/o cultural "allá" that the performer then collapses into the safety and familiarity of "aquí." Further manipulating the fast-food giant's status as the epitome of Americana, Tía Cuca demands that her server "supersize the lengua," bringing Spanish and English, Mexican meat and U.S. gluttony, and the all-powerful capitalist machine into a single indigestion-inducing order.

### Just Comadres?

Plucked from Palacios's own richly musical childhood, her performance of "Cu Cu Ru Cu Cu Paloma" details the homoerotic undertones of a favorite family memory, a passionate duet between comadres Lala and Trini. Cast in melodramatic and overtly essentialized depictions of Chicana lesbian eroticism, the staging of this particular piece offers two versions of the song, one with play-by-play explanations for her audience, and a second performance lip-synching with the actual audio track sung by Lola Beltrán. In the first manifestation, Monica sets the scene as passionately charged: "They would get to that one point where they would be really close together, looking into each other's eyes, like only Mexican women can who sing together." She provides a narration throughout her account of the duet, as the women exchange verses and powerfully held the notes. Palacios interprets the ranchera style of singing for her audience, explaining:

> ...they would both sing: *Palomaaaaaaaaaaaaaaaaa!*
> Holding it on that one note: *Aaaaaaaaaaaaaaaaaaaaaaa!*
> Because this is what you do with these *rancheras*: *Aaaaaaaaaaaaaaaaaaaaa!*

The layers of performance help to stage Palacios's multisided transfronteriza subjects. This Chicana performer of one generation embodies the two Mexicana comadres of another generation, emphasizing their shared knowledge of the cultural tradition of Mexican music and particularly the stylings of ranchera songs, where all three understand the importance of "holding it on that one note...because this is what you do." Monica's access to the music, its traditions, and the community that keeps it alive form a bridge from her performative persona's Mexican origins and familial legacy to Palacios's contemporary performance practices and positionality within the United States. Coded within her knowing "what you do" is her proximity to the cultural centers that define tradition and her belonging within this Mexican-origin Chicana/o music-savvy community. Everything about this scene and the comadres' performance suggests closeness and sameness, in stark contrast to the experiences of distance and difference from a heterosexist and homophobic Anglo-dominant norm in Palacios's experiences with the mainstream entertainment industry and its reception of her work.

The women's gradual build to a climactic finish finds the two comadres mere inches apart, "and their lips would be really close together—quivering like this. Full of passion and ruby red lipstick." Since the account is offered as Monica's childhood memory, her childhood self reads the multiple layers, or sides to the comadres' duet. She initially identifies the tone of their performance as something distinctly Mexican and female, especially when they "would get to that one point where they would be really close together, looking into each other's eyes, like only Mexican women can who sing together." The women's proximity to each other, their locked gaze, and their shared ethnic and gendered positionalities come together to create a transformative musical medium.

Yet when considering the possibility that the comadres performance is purely heteronormative in nature, the performer doubts aloud: "Just *comadres*? I don't think so" (371).[19] Sandoval-Sánchez and Saporta Sternbach liken the comadres' performance to a sexual act, complete with crooning climax (116). The dramatic Mexican standard and the performance by the two supposed comadres are decoded by the performer's gaze. She understands the silent language of Lala and Trini's bodies, from their quivering lips to their locked gaze. Even as a child, Monica claims her connection to a community defined in difference and desire, and the emotional excess with which Palacios performs this scene is an exemplification of both Chicana and lesbian identities as performance.

Palacios's staging of the song provides an especially interesting transnational take on queer Chicana identity, since as a solo performer she not only embodies both the older generation of Lala and Trini in their call and response delivery of the emotional lyrics but also becomes the young Chicana girl—coming of age in the presence of Chicano community, comadrazgo, and displays of female sensuality and desire. This young girl's ability to "queer" the Mexican and the female cultural practices around her allow for the emergence of an adult queer subject and the continuation of a familial legacy of difference and desire across nations and generations.

## Conclusion

Performance critic Kate Davy posits, "An understanding of how the lesbian performer represents herself on-stage is useful not to separate and valorize her forms of expression as unique from those of everyone else, but to understand how some lesbian performance has begun to push at the boundaries of representation itself" (43). Certainly Palacios pushes at boundaries of gendered and sexual representation, but also of language, ethnicity, and nation. Palacios utilizes elements of performance and performativity to stage the complications of singularly defined minority subjectivity, to resist a static aesthetic of queer and/or Chicana artistic production, and to complicate the politics of identity formation and representation afforded to subjects defined in difference from dominant spheres due to racial, ethnic, gender, or sexual identities. In this chapter I have outlined how one Chicana solo performer's work subverts heterosexist, misogynist, and racist paradigms among Latino, lesbian, and Anglo communities. For the purposes of my scholarship, then, it is most productive to understand transborder subjects as those individuals who actively engage with the direct or indirect cultural, political, and social consequences of border crossings. Palacios's work stages a queer Chicana transfronteriza body and in doing so constructs new worlds that resist the marginalization of multiplicity and speak the fluidity of all "trans" subjectivities. Palacios's transborder subjects need not have stepped across any geopolitical boundary—though some have. Neither have they all communicated or exchanged goods across national boundaries in order for the impact of such movement to have shaped their experiences or identity as transfronteriza. Mexican music, food, and cultural traditions uniquely inform Palacios's representation of queer Chicana identity. Her work demands an understanding of "transborder" that is equally as fluid and transgressive as human experience itself. Palacios's work performs the possibilities of a transfronteriza subject to stage her multiple and simultaneous sides of identity and transform the meanings of distance and difference within her own borderlands being—aquí, allá, and everywhere in between.

## Notes

1. *Borderlands: The New Mestiza*. 2nd Edition, 1999, 25.
2. Mexican of/from this side.
3. Here, transnational, as used by Louis DeSippio (2003), suggests an active involvement with a country of origin via the movement of goods, bodies,

and/or communication across geopolitical national boundaries. I invoke transfronteriza/o to suggest a connection to discourse being produced at and around the U.S.-Mexico border, in Spanish as well as English, and allow for gender-specific discussion of Chicana/Latina subjectivity.
4. Of/From neither here nor there.
5. In a 2008 lecture, Gutiérrez traced the phrase's trajectory in popular production over the last several decades. All subsequent discussion of Gutiérrez's work references this public presentation.
6. W. E. B. Du Bois's theory of double consciousness maps the strategic multiplicity being demanded of African American subjects when seen and categorized as other by dominant Anglo society. While certainly in conversation with Du Bois's conceptualization of "two-ness," Anzaldúa's and more recently Gutiérrez's theoretical discussions additionally suggest modes of multiplicitous interstitial being that transcend the dichotomous divides of either/or and aquí/allá paradigms and posit myriad possible performances of self.
7. For alternate theorizations of sidelessness, see also Eliana Rivero's discussion of márgenes (1996) and hovering (2000).
8. To differentiate, I will refer to the artist by her last name, Palacios, and her performative persona, by her first, Monica.
9. All subsequent references to Palacios's Arizona State University performance are taken from the event videotape and the artist's unpublished script. Please note that this version of "Greetings" contains significant edits/additions from the 2000 published script.
10. All references from unpublished interviews with Palacios, July 7, 2008.
11. For additional research on the evolution of Culture Clash, see David Gumaro García's dissertation "The Evolution of a Critical Race Theater: Culture Clash and Chicana/o Performance Art, 1965–2005" (2006).
12. *Greetings From a Queer Señorita*. Arizona State University. Tempe, AZ. November 2, 2007.
13. Ibid.
14. Artist's blurb that appeared in ASU promotional materials and on the university website prior to her campus appearance.
15. Unpublished interview with Palacios. January 9, 2009.
16. For an analysis of Palacios's latest performative work on California Proposition 8 and the same sex marriage debate, see Marivel Danielson's "Loving Revolution: Same-Sex Marriage and Queer Resistance in Monica Palacios's Amor y Revolución" (2010).
17. On November 4, 2008, California voters elected to accept Proposition 8, which declared marriage an institution between a man and woman, seemingly nullifying future same-sex marriages and overturning the California Supreme Court's earlier ruling. On August 4, 2010, U.S. District Judge Vaughn Walker struck down Proposition 8 as unconstitutional in its restriction of marriage to opposite sex couples. Both sides of the debate anticipate the issue of same-sex marriage legality to come down to a ruling in the U.S. Supreme Court.

Days after the ruling, a federal appeals court imposed a stay on performing same-sex marriages until the case is heard by the appeals court in late 2010. For additional information, see Equality California's official website at: http://www.eqca.org.
18. See Wolff, Janet. *The Social Production of Art: Second Edition* (1993).
19. This direct dismissal or negotiation of comadrazgo in favor of explicit lesbian desire also appears in the narrative work of historian and novelist Emma Pérez. See *Gulf Dreams* (1996); and Catrióna Rueda Esquibel's "Memories of Girlhood: Chicana Lesbian Fictions" (1998).

# 8

# Selena's "*Como la Flor*": Laying the Sound Track of *Latinidad* [Latinness]

*Deborah Parédez*

Throughout the 1990s, amidst prevailing anti-immigrant, English-Only, and welfare reform legislative acts that threatened the citizenship rights of many Latina/os, the conspicuous exaltation of the Latin crossover star marked U.S. popular culture. Before her tragic death at age 23 in March 1995, Tejana superstar, Selena Quintanilla Pérez, was touted as the prototype of the Latin music crossover artist.[1] In the music business, the term crossover generally implies a unidirectional, assimilationist move from a racially marked "regional" genre to the realm of English-language pop music defined by a strategically unmarked Anglo-American standard.[2] As such, the notion of crossing over serves to reify hegemonic notions of whiteness by charting a teleological journey toward "American" culture, thereby effacing the complex dynamism of, and cross-cultural borrowings among, the multiple and often undervalued communities that compose the diverse range of popular cultures in the Americas.[3] This discursive frame also strategically obscures the profound impact that the multinational recording industry has had on regionalized musical genres such as Tejano music.

The story of Selena's career has been locked within this crossover narrative trajectory.[4] From official commemorations approved by her family to the narratives that frame the Selena musical, the biopic, the *Behind the Music* episode about her, obituaries, tribute shows, and magazines chronicles, Selena is often remembered as a Latin music star who was on the cusp of crossover stardom when she died. The story usually goes something like this: Selena successfully crossed over from the regional Tejano music market into the multinational Latin music market and then tragically died just at the moment that she was poised to cross into the U.S. English-language pop music market. Within this crossover frame, Selena is positioned outside of the boundaries of popular U.S. music due to the regional "obscurity" of Tejano music, its linguistic categorization (predominately Spanish-language lyrics), and its working-class affiliations. Most pointedly, the crossover narrative fails to account for the ways that Selena's distinctly American pop music provided a sonic and performative space in which the transnational formulations of U.S. *latinidad* coalesced.

## Selena and Latinidad

Selena's transnational Latin/o American success resulted from both her adept fusing of pan-Latina/o musical sounds and from the entrance of multinational record companies who had begun to sign on and distribute a number of Tejano acts during the 1980s. Selena's success during these years coincided with and was undeniably linked to increased grassroots assertions of and multinational corporate attempts to capitalize upon latinidad. As a result of these forces, Coca-Cola signed on Selena for a promotional deal in 1989.[5] In return, the company provided crucial financial support for underwriting her touring career during this time. Months after signing on with Coca-Cola, Selena secured a deal with EMI Latin Records who began promoting her as a Latin music star by capitalizing upon the transnational "Latin" sound already present in her "regional" Tejano music and by encouraging her to continue improving her Spanish-language skills.[6] EMI Latin thus had a large part in engineering Selena's successful "crossover" from a regionally-identified Tejana to a nationally marketable Latina. During her tenure with EMI Latin, Selena's concert tours and television appearances throughout Latin America and her musical collaborations with Honduran pop singer Alvaro Torres and the Nuyorican boy-band Barrio Boyzz further facilitated her Latin/o American appeal.[7] The transnational reach of Spanish-language networks such as Univisión also contributed to her widespread popularity by broadcasting a number of Selena's concerts across the western hemisphere.

But recording and media industry engineering did not solely account for Selena's inter-Latino popularity. Selena's remarkable stage charisma, vocal power, and deft inter-Latino choreographic moves during her live performances contributed substantially to her widespread acclaim. Selena's fulsome and emotive vocal quality evoked the *filin*, or deliberately performative, singing styles of Latin/a American female *bolero* and *ranchera* performers whose melodramatic flair and world-weary resiliency secured their positions as queer Latina/o icons.[8] But unlike many Latina divas who came before her, Selena channeled her throaty, teardrop-in-the-voice musical stylings within an unabashedly crossover-pop casing. The "synthetic" pop playfulness that framed the "soulful" qualities of Selena's voice distinguished her as a specifically plebeian diva. She delighted in the shiny plastic accoutrements of pop while refusing to succumb to its historically whitening effects. She did, after all, perform Tejano-style cumbias—a musical form regarded by dominant U.S. culture and by a range of Latina/o communities as derivative pop-schlock with a "lower class" country twang.

These explicitly working-class Tejana markings in some ways made Selena and her music counterintuitive symbols of latinidad. Selena's popularity among a range of Latina/os and her promotion (both corporate and personal) as a Latina star conspicuously occurred even as she cultivated a proud Tejana persona through her style, linguistic markings, and decision to continue residing in the working-class Tejano neighborhood in which she was raised. Selena's simultaneous maintenance of her Tejana identity and her claims to the space of latinidad, as Frances Aparicio argues, "defy the linear conceptions of identity shifts" that have often pervaded discussions of Latino identity formation.[9] Selenidad undeniably raises critically productive questions about the tensions that disrupt and affiliations that enable latinidad. Indeed, by most accounts, Selena helped inaugurate the "Latin Music Boom" that exploded in the 1990s—an ironic fact, given the conspicuous erasure of Mexicans and Tejanos within both dominant representations and within the Latin/o music industry itself, as the controversy over the first annual Latin Grammy's made clear.[10] Given that Tejana/os historically have been (dis)regarded as decisively unhip, blue-collar country cousins within larger Latina/o imaginaries, how and why did Selena, with her proudly proclaimed Tejana markings, become a transnational Latina icon among often divided Latina/o communities across the Americas during the 1990s?[11] This chapter addresses this question by tracking and closely examining Selena's performances of one of her most notable signature songs, "Como la Flor" [Like a Flower]. Selena's music operates as one of the most frequently traversed sound tracks of latinidad, and her performance of "Como la Flor" affords us the opportunity to listen to the ways that the staging of racialized sexuality often provides the bass-line for the sounds and gestures of (trans-)national citizenship and migration. In this way, Selena's concert version of this distinctly American pop song charts the emotional registers and cultural codes of latinidad.

## Como la Flor

"Como la Flor" circulates frequently within Selenidad—from video clips posted on YouTube and tribute websites to reenactments performed by young girls and drag queens. This song famously closes the Astrodome concert recreated in the opening moments of Gregory Nava's 1997 biopic and documented on the 2003 DVD release, *Selena Live—The Last Concert*.[12] A close look at Selena's final concert rendition of "Como la Flor" reveals how this signature song offers a site wherein expressions of Latina/o longing and belonging are palpably felt. Through both musical components (tempo, rhythm, lyrics, and song structure) and performative skills (easy charisma, choreographic virtuosity, velvety voice), Selena's performance of "Como la Flor" creates a circuit for navigating Latina/o grief and survival. This song provides emotionally useful modalities— what Jill Dolan would call utopian performatives or what Josh Kun identifies as audiotopias—that posit new possibilities for latinidad beyond the homogenized categories of market segment, political constituency, or national threat that characterized constructions of Latina/os at the turn of the twenty-first century.[13] Instead, this song measures and directs the affective labor of latinidad, invoking the pleasures and punishments resulting from "feeling" Latina/o. Within this performance, we can hear the sounds of Latino desire, witness the improvised steps marking Latino loss, and sing along and follow the lead of the audiotopic possibilities for queer latinidad or Latina agency that they offer. "Como la Flor" thereby tunes us in, so to speak, to the affective frequency of latinidad and to the echoes of its lasting political effects.

Selena closed her 1995 Astrodome concert with "Como la Flor," the hit that has circulated throughout Selenidad as her trademark song. Most of the songs Selena performed between her opening "Disco Medley" and "Como la Flor" were drawn from her 1994 triple platinum album, *Amor Prohibido*.[14] A few weeks before the concert, Selena was nominated for a Grammy in the Mexican-regional category for *Amor Prohibido* (the previous year, she had won the "Best Mexican American Performance" award for her album *Selena Live*, making her the first Tejana artist ever to win a Grammy).[15] Given the number of hit singles cut from *Amor Prohibido* and from Selena's previous albums, the positioning of "Como la Flor" as the concert's closing song underscores its special status within the repertoire of Selena's songbook. As the final song in her final concert, "Como la Flor" has emerged as Selena's swan song, as the aural signifier for both Selena's creative vitality and her untimely death. Given its literal translation (like a flower) and its clichéd associations with beauty and ephemerality, the song title has also become Selena's posthumous epithet, inspiring the name of her biography, a drag contest tribute, and countless other commemorative acts, including the musical tribute, *Selena: A Musical Celebration of Life* (2001) and the ten-year anniversary tribute, *Selena ¡Vive!* (2005) that both showcased the song as their rousing final number.

A pivotal scene in Gregory Nava's biopic recreates an iconic staging of "Como la Flor" that depicts both the effects and affect of Selena's concert versions of the song. In the scene, Selena and her band are performing before an unruly crowd at an outdoor concert in Monterrey, Mexico in 1993. In an effort to manage the mass of overcrowded fans, Selena turns to her brother as they huddle backstage and says, "Let's do 'Como la Flor,' but start it slow, OK?" She demonstrates for him, singing the traditional cumbia melody of the tune in a soothing, elongated tempo, "*Co-o-o-mo la flo-o-o-r.*" They walk onstage, and after the opening chords crest and fall, Selena starts to croon the song's chorus, taking her time with each phrase. Just before the final line, she pulls the microphone away from her mouth and deliberately pauses. In this interlude, she lifts her hand and waves sweetly to the audience and then draws her hand toward her mouth, pressing her index finger against her lips, encouraging the crowd into a hush. The audience, entranced, stands together peaceably, listening intently as Selena finishes the chorus in a measured cooing—casting her performative spell—before gently guiding the crowd back toward the song's trademark cumbia rhythm.

In the narrative arc of the film, the concert follows a frequently chronicled scene from Selena's biography at a Monterrey press conference wherein she defied the odds, overcoming her lack of Spanish-language fluency and the prevailing stereotype in Mexico of Tejana/os as assimilated, uncultured Latinos, and charmed the Mexican reporters with her charismatic charm and gracious decorum.[16] Following the "Como la Flor" performance scene, the camera cuts to an image of Selena's tour bus crossing a river—presumably the Rio Grande—semiotically representing the movement of successful crossover. The next scene takes place inside the bus where Selena's band and family are reading several Mexican newspapers that feature Selena on the front page. Selena's father, Abraham, who reads from a paper with the headline, "*PROVOCA SELENA HISTERIA EN BAILE*" [Selena provokes hysteria at dance], exclaims, "Listen to this: 'Selena is a genuine artist of the people.'" Selena responds giddily, "*¡Que viva México—Monterrey!*" as the rest of her band and family squeal with delight. This series of scenes collectively convey the preliminary moments of Selena's transformation from a regional Tejana into a transnational Latina star. Within this process of Selena's cross-border acceptance, "Como la Flor" emerges as the auditory marker of *pocha/o* triumph, its drawn-out chorus momentarily invoking a community of listeners across various divides.[17]

The filmic placement of "Como la Flor" within its story of Selena's transnational achievements underscores the transformative power of the song (the rowdy audience quelled, the Tejana girl accepted in Mexico) and the song's own transformation (from synthesizer-driven pop cumbia to captivating ballad) in performance. As an amalgam of various live versions of "Como la Flor," Nava's concert re-creation specifically alludes to Selena's Astrodome concert in the moment when Selena waves coyly to the audience. The scene highlights the emotional investments and interactive participation encouraged by the song and enshrines the song securely within Selena's memorial terrain. But how and why exactly did "Como la Flor" achieve this status? What is it about Selena's performances of "Como la Flor" that has inspired such valedictory reverence, pleasurable engagement, and gestures of identification across the space of Selenidad?

A pop cumbia written by A. B. Quintanilla and Pete Astudillo, "Como la Flor" was Selena's first hit single when it was released on her 1992 album *Entre a Mi Mundo*. The lyrics of the song, like many pop tunes, ramble along with a tale of heartbreak, its catchy chorus crowing *"Como la flor (Como la flor) / Con tanto amor (con tanto amor) / Me diste tú / Se marchitó / Me marcho hoy / Yo sé perder / Pero, ay-ay-ay, cómo me duele / Ay-ay-ay, cómo me duele"* [Like the flower / With so much love / You gave me / It withered / Today I leave / I know how to lose / But, oh, how it hurts me / Oh, how it hurts me]. The song invites participation; the call-and-response lyrical structure of its chorus and the narrow range of its *tessitura* seduce listeners into singing along, while its transnational cumbia beat welcomes a wide range of Latina/o dancers to move in the side-to-side slide of its galloping tempo. The song's upbeat pop cumbia melody works as a crosscurrent against its self-abnegating and lovelorn lyrics, not unlike a number of cumbia, salsa, and other dance tunes within Latin/o music whose melodic tempos and the quick-paced choreography they inspire seem at odds with lyrics of unrequited love, political commentary, or tragic loss.[18] There is, as a result, a tensive pull built into the song as the aching proclamations of loss strain against the cumbia's playful pop synthesizer-driven charge.

"Como la Flor's" melodic classification as a cumbia was a large part of the song's inter-Latino appeal. Many Latin music industry executives and experts agree that, as Arista Records producer Cameron Randle asserts, "Cumbia's what opened the door for Selena.... It's considered the musical passport to Latin America, you know—the cumbia."[19] Indeed, cumbia had by the 1980s emerged as a transnational symbol of working-class latinidad. Whereas in Colombia, the cumbia was often played in a big-band style, Tejano musicians stripped the form down into an accordion-driven conjunto sound. Selena and her band continued to transculturate the Tejano cumbia with elements from ska, reggae, hip hop, and funk, thereby revealing one of the ways Selena's music represented an "index of interlatino articulations and of the transnational circulations of sounds that made them possible."[20] As Selena's brother and band mate A. B. Quintanilla stated, "They call us Tejano, and yes, we are from Texas. But a lot of the music we're playing is from Mexico and South America [and is] a mixture of tropical, reggae, cumbia, all these things. It's got pop influences to it, too."[21] This synthesis of sounds from across the Americas is not altogether surprising given the Afro-diasporic cultural roots shared by the cumbia, tropical, and hip hop music and dance styles. In this way, Selena's music also, as Deborah Vargas notes, "captured the underexplored cultural dialogue between Mexican American and African American communities" in addition to other Latin/o American musical traditions.[22] In its transculturated structural components and lively tempo, "Como la Flor" ultimately exemplified a contemporary, classic pop cumbia crafted from and aimed at a range of Latina/o aesthetic tastes.

Selena often began her live renditions of "Como la Flor" by singing the chorus as a mournful attenuated cadenza, breaking from the song's pop cumbia melody (as depicted in the scene from Nava's film). In concert, "Como la Flor" pulled its audience in the undertow of its marked Latina sorrow, only then to buoy them up on its bouncy cumbia rhythm. The sing-along seduction of its emotive opening with its direct address—*"me diste tú"*—and its easy-to-follow dance beat called upon the audience to interact with their whole bodies—as harmonizing chorus and as exuberant dancers. Selena often expanded the song's participatory ethos by using it as the moment in performance when she engaged directly with the crowd, encouraging a call-and-response echo or moving beyond the borders of the stage to share the microphone with her adoring fans. In one such engaging moment during a 1992 concert at Rosedale Park in San Antonio Texas, Selena invited young women onstage to sing the chorus, offering them a moment to showcase their own talents and performative aspirations. After assembling the girls in a line onstage, Selena instructs one of them, "You know the words? OK. You wanna take it by yourself? I want you to put emotion into it. This is your debut. Tonight you are a star!" When she turns to the final girl, who appears to be no older than five years old, she proclaims to the audience, "All right, can y'all see her? This is the next Selena-to-be! *Está chiquita pero picosa* [She's small but she's spicy]."[23] Throughout the solos, Selena claps encouragingly, standing close and guiding them on the beat when necessary or standing outside the spotlight when they hit their marks. These interactive moments staged repeatedly during live performances of the song are suffused with an almost prescient sensibility, as Selena appears to be conducting rehearsals for her own replacement. The song continues to carry this sense of promise and loss. The performances of "Como la Flor" have thus come to signal the capacious and participatory space for self-assertion created by Selena's stardom and her death.

**Swan Song**

Selena's Astrodome performance of "Como la Flor" evocatively captures this sense of Latina/o belonging that arises from the "affective investments" the song encourages from its audiences.[24] By the time Selena performed "Como la Flor" at the Astrodome in 1995, her fans had already come to associate the song with a multivalent emotional register and communal sensibility. As a result, an anticipatory energy and a self-conscious theatricality pervade the performance; Selena and her audience know their parts: she knowingly beckons, and they gather. In the crosscurrent pull from emotive chorus to ebullient choreography, "Como la Flor" captures and conveys what Roland Barthes calls "the grain" of Selena's voice, or the "body in the voice as it sings."[25] Or as Jose Behar, president of EMI Latin Records, frequently noted, Selena had "that teardrop...in her vocal chords."[26] Precisely because of its residue of materiality and its melodic shifts, the song successfully evokes Selena's presence in the elegy marking her absence, and thus offers an auditory—or in Kun's words an audiotopic—space for moving through tragedy and occupying the afterward of survival. But the song not only carries the body of Selena's voice—the sensuous textures of her style, the violet blur of her backspins, the unleashed teardrops in her voice; in its interactive ethos— "Como la Flor" also carries the *bodies* in her voice, or to paraphrase the legendary Abbey Lincoln, the song carries the people in her. "Como la Flor" provides an anthem for a collective Latina/o grief, lyrically offering its plangent expressions of loss while marking the time, in pop cumbia tempo, toward the other side of sorrow.

In the closing moments of her Astrodome concert, Selena introduces "Como la Flor" as her final song, speaking rapidly, "Ahora, me gustaría dedicar esta canción a todos ustedes porque ustedes hicieron esta canción un éxito—el primer éxito para nosotros aquí en los Estados Unidos, igual como en México. Esperoque se recuerden esta canción" [Now, I would like to dedicate this song to all of you because you made this song a hit—our first hit here in the United States and in Mexico. I hope you all remember this song]. She then slows down her pace, shifts her gaze toward her raised right hand and begins her signature move associated with this song: a flamenco-inspired floreo hand gesture, turning her wrist in three beckoning waves, elbow to fingertips twisting in serpentine motion, fingers elongated, as she languorously belts, "Como la flo-o-o-o-o-r." The crowd roars as she continues, "Con tanto amor," taking her time with each line, "Me diste tú," drawing us languidly through the chorus toward the phrase, "Yo sé perde-er-er-er-er." And then she pauses. She pulls the microphone slowly away from her mouth to revel in a smile, and the crowd roars once again as she beams in this smiling pose, inviting us to stand with her a while in this musical rest. When she breaks the pose, it is to acknowledge the future, as she turns directly to the camera recording the event and waves with her right hand, index finger bandaged, thumb encircled by a gold ring. She is smiling broadly and waving knowingly in an aside that conveys intimacy and anticipation. She finishes the chorus, "Pero"—another pause—"Ay-ay-ay," left hand clenched into a fist over her heart as she finishes, "Cómo me duele." The tempo then quickly shifts into the recognizable gallop of the synthesizer-driven melody as Selena repeats her signature hand gesture and the lights brighten to showcase her famous back spins and shuffling steps that smoothly mark the 4/4 time of the cumbia. She then launches into the first verse of the song, carrying us along toward the chorus again, inviting a response to her call, "¡Con ánimo, raza. Vámonos!" [With feeling, my people. C'mon!], and the crowd echoes, "Como la flor."

 This performance of "Como la Flor" captures the affective tenor of Latina/o belonging. Before the song begins, Selena marks out a space for latinidad with her Spanish-language introduction, spoken without the traditional twang of a Tejano Spanglish or the rapid-fire cut vowels of Caribbean accents. Both the pace and the pitch of her sentences evoke a hybrid U.S. Latina/o Spanish that offers a familiar invitation to listeners from across the transnational divides of latinidad. Her Spanish introduction, with its cross-border signification ("el primer éxito ... en los Estados Unidos, igual como en México"), discursively marks the song as a space for transnational Latina/o identification. This moment highlights how, even while she is performing at the rodeo's designated Tejano Night, Selena deftly navigates the affirmations of Tejana/o culture and identifications across the spectrum of latinidad.

 Having established the pan-Latina/o parameters of the song, the performance proceeds to embody the emotional register of Latina/o mournfulness. The achingly melancholic tone of Selena's opening, improvisatory vocal stylings is evocative of the doleful, booming voices of Mexican female ranchera singers who sang with melodramatic flair about themes of longing and despair.²⁷ The elongated cadenza, with its self-consciously exaggerated grieving punctuated by dramatic pauses, also resonates with the filin styles of female bolero singers such as Chavela Vargas or La Lupe whose powerfully throaty vocal styles and hyperbolic stagings of sorrow and betrayal historically served as outlets and templates for Latina/o grief.²⁸ The tempo of this introductory improvisation and its lyrics of exposed heartbreak combined with Selena's repeated flamenco-esque floreo gesture suggest both the overwhelming force of Latina/o sorrow and the staggering power of the Latina diva to guide us through it. The incorporation of flamenco choreography here does not signal an attempt to gain cultural capital with a gesture toward Spanish performance forms, but rather, in its transculturated fluidity, evokes the emotional landscape of the duende—the "shadowy, palpitating," soulful, creative force—central to flamenco practice.²⁹ This moment of performance is thus aurally and visually saturated with the intense, emotive colorings of Latina/o longing that pulse in the closing phrase of the chorus, "Yo sé perder," the final word made performative with the aching, attenuated moan of its second syllable.

And then there's the pause. The breath taken in the midst of so much loss. The dramatic silence before the final enunciation of agony, "Pero, ay-ay-ay, cómo me duele." The moment perched on the brink of sorrow's end. The unpredictability of the pause and the uncertainty of its duration grip the audience in the magic of the performance's present tense and emotional presence. The pause takes its time, suspending the audience in the now. But the pause also provides a break from the temporal space of the now in the instant when Selena shifts from her mournful, anguished pose to smile at the audience and then wave at the camera recording the event. Her knowing smile—a clear and self-conscious "break" in character—acknowledges the act, or the deliberate staging of grief performed, and creates an opportunity for reveling in self-reflexive appreciation of her skills at staging the act. The aside of her wave, like the song itself, is imbued with juxtaposed meanings, signaling an assurance in a time and space beyond this moment of sorrowful lament, while also presaging her imminent death. The wave acknowledges and welcomes an audience beyond the Astrodome even if only to offer them a way to say goodbye. The pause is infused with generosity, inviting its spectators to join in—to applaud at the virtuosic skill, to beg with knowing anticipation for the finish, or to bellow out their own cries of grief. In this way, the pause maps out an audiotopic space wherein Latina/o voices are encouraged to resound.

The movement from pained outcry to playful pop melody is what makes this performance of "Como la Flor" especially conducive to the expression of Latina/o sorrow. Selena's break from her melodramatic belting into her signature cumbia-backspins not only charts a path through and beyond Latina/o sorrow but also conveys an irreverence toward grief itself. As the song's self-abnegating lyrics are repeatedly undercut by Selena's self-asserting skills as a performer, the performance increasingly appears to be winking at itself, self-consciously turning its back on its themes of despair in a way analogous to the repeated 360-degree turns Selena effortlessly executes throughout the song. This irreverence toward loss is evocative of the playful mockery of death expressed in Mexican and Mexican American rituals commemorating the Day of the Dead and other Latina/o mourning practices.[30] The interplay between reverence and reverie enacted within the performance of "Como la Flor" thus registers as a recognizable template for and mode of expressing Latina/o grief.

The citational style of the performance and its dancerly approach to longing and loss are also, of course, what make this version of "Como la Flor" decidedly queer. The unabashed delight with which Selena appears to be quoting her own exceptional skills as a performer—within the plaintive tone and measured pace of the opening chorus and the kinesthetic verve of the cumbia choreography that together showcase her range as both mature, full-voiced songstress and dancing pop star—and the knowing sense with which Selena plays up her range establish her as an undeniable diva within a queer pantheon.[31] In its queer aesthetics, "Como la Flor" possesses a particularly disco sensibility—and not simply because Selena performs the song while costumed in her purple-spangled disco diva pantsuit. The performance's simultaneous articulation of deliberate lament and propulsive pop beat resonates with, as Walter Hughes observes, "disco's representation of desire [that] always included the element of loss."[32] Relinquishment to the "disciplinary, regulatory discourse" of disco's insistent four-on-the-floor beat was, according to Hughes, a performative practice by which gay male identity was produced and wherein gestures of mourning and survival in the fallout from AIDS has been enacted: "the lyrics [of disco] remind us that grief can control us as tyrannically as desire, and so our submission to the beat is still a necessary practice."[33] "Como la Flor" shares this queer dialectic of lyrical longing and conditioning beat. The song's cumbia gallop rides roughshod over its grieving lyrics, providing a disciplinary practice whereby Latina/os dance through and beyond dolor. In particular, the disco ethos that permeates this performance of "Como la Flor" foregrounds queer ways of knowing within a sonic and kinesthetic practice of Latina/o belonging. Through its disciplining beat, grieving diva excess, and gender ambivalent vocal address, "Como la Flor" queers the cumbia—that "musical passport" to pan-Latino affiliation—recalibrating the hetero-normative logic that often constrains the rhythms marking latinidad.

In fact, it was in part due to the ways Selena queered the cumbia that she garnered such a following among a range of queer fans from across the Latina/o spectrum. Historically, the role of the Tejano (and it was invariably a Tejano and not a Tejana) cumbia performer was to "manage" the movements of the dancers on the dance floor through a measured pacing and tempo.[34] Thus, Tejano cumbia singer/musician(s) often maintained a discrete boundary between the orchestrations onstage and the revelry of the dance floor. Selena's live performances, in addition to challenging the entrenched masculinist performance history of the Tejano cumbia, refused such a spatial distinction. Selena, known as much for her dancing skills as for her musical range, used her choreographic solos during her cumbia performances to "lead" and to provoke improvised movement among the dancers on- and offstage. By foregoing the conventional hetero-coupling of partner dancing, her solo dance moves not only disrupted the traditional female Tejano dance position as "follower" but brought the desirous pleasures and kinesthetic negotiations of a queer dance floor ethos to the stage. Selena queered the cumbia by using the musical form to boldly stage a frequently derided sexuality (in this case, working-class Tejana) as a position of power—evidenced through choreographic virtuosity—and as a catalyst for respatializing the gendered and sexual confines of Tejano music.[35]

"Como la Flor" makes room for a multitude of Latina/o bodies in Selena's voice, rehearsing their arrivals in the capacious space of her brand of Américan pop music. The performance history of the song reveals the ways in which "Como la Flor" had been preparing Selena's audiences for her departure all along; it is therefore no surprise that participants in Selenidad take up the song, partake in its offerings, swoon and slide and succumb to its sorrow as a way of feeling their way through latinidad. To perform the longing of "Como la Flor" was to share in the collective grief around which latinidad cohered at the close of the twentieth century. In its simultaneous enunciation of arrival and loss, the song expresses and modulates the way latinidad felt in the years marked by English-only propositions, immigration and welfare reform, and the disproportionate losses of Latina/os to AIDS. The Astrodome performance of "Como la Flor" captures the grain of Latina longing in Selena's voice as it achingly elongates the perder, and in its kinesthetic directives to survive the duele by audaciously occupying the dance, the song also continues to carry the resilient choreography of latinidad in her voice. In the years since the Astrodome concert, in the midst of celebrations of "Latin culture" and legislation against Latina/o bodies, it is no surprise that many Latina/os accept the invitation to move creatively within "Como la Flor's" generous dimensions.

## Notes

1. Cepeda addresses the decontextualized and de-historicized construction of Latina/o performers as crossover acts in "'Columbus Effect(s)': Chronology and Crossover in the Latin(o) Music 'Boom'" (2001).
2. In an interview with Manuel Peña, Arista Records' executive Cameron Randle notes, "'Crossover' is pretty much one concept...which is to crossover from a more obscure genre, a more confined genre of music, into a mainstream awareness or consciousness." Qtd. in Manuel Peña, *Música Tejana: The Cultural Economy of Artistic Transformation* (1999), 195.
3. More on the ideological repercussions of the musical crossover narrative can be found in Garofalo, *Rockin' Out: Popular Music in the USA* (1997), and Lipsitz, *Dangerous Crossroads: Popular Music, Postmodernism and the Poetics of Place* (1994).
4. For a commentary on Selena and the crossover narrative, see Vargas, "*Cruzando Frontejas*: Re-mapping Selena's Tejano Music Crossover" (2002).
5. Due to their desire to capitalize upon the growing Latina/o market, Coca-Cola renewed Selena's contract after 1992, the year in which it dropped celebrities from its ad. campaigns. See Patoski, *Selena: Como La Flor* (1996).
6. The category of Latin music requires that at least 50 percent of an album's tracks must be in Spanish. The promotion of this music occurs largely in Spanish-language media, underscoring the ways that Latina/os are primarily defined by language. See Cepeda, "*Mucho loco* for Ricky Martin; or The Politics of Chronology, Crossover, and Language within the Latin Music 'Boom'" (2000).
7. The video for "*Buenos Amigos*," Selena's 1991 duet with Honduran pop singer Alvaro Torres, introduced Selena to audiences on the East and West coasts and helped the ballad reach number one on the Billboard Latin tracks chart. Selena followed this with a guest appearance on the video for "*Donde Quiera Que Estés*" wherein she sang and danced in hip-hop formation against an urban backdrop with the Nuyorican boy-band, Barrio Boyzz. Freddy Correa, one of the members of Barrio Boyzz, went on to tour with Selena as one of her backup singers/dancers.
8. Knights writes, "Through the explicit emphasis on deliberate performance, *filin* provides a queer cultural space in which gender identities and sexual roles can be destabilized" (2006), 87.
9. Aparicio, "Jennifer as Selena: Rethinking Latinidad in Media and Popular Culture" (2003).
10. The First Annual Latin Grammy's took place on September 30, 2000 in the midst of public criticism expressed by Gilberto Moreno, general manager of Fonovisa, the California-based Latin music label known for releasing regional

Mexican recordings. Moreno's comments, initially printed in the Spanish-language newspaper, *La Opinión*, and reported on in major papers across the country, reflected larger sentiments among many Mexican Americans that despite their demographic status as the majority group among Latina/os, they continued to be absent or underrepresented in English- and Spanish-language media outlets. These conflicts belie the inter-Latino tensions that arise along lines of race, class, and region within the United States. See Arroyo, "Una falta de respeto total," *La Opinión*, September 1, 2000, 9C; Arroyo, "ARDE TROYA! Pepe Aguilar y muchos nominados no aceptarían el premio; 'Es una fiesta de Sony y Emilio Estefan,'" *La Opinión*, August 29, 2000, 1B.
11. Arista Records' executive, Cameron Randle, makes this point clear: "We just came back from the *Billboard Magazine* Latin conference in Miami. And you go down and get a sobering reminder of Tejano's place within the Latino family, musically. It's still treated essentially as a blue-collar, secondary genre of music that is confined to a geographical area." Qtd. in Peña, 196.
12. *Selena Live—The Last Concert.* 55 min. Image Entertainment, 2003, DVD.
13. Dolan (2005) defines utopian performatives as those moments in performance that, "in their doing, make palpable an affective vision of how the world might be better" (6). According to Dolan, utopian performatives are "most effective as a *feeling*," and, as such, their political and social efficacy resides in creating "the *condition* for action" in the spaces beyond the now of the performance (20, 169, emphasis in the original). Kun (2005) writes about both the spaces within and produced by music—the structural components of song and sound as well as the social, political, and imaginative worlds music makes. Kun calls our attention to what he calls audiotopias, those "small, momentary lived utopias built, imagined and sustained through sound, noise, and music" (21).
14. A large part of *Amor Prohibido's* appeal to a range of Latina/o listeners was its mixed repertoire of sounds that represented the culmination of Selena and her band's creative efforts to combine traditional Tejano forms with other Latin/o and African American sounds and instrumentation. See Cepeda, "*Mucho loco* for Ricky Martin," for a discussion of mainstream chronologies of the Latin Music "Boom."
15. The first Tejano artist to win a Grammy was Flaco Jimenez, who, in 1986, garnered an award for a remake of his father's song, "Ay te dejo en San Antonio."
16. In the logic of the recording industry, Tejano artists such as Selena had to acquire commercial success in Mexico as a means of proving their potential to reach pan-Latino U.S. audiences and of assuring an eventual ranking within Billboard's Mexican regional (Mexican American) and Latin charts. Not unlike many third-generation, working-class Tejanos, Selena was not entirely proficient in Spanish. In fact, early on in her career, Selena was unable to conduct interviews with the Spanish-language media without an interpreter and was often derided for it. Moreover, Selena's morena features

further entrenched her affiliation with the working class. It was thus necessary for Selena to "cross over" linguistic and class borders in addition to musical and cultural ones.
17. Historically, the term *pocha/o* was deployed as a derisive epithet to describe Mexican Americans who did not possess fluency in Spanish or was thought, in general, to be too "Americanized." The term has been appropriated by recent generations of Chicana/os as an assertion of bicultural pride. See, for example, the work produced on www.pocho.com.
18. See Aparicio, *Listening to Salsa: Gender, Latin American Popular Music, and Puerto Rican Cultures* (1998), for an analysis of salsa lyrics.
19. Qtd. in Peña, 197.
20. Aparicio, "Jennifer as Selena," 97.
21. Qtd. in Mitchell, "Selena," *The Houston Chronicle*, May 21, 1995, Magazine Section: 6.
22. Vargas, "Bidi Bidi Bom Bom: Selena and Tejano Music in the Making of *Tejas*" (2002).
23. Personal video of Selena in concert, Rosedale Park, 1992, in collection of author.
24. I borrow the concept "affective investments" from Grossberg's "Is there a Fan in the House?: The Affective Sensibility of Fandom" (1992). Knights offers an insightful application in "Tears and Screams: Performances of Pleasure and Pain in the Bolero" (2006).
25. Roland Barthes' "The Grain of the Voice" (1977).
26. Qtd. in Rohter H39.
27. For a feminist analysis of rancheras and their reception, see Nájera-Ramírez, "Unruly Passions: Poetics, Performance, and Gender in the Ranchera Song" (2003).
28. In her queer analysis of Chavela Vargas and La Lupe, Knights describes *filin* ("feeling") as "an explicitly emotional or expressive style of singing achieved through various techniques...[that include] its gestural performance style incorporating silences and pauses for dramatic effect" (87). For more on La Lupe and Chavela Vargas, see Aparicio, "La Lupe, La India, and Celia: Toward a Feminist Genealogy of Salsa" (2000); Aparicio and Wilson's "Memorializing La Lupe and Lavoe" (2004); Yarbro-Bejarano's "Crossing the Border with Chabela Vargas: A Chicana Femme's Tribute" (1997).
29. García Lorca, "Play and Theory of the Duende" (1998).
30. For more on the commemoration of the dead and its relationship to Mexican American folkways, Mexican national identity, and Latina/o expressive culture, see Brandes, *Skulls to the Living, Bread to the Dead: The Day of the Dead in Mexico and Beyond* (2006), and Carmichael and Sayer, *The Skeleton at the Feast: The Day of the Dead in Mexico* (1992).
31. For more on diva singers and queer spectatorship, see Koestenbaum, *The Queen's Throat: Opera, Homosexuality, and the Mystery of Desire* (1993), and Leonardi and Pope, *The Diva's Mouth: Body, Voice, Prima Donna Politics* (1996).

32. Hughes, "In the Empire of the Beat: Discipline and Disco" (1994).
33. Hughes 148, 156.
34. Vargas "*Las Tracaleras*: Texas-Mexican Women, Music, and Place" (Ph.D. diss., University of California – Santa Cruz, 2003).
35. My thanks to Deborah Vargas for helping me develop this insight.

Part IV

# *De Imágenes y Sueños* [Of Images and Dreams]: Transnational Border Visual Cultures

# 9

# De Imágenes y Sueños [Of Images and Dreams]: Transnational Mexican Visual Culture

*Tomás Ybarra-Frausto*

The opening page of the canonical Chicano novel *Y no se lo tragó la tierra* [*And the Earth Did Not Devour Him*] by Tomás Rivera begins:

> These things always begin when he would hear someone call him by name. He would turn around to see who was calling, always making a complete turn, always ending in the same position and facing the same way. And that was why he could never find out who it was that was calling him, nor the reason why he was being called.
> He would even forget the name that he had heard. Once, he stopped himself before completing the turn, and he became afraid. He found out that he had been calling himself. (Rivera 6)

This call to self occurs to individuals, communities, and nations at strategic and transformative moments in their history. As we round the corner of the twenty-first century, some despair sensing that the center is not holding—that everything solid seems to melt into thin air. For many others, especially U.S. Latinos who now constitute the largest ethnic group in the country, the present is a heady moment of introspection, analysis, and action.

The Latino imagination expressed in visual art, literature, and the performing arts provides new and expanded narratives of the American experience. The dreams and aspirations of native-born Latinos and newly arrived immigrants from throughout the Americas inform the current cultural production of U.S. Latino artists. Their ardent images and forceful narratives underscore the reality of contemporary society as multilingual and multicultural.

Today, migratory flows and escalating exchanges of goods, economies, and ideas across hemispheric borders position contemporary U.S. Latino experience and cultural expression as part of an incipient transnational imaginary. Transnationalism is here defined as the circular flow of people, ideas, practice, and cultural and economic resources that occur when individuals or families embark on earning a living and making a life across national borders.

## Contact Zones

The borderlands on both sides of the U.S.-Mexico border share many of the attributes of what Mary Louise Pratt labels as "Contact Zones." Pratt explains, "'Contact Zones' are not geographic places with stable significations, but are simultaneously sites of multi-vocality, of negotiation, borrowing and exchange." She further explains, "These are social spaces where disparate cultures meet, clash and grapple with each other, often in highly asymmetrical relations of domination and subordination. A 'Contact' perspective emphasizes how subjects are constituted in and by their relations to each other. It stresses copresence, interaction and interlocking understandings and practices" (Pratt 7). The contemporary "Contact Zone" between Mexico and the United States continues a long trajectory of commodity and cultural exchange between people living in adjacent geographies.

From the dawn of Mesoamerican civilizations, there is a mythic discourse of departure and return between Mesoamerica and what is now the American Southwest. Archeological evidence describes trade routes and diverse forms of cultural exchange, including pottery, textiles, and jewelry, between the northern mythic Aztlán and Mesoamerica. These primordial indigenous encounters, contacts, and interchanges are the prologue to later centuries of contiguous engagement.

During the colonial period, key conduits for cultural contact and exchange were the "Caminos Reales," the roadways linking central Mexico and the American southwest. The "Caminos Reales" created "Contact Zones" for the reciprocal movement of people and the exchange of cultural goods such as decorative arts, textiles, furniture, and musical instruments. In the twentieth century, the Mexican Revolution (1910–1920) was a historical junction that augmented sociocultural links between Mexico and the United States. The hundreds of thousands of Mexicanos emigrating north brought with them the norms and cultural values sorted in the distinct regional culture of Mexico. This cultural diversity invigorated the long-established Mexican American culture and cities such as San Antonio, Los Angeles, and Chicago, among others.

Today, the "Contact Zone" linking Mexico to the United States is a strategic social space of cultural entanglements. Within intensifying processes of circular migration, sending-communities in Mexico and receiving-communities in the United States forge dense and strong social and cultural networks based on solidarity and shared aspirations. New scenarios of identity and belonging subvert traditional national narratives of cohesion and homogeneity. As people move back and forth between the United States and Mexico, vital and innovative cultural expressions respond to intertwined economies, new communication technologies, and interacting social systems on a multidirectional flow of culture.

## Martín Ramírez

In the long continuum of borderlands cultural exchange, the artist Martín Ramírez remains a precursor to contemporary artists delineating a transnational sensibility. In 1924, Ramírez, a self-taught visionary artist, migrated to California from Los Altos de Jalisco to work in the mines and railroads. He abandoned a Mexico destabilized by the carnage of the Mexican Revolution and the religious persecutions of the Cristero rebellion. When Ramírez arrived in California he saw shanty towns and shuffling lines of people in the tatters waiting for a piece of bread and soup from makeshift soup kitchens. The shadow world of the Great Depression and its stark human scenarios parallel Ramírez's fragile psychological frame of mind.

In 1931, Ramírez is picked up by the San Joaquin County Police and committed to Stockton State Hospital, where he receives a preliminary diagnosis of manic depression. From 1948 on, he begins a lifelong confinement in the psychiatric ward at the De Witt State Hospital in Auburn, California, assessed as suffering from *dementia praecox*.

Completely deracinated from his family and his culture, unable to speak much English, and totally isolated from the world at large, Martín Ramírez brings into being a redemptive artistic project. Refusing victimization, he starts the prodigious task of creating a rich symbolic universe that negates his isolated reality.

Ramírez's artwork is an astonishing output of multilayered drawings and collages executed with rigorous control of line, space, and rhythm. Moving seamlessly between real and imagined worlds, his drawings are visions of a remembered rural Mexico of ranchitos, colonial towns, and religious practices. Simultaneously he projects a complex interior world of labyrinths, tunnels, and fantastic architecture.

A true original, Martín Ramírez is slowly being rescued from marginality by art historians who move beyond the normative categories and rigid taxonomies of mainstream art histories. One such scholar is Victor Zamudio-Taylor, whose pioneering research and publications have vindicated the art of Ramírez and its place in Mexican American art and cultural studies. Zamudio-Taylor writes:

> Instead of being an outcast—one who has never really been an integral part of any community because of his hospitalization—Martín Ramírez would be viewed and honored as a heroic figure of resistance and cultural affirmation, an artist who preserved in the most hostile of conditions, a figure who should be the source not of shame but of pride, a pioneer Mexican American artist whose oeuvre outlives time and speaks to us today in a most relevant and contemporary way. (Zamudio-Taylor, 66)

Postrevolution, immigration continued unabated. The journey was always dangerous and often humiliating. Documents show that, beginning in the 1920s, officials of the U.S. Public Health Service in El Paso "deloused and sprayed the clothes of Mexicans crossing into the U.S. with Zyclon B. The fumigation was carried out in an area of the building that American officials called ominously enough the 'gas chamber'" (Romo, 223).

Raúl Delgado, who came to the United States as a bracero in 1958, described being deloused by U.S. customs agents at the Eagle Pass Border:

> They put me and the other braceros in a room and made us take off our clothes. An immigration agent with a fumigation pump would spray our whole body with insecticide, especially our rear and our *partes nobles*, some of us ran away from the spray and began to cough. Some even vomited from the stench of those chemical pesticides...the agent would laugh at the grimacing faces we would make. He had a gas mask on, but we didn't. (Romo, 223)

Such traumatic indignities and suffering are themes in the lore of "El Cruce," the crossing over "pa'l norte." In rural villages and towns through Mexico, the epic journey north has become a rite of passage, a defining life experience for young men, and more recently for women and entire families.

Artists and writers continue to be crucial in giving voice and a human face to the anonymous border crossers often only mentioned as "mano de obra." Whether through documentary photography, oral and written testimonies, corridos, visual arts, and performative artistic expressions, artists depict the exploitation as well as the aspirations and agency of migrants in their obstinate quest for well-being.

### The Archive and the Repertoire

In the contemporary period within the United States, from the Chicano cultural and civil rights reclamation project in the mid 1960s to the emergence of a pan-Latino consciousness at the turn of the twenty-first century, the U.S.-Mexico borderlands function as an intense "cultural incubator" and a sedimented locus of cultural production.

Within this liminal "contact zone" of attraction and repulsion I want to extend the notions of "the archive" and "the repertoire" as theorized by Diana Taylor in her groundbreaking book, *The Archive and The Repertoire: Performing Cultural Memory in the Americas*. Taylor convincingly explores the histories of North and South America through literary and historical documents (the archive) and forms an embodied performance (the repertoire) as she states that "not everybody comes to 'culture' and 'modernity' through writing" (Taylor, 21).

In the U.S.-Mexico "contact zone," enacted knowledge passed on by repeated embodied practices such as storytelling, cooking, singing, and dancing, as well as patron saint feasts and civic festivals, transmit memories and social identities. Written documents (the archive) are constantly revitalized by such notable scholars as Américo Paredes, Jovita González, José Limón, Gloria Anzaldúa, Manuel Valenzuela Arce, Amelia Malagamba-Ansótegui, María Herrera-Sobeck, Norma Cantú, among many others, who have studied the embodied and performative practices of "the repertoire" and preserve them in "the archive."

The archive and the repertoire together function as social epistemes (ways of knowing that transmit knowledge). Discursive written documents and embodied knowledge passed on by physical performative actions are in a constant state of interaction throughout the borderlands. Scholars such as Jacques Le Goff propose "that writing and the archive provide historical consciousness while performance and the repertoire provide mythical consciousness" (Taylor, 21). Within this framework of "the archive" and "the repertoire" we can glance backward to the recent past to recall core interventions in the process of arte fronterizo.

In his 1976 book, *A Texas-Mexican Cancionero*, Américo Paredes posits the notion of "Greater Mexico," referring to the borderlands as a social space where transnational communities can enact new identities, politics, and culture outside the realm of "lo nacional." The Paredes concept of a "Greater Mexico" establishes an imagined cultural bridge permitting encounters and rescue of common origins, traditions, and values linking cultural workers on both sides of the U.S.-Mexico border.

In the 1980s, with the rapid growth and increasing impact of border economies and demographics, the Mexican government begins to decenter Mexico City as the sole arbiter and definer of "la cultura nacional." Financial and intellectual resources are channeled to support "Casas de Cultura" along the length of the border. Cultural programs and projects in the Casas de Cultura focus on articulating and validating a "fronterizo" consciousness and a border cultural discourse. Scholars such as Amelia Malagamba-Ansótegui and José Valenzuela Arce, both professors at the Colegio de la Frontera Norte in Tijuana, Baja California, arranged convocations and established networks and collaborative projects between artists/activists along the border. "Festivales internacionales de la Raza" held in various border towns showcased border cultural production for over a decade, starting in 1983.

Binational awareness was further animated by notable exhibitions such as "A través de la frontera," mounted in Mexico City in 1983. Critics, curators, and artists from "La Capital" and the borderlands engaged in heated debates on how to interpret and integrate "arte fronterizo" into official canons of "la cultura nacional." On the American side, a key animator of border art was the Border Arts Workshop, Taller de Arte Fronterizo (BAW/TAF), an interdisciplinary group of artists, scholars, and cultural artists founded in 1984. Over time, the group included David Avalos, Elizabeth Sisco, Guillermo Gómez-Peña, Victor Ochoa, and many other borderland artists. In the collective art practices, the BAW/TAF integrated exhibitions, performance, community dialogue, and media interventions to create awareness of border social realities.

## Malaquías Montoya

Malaquías Montoya is a decisive figure in the debates about the social meanings of fronterizo art and the search for contact and exchange with border artists and cultural organizations. Montoya participated in both A través de la frontera and in several editions of the Festivales internacionales de la Raza. In 1985 Malaquías Montoya's paintings and graphic art were selected for a comprehensive exhibition in Tijuana. Originally scheduled for one month, the exhibit garnered such positive critical and popular acclaim that it was extended for an additional three months. Montoya was also invited to paint a portable mural with the theme of "El barrio, primer espacio de la identidad cultural" in Tijuana, Baja California. The mural was completed in the summer of 1986 and is acknowledged as the first Chicano mural painted in Mexico.

As an artist and cultural activist, Malaquías Montoya "has dedicated his life to informing and educating those neglected and exploited people whose lives are at risk in milieus of racism, sexism and cultural oppression" (Zirker, 10). He seamlessly moves from representing the local concerns of farmworkers and poor Chicanos in California to rendering images of global struggles for cultural equity and social justice.

Montoya's art includes drawings, acrylic paintings, murals, and posters. He is internationally recognized for his bold silkscreen prints that are forceful combinations of vital images, subtle coloration, and text. The image and text composites simultaneously delight and focus the viewer's attention to pressing social concerns. In all his creations, Malaquías Montoya exhorts viewers to move beyond aesthetic contemplation to direct social involvement.

Continuing the great Mexican tradition of graphic art, in the footsteps of masters such as José Guadalupe Posada, Luis Arenal, and Leopoldo Méndez, Malaquías Montoya is also recognized as a "veterano" Chicano artist. He has inspired and mentored legions of cultural workers on both sides of the U.S.-Mexico border to make art that educates, communicates, and can be valued for its social utility beyond its commodity value. At the turn of the millennium, new "Contact Zones" are being created as immigration increases from non-border "sending communities" in Mexico to "receiving communities" in the south and midwestern regions of the United States.

### Alejandro Santiago, 2501 Migrants

Alejandro Santiago, master artist, lives and maintains a studio in the valley of Etla in Oaxaca. A self-described nomad, Santiago has lived and worked in Mexico City, Paris, and has traveled throughout the United States and Europe, always returning to his "patria chica" in Oaxaca. The project 2501 migrants took root when Santiago, newly returned from Europe in the early 1980s, saw many villages being abandoned and fields left fallow as local campesinos immigrated to California. In a serendipitous gesture, a friend offered him a one-way plane ticket to Tijuana. From there, with false identification papers obtained from a coyote, Santiago crossed illegally to Oceanside and from there to San Francisco.

Having experienced the indignities and trauma of being a "mojado," Santiago returned to Oaxaca with the idea of memorializing the 2,500 members of his community in Teococuilco who are transnational immigrants. The extra one in his "2501 Migrants" represents the next person already preparing to leave. Each of the absent community members would be evoked by a life-sized, three dimensional terra cotta sculptural figure with painted and glazed features. The aim was not to create individual portraits but figural representations marking a void or an absence.

Working with clay obtained from pits around the community, Santiago molded his figures by hand. Next the artist was confronted with the difficult task of having to find commercial ovens to bake the fragile clay statues. After importing large custom-made ovens, local elders and youth were hired in teams to mold and paint each particular figure under the guidance of the artist. Each personage has an individual personality reflected in his/her shape, body stance, and attitude. The creation process took over three years.

Alejandro Santiago wanted to have all the figures sited in the village to welcome the returning migrants coming home to celebrate the yearly "fiesta patronal." The clay figures would be placed in the windows of empty houses, in the belfry of the abandoned church, in the cemetery, and in all street crossroads of the village of Teococuilco.

Functioning as guardians, the figures remind the returning workers that they have not been forgotten, and that they occupy a space in the memory of those who stay behind. The sculptures mark the space of those returning and those who will be absent forever. In Oaxaca, the 2501 migrants stand amidst "mainly empty houses where only an old grandmother remains, an ancient woman who sweeps the bedrooms remembering the names of the sons she has not seen again, of the grandchildren whom she does not know" (Villareal, 14–15).

## Enrique Chagoya

Born in Mexico City in 1953, Chagoya is currently professor of art at Stanford University. While serving as Artistic Director of Galería de la Raza in San Francisco in the mid 1980s, he advanced the Galería's goal of promoting a hemispheric exhibition program. Chicano/a, Mexican, and Latin American artists were invited to present their art, give gallery talks, and debate the aesthetic and sociopolitical implications of the transnational, especially the mobility of iconographies and styles between the Americas.

In his own idiosyncratic work, Chagoya engages a process he labels as "reverse anthropology." His imagery pushes hegemonic cultures to the margins and he reinterprets official histories and dominant cultural paradigms by replaying them from the point of view of the dispossessed. "Chagoya rewrites, redraws, and collages playful and violent alternative histories in an inexhaustible collection of signs, symbols, imagery and languages" (Hickson, 16).

Chagoya describes his artistic credo: "My work is a product of collisions between historical vision and contemporary paradigms. It is a thesis and an antithesis that ends in a synthesis in the minds of the viewer. I seek to create a nonlinear narrative with many possible interpretations" (Chagoya, 180). Depending on specific content, he works in different media, painting, drawing, print-making, video animation, and installations.

In Chagoya's art, collisions and encounters fuse illustrations taken from Old World books and manuscripts and new world codices. With superb drawing skills, an acute color sensibility, and a masterful compositional sense, Chagoya's paintings, drawings, and prints intermingle pre-Columbian mythology, Catholic icons, superheroes from American comics, and media ethnic stereotypes. Brimming with wit, irony, and biting humor, Chagoya employs social satire as an organizing theme of his visual narratives. For the past decade, Enrique Chagoya has been producing contemporary renditions of pre-Columbian codices.

In ancient times, the codices were made from amate paper, hand-colored and folded in accordion-like extensions. They were read from right to left and functioned as compendiums of historical, astronomical, ritual, medical, and genealogical indigenous knowledge. "A mere twenty-two [original codices] survive—three Mayan, nineteen Mixtec/Zapotec and no Aztec—and for the most part continue to reside in European collections, far from their lands of origin" (Hickson, 17).

For his postcolonial codices, Chagoya appropriates illustrations from reproductions of indigenous codices and images from Mexican and American comic books, religious imagery from Catholic catechisms, and illustrations from old books found in flea markets. The codices present unexpected juxtapositions of images from vernacular and high culture to subtly comment on social issues of the moment. Chagoya's drawings, paintings, and prints bristle with ambiguity and multiple cultural references, constantly reminding us that being a border crosser is a permanent process of reinvention.

### Dulce Pinzón

The five boroughs of Manhattan have a steadily growing population of Mexican immigrant workers. Many come from Puebla, and they have

**Figure 9.1** "Minerva Valencia from Puebla," by Dulce Pinzón (Courtesy of the Artist).

baptized the area as Pueblatitlán. Living in Brooklyn, Mexican-born photographer Dulce Pinzón pays homage to immigrant workers in her *Superheroes* series. The project consists of 20 color photographs of Mexican immigrant workers costumed as comic-book superhero characters. Posed in their work environments—Superman delivering food on a bicycle, Catwoman babysitting children, Spiderman cleaning windows on the side of a building—the photos include text naming the real worker depicted and detailing how much money each sends home to Mexico every week. The money "remesas" (remittances) sent home by immigrant workers in 2006 were estimated at 16.6 billion dollars. After oil and tourism, "remesas" constitute the third-largest component of the Mexican economy.

Pinzón's *Superheroes* series shines a spotlight on the silent, largely unseen Mexican immigrant workers steadily more present and visible in all sectors of the New York economy. Working long hours for low wages in dire conditions, the workers scrimp and save to frequently send as much money as they can to families in Mexico who rely on these "remesas" to survive. Increasingly, the U.S. and Mexican economies are becoming interdependent. Mexico is dependent on immigrant workers' "remesas" and the United States is equally dependent on Mexican immigrant labor. Dulce Pinzón's staged and colorful photographs juxtapose real work environments and theatrical, stylized actions in the manner of comic-book storyboards. With a wistful humor, *Superheroes* helps restore humanity to the largely anonymous immigrant workers and restores the topic of work as a heroic subject for artistic creation.

## Margarita Cabrera

Margarita Cabrera lives and works in the binational social space of Ciudad Juárez and El Paso, Texas. Her artwork is inflected with a binational sensibility in themes, materials, and art-making process. Cabrera's sculptures allude to Mexican artisanal traditions as well as to U.S. consumer culture and pop art. A laborious and meticulous concern for detail is a hallmark of women's craft production seen in needlework, embroidery, and weaving. The site-specificity of the U.S.-Mexico border allows Cabrera to pay homage—through her process and materials—to barrio "costureras" (neighborhood seamstresses) and to the precise handiwork of maquila workers in border assembly plants.

These low-wage assembly-line jobs are part of a complex global economy that prompted the artist to create handcrafted soft sculptures alluding to women's labor on both sides of the border. Maquiladora factories mainly employ young women to assemble many of the component parts in home appliances such as vacuum cleaners, toasters, and blenders. These appliances are destined for U.S. consumers to ease household chores and provide more leisure time. The Mexican workers who help assemble the appliances with parts made elsewhere will not have access to the finished product, nor will such products ever lighten their workloads.

Cabrera's soft sculptures of home appliances, cars, and plants are all made to scale. First the artist removes all the non-Mexican parts in the armature of the original objects, creating a facsimile soft sculpture constructed around surrogate supports and parts crafted from hand-sewn vinyl elements. The artist's actual-sized butter-yellow soft Volkswagen sculpture is a whimsical, nostalgic homage to the beloved Volkswagen beetle, called a "vocho" in Mexico. This compact "people's car" was ubiquitous in the daily life of all classes of Mexicans and was especially beloved because it was assembled in Mexican factories until 2003. In contrast, her gigantic Hummer comments on the gasoline-guzzling macho speed machine modeled after military vehicles and used in protecting American interests abroad.

**Figure 9.2** "Vocho (Paprika-Red Orange)," by Margarita Cabrera, 2004 (Collection of Jerry Speyer. Courtesy of the Artist).

Another subtle critique is launched in Cabrera's meta-realistic replicas of agave and other border plants. Close inspection reveals that these plants are crafted from remnants of Border Patrol uniforms, with zippers, buttons, and even patrol patches left in the fabric. Viewing the plant sculptures triggers associations of the thousands of immigrants crossing the hostile border full of natural and human obstacles. At once serious and whimsical, Margarita Cabrera's sculptures delight viewers with their sensuous materials, fastidious handiwork, and strong commentary on transborder social realities.

## Paradigmatic Border Interventions

The border is a geographical and material site as well as a discursive terrain. From the mid 1980s onward, artistic and theoretical interventions defined border subjects as multilingual, hybrid, and binational. Forms and content of visual culture rearticulated the sociocultural processes of "mestizaje" and "transculturation." Artworks fused iconographies, forms, and styles from elite and vernacular culture on both sides of the border. The spaces "in between" languages, cultures, genres, and geographies were considered nutrient sources within which to envision new social scenarios.

By the late 1980s "la frontera" was being compared and linked to worldwide sites of migration, displacement, and rearticulation of identities and culture. Simultaneously, border sociopolitical struggles were also associated with international struggles for equity, participation, and human rights. Looking back at the immense artistic interventions that have defined the substance of transnational visual culture, specific pieces sited in public spaces remain etched in collective memory long after their exhibition. These memorable public artworks still resonate with dense cultural referents and deep emotional power. A short list of such memorable artworks is described below.

### Border Door

In 1988, Richard A. Lou, then a member of BAW/TAF, created Border Door, an installation sculpture precisely on the U.S.-Mexico border line, a quarter mile east of Tijuana's Rodríguez International airport. Border Door was installed at a grassy plot where the border fence had been trampled down by the passage of undocumented workers. The artist says:

> It was a freestanding door and it worked.... And there were 134 detachable keys on the south side. They're on nails on the door. It was an installation but was also a performance piece, because in addition to installing it, the other aspect of this performance was going to be the neighborhood where I grew up, the Colonia Roma, starting at the house where I grew up, where I handed out between 200 and 300 keys and invited people to use my border door, to open it with a key and cross the border with dignity. The keys on the door were for people I couldn't encounter.... It really was a way to counter the image of the undocumented migrant running through the night, cutting through wire, being illegal. If you have the key to a door and you enter through it, then you're legal, you're walking into a place to which you have a right. (Berelowitz, 164)

The powerful presence of the sculpture and its performative, conceptual elements gave resonance to the local experience of border crossing as an international fact.

### La Mona

Five stories high, the sculptured and audacious nude form of La Mona (The Doll) rises up in the suburb of Colonia Aeropuerto in Tijuana. She is the home of Armando Muñoz García and his family. With bifocal references to official statues of "La Madre Patria" and The Statue of Liberty, La Mona expresses the exuberant ingenuity of an urbanist's fervid imagination. It is an invention somewhere on the delirious spectrum between modernist conceptual art and a vernacular rasquachismo.

This provocative residence negates all building codes and architectural paradigms. It is a hollow structure made of cement except for the head and arms, which are built out of fiberglass. The kitchen is in La Mona's belly, the bedroom with a visible window is within her bosom, and there is a tiny artists studio in her head. Standing proudly as an Amazon, La Mona has become a landmark registering the ingenuity of improvisation and bricolage. She exemplifies the spirit of abandon and creativity found in the dynamic vernacular context of Tijuana itself.

### Trojan Horse: *Toy an Horse*

Marcos Ramírez Erre, long engaged with Tijuana's art groups, created a monumental two-headed wooden horse as a site-specific installation for In Site in 1997. Standing 30 meters tall, the sculpture was installed prominently at the San Diego/Tijuana Border Inspection Station where it was visible to all border crossers coming North or going South.

Bifocality is the essence of the piece. The Horse's two heads are mirror images of each other, one looking toward Mexico and one toward the United States, suggesting the complex and contradictory dualities of the border. As José Manuel Valenzuela Arce writes: "Erre's project underscores some of the concerns...where two-headedness emphasizes a dual perspective, a dual identity and as a result, ambiguity. Who is the invader, who is the invaded? Who is dependent, who is being depended upon? Does this border separate us or unite us? Duality also provides the answer. The border neither separates nor unites. We remain linked" (Canclini, 39).

Unlike the original Trojan Horse, this one has a hollow, see-through armature (no one could hide inside). The transparency suggests that binational relations, questions, and solutions must also begin with recognition of interconnectedness and transparency of actions on both sides of the border. There is a wide-ranging legacy of artistic interventions by border artists concentrated in two frameworks: on the one hand, public art projects that explore the anchored identities and sensibilities of people who live and work in the border zone, and, on the other hand, the border as a site of crossing, a space of transit, of de-territorialization and nomadism. Both frameworks are integral components of border image-making in Mexico and the United States.

## Fulana

In the global present, the legacy of transnational visual culture continues with experiments in virtual space. Far from the U.S.-Mexico borderlands (for the most part), a collective of Latina media artists are expanding the scope and meaning of transnational visual culture.

Founded in 2000 in New York City, Fulana is one of the few Latina media collectives in the United States. It is composed of a pan-Latina coterie of artists/activists: Marlène Ramírez-Cancio (Puerto Rican from the island), Cristina Ibarra (Chicana from El Paso, TX), Lisandra Ramos-Grullón (Dominican from New York City), and Andrea Thome (Chilean/Costa Rican from Madison, Wisconsin). The group creates video and print media projects fusing bilingual humor, parody, and satire to critically analyze and comment on themes and issues relevant to U.S. Latinos.

Fulana derives its name from the ancient Arabic word "fulán," meaning "anyone." In Spanish, "Fulano/a" or "Fulano/a de Tal" is a made-up name that refers to an anonymous "anybody." Fulana takes its name to heart. It is a nonhierarchical collective where anyone in the group can assume any role or responsibility during the creative process. The writing of scripts, as well as the oversight of video direction and production, is done by all members together. Furthermore, anyone can access their work around the world by visiting their website, fulana.org, where their videos are freely available for viewing by transnational audiences (Ramírez-Cancio).

A representative example of their work is *Amnezac*, a one-minute mock television commercial for a pill that markets itself as "The Most Powerful Anti-Historiamine on the Market™." The video—which begins by asking viewers: "Do you feel anxiety about world events you cannot change? Are your political concerns interfering in your patriotic activities, like shopping and paying taxes?"—examines how belonging and citizenship in the United States are equated with consumerism. If you are not shopping and consuming beyond your means, you are not doing your duty as a loyal, uncritical citizen. In the throwaway, disposable economy of American society, you will find happiness in things rather than in thoughts.

A concurrent meta-commentary in the video posits that the United States has become a "pill society." No matter what the malady, a pill can relieve your symptoms. The soothing voice in the commercial asks: "Does the Iraq war remind you of U.S. invasions of Latin American countries, including your own?" Amnezac (*"amnescilin/atrocitate oblivium"*) promises to dull your anxiety and eradicate your long-term historical memory, relieving all symptoms of your "historical memoritis." This historical amnesia could prove a handy antidote for Latinos who feel they must dismiss thinking about historical and ongoing aggressions against Latinos,

**Figure 9.3** "Unblock Your Chimichanga," Part of the *Lupe & Juan Di from the Block* Project, Fulana 2003.

from colonization, invasions, and racialization, to current immigration debates wanting to close borders to further Latino immigration. The *Amnezac* video seamlessly employs the cool, detached techniques of television pharmaceutical commercials, sprinkled with mordant bilingual satire, to zero-in on the perils of historical disavowal.

Other videos in the Fulana repertoire include: *Latino Plastic Cover*, a spoof on the ubiquitous use of clear plastic to protect and conserve objects—and in Fulana's imaginary, even people and cultural practices—within the Latina domestic sphere. *Lupe and Juan Di from the Block*, a mock music video parodying J-Lo's pop hit "Jenny from the Block," uses the Virgen de Guadalupe and Juan Diego to comment on the hyper-commercialization of Latino cultural icons, the social processes of "crossing over" or "selling out" to the mainstream, and the transcendent meaning of racial and cultural "mestizaje." *Operation Blue Blood*, a video that remixes images taken from the web during Hurricane Katrina, remarks on the American social structures that separate and protect the "haves" from the "have-nots," as exemplified by the government's slow response to Katrina's working-class victims. The video was uploaded six days after Katrina and received one hit per minute during its first week online, as people all over the world followed the aftermath of the hurricane. *Tercer Impacto: Hispanacea*, a parody of Univisión's news show Primer Impacto, touches upon the delusions of American society and its manic fears of a Latino cultural invasion. Since Latina women live longer, have more children, and resist oppression, merchandizing experts develop "Hispanacea," an elixir derived from the survival essence found in Latina bodies, allowing the Anglo market to commodify the "essence" of their resistance and endurance. So Hispanacea shows—among other things—how the powerful sustain themselves by drawing vitality from those they oppress.

Appropriating the form and content of mainstream media commercials, the Fulana collective filters and reformats their formal elements through a critical Latina sensibility. The images, pacing, and narratives of Fulana's mock television commercials, their music videos, and their print interventions include precise elements drawn from Latino popular culture. Telenovela melodramatics, comedic effects from bilingual code-switching, and layered cultural referents blur the line between art, advertising, and popular entertainment in Fulana productions. As their mission statement declares, "We respond to the ways ideologies and identities are marketed to us, sold to us—and how we sell ourselves—through the mass media" (Fulana website).

## Conclusion

Desde siempre, from time immemorial, the U.S.-Mexico borderlands have been a zone of "carga y descarga," a "contact zone" that remains a route for trading, cultural exchange, and a major pathway for immigration. La frontera has always been and continues to be a geographic and symbolic site for encounters, transformations, and death.

Thousands have died or been killed in the epic crossing al Norte. The journey itself has always been a supreme act of courage and the maximum test of human will and hope. Immigrants must traverse a geography of grave natural and human obstacles. Each crossing is a saga of danger and insecurity. Some migrants swim across a treacherous river, others walk across the scorched bleakness and unbearable heat of the Arizona desert. Immigrants crawl through underground tunnels, huddle in suffocating freight cars in trains, and become human cargo routinely stuffed into the trunks of cars and trucks. And always, there is the constant running and hiding from "la migra." The despised border patrol potently equipped with the latest surveillance technology, such as infrared detectors, human tracking sensors, helicopters with blinding searchlights, vicious dogs, and guns.

The multigenerational migrant stream continues and now includes more women and entire families. New migration routes bring transnational voyagers into the heartland of our country, into states such as North and South Dakota, Georgia, and Missouri, among others. In these geographies far removed from the homeland, technologies like the cell phone, the digital camera, and the Internet have become prime conduits for maintaining social and cultural ties across spatial divides. Hometown Associations and other transnational political organizations have emerged and established forums through which documented and undocumented immigrants can enfranchise themselves.

The elemental struggle to survive against all odds, to work and seek a space of belonging, is a transformative human experience. Border crossers and their efforts to endure in unfriendly environments in the United States provide never-ending inspiration for pictorial expression. With assurance, conviction, and mastery, transfronterizo visual artists have left us a significant and growing "image bank" as well as an archive of documents and a repertoire of embodied knowledge that preserve collective memory. Like border crossers worldwide, we all seek refuge, work, and options for our well-being. The hope (la esperanza) to finally secure a place of safety and belonging.

I will end my article as I started, quoting another fragment from Tomás Rivera's *Y no se lo tragó la tierra/And the Earth Did Not Devour Him*. In it we hear the voice of a woman who is standing with other migrants in a "troca de carga" traveling pal norte, a los trabajos en Minnesota:

> When we arrive, when we arrive, the real truth is that I'm tired of arriving. Arriving and leaving, it's the same thing because we no sooner arrive and...the real truth of the matter...I'm tired of arriving. I really should say when we don't arrive because that's the real truth. We never arrive. (Rivera, 145)

# 10

# Coming and Going: Transborder Visual Art in Tijuana

*Norma Iglesias-Prieto*

(Translated from Spanish by Rita E. Urquijo-Ruiz)

In this chapter, I reflect upon the characteristics of contemporary visual art in Tijuana, emphasizing the fact that it is produced in a transborder space that marks its subjects and practices. One cannot understand these transborder artistic practices outside of the global context that is currently creating and defining new social relations and imaginaries. As Tomás Ybarra-Frausto's chapter (chapter 9) indicates, reality is now marked by a massive migratory flux, given the growing exchange of goods, capital, and ideas that confluence to create a new transnational imaginary.

## Transborder Contexts under Transnational Frameworks

With the so-called globalization process, we come to an accelerated change in the World where, on the one hand, the economic interdependence and internationalization seem to shrink it, to erase borders, to standardize culture, and to question the sense of belonging as well as the concepts of time and space (geographical dislocation). On the other hand, we experience the process of accumulated capital and an increased marginalization that deem almost inconceivable the contrast between those who have and those who do not have access to information, technology, capital, and the job market. After the terrorist acts of September 11, 2001, we have lived through the fortification of national borders, the intensification of the discourses regarding fear of the "other," as well as the embellishment of local cultures and nationalism. These apparently contradictory processes occur around the world but are particularly experienced in an intensified and graphic manner along international borders, especially the one between Mexico and the United States. This is due to the fact that, among other factors, this is the most unequal and asymmetric border in the world, with the highest degree of interdependence and dynamism, and one of the biggest geographically (more than 2,500 kilometers long) and in terms of population (83 million inhabitants). Such border has been classified by renowned academics (Canclini, Appadurai, Bhabha, Dear, among others)[1] as the "laboratory of globalization," the "laboratory of postmodernity," and as "an inconspicuous example of the glo-cal." Within this extensive border, the one between Tijuana (Mexico) and San Diego (United States) is especially interesting due to its highest level of asymmetry, dynamism, and interaction. It thus becomes the ideal space to consider the challenge that globalization presents to us and the role that art is playing in questioning such global tendencies. It is critical to consider the interrelations between conflicts and the multiple points of discussion between the global/local, the public/private, individualism/community, the "we"/"other," north/south, rich/poor, control/opportunity, as well as conflict and the development of a consensus.

In this sense, it is important to debate the differences assumed between the concepts of *transnational* and *transborder*, given that this allows us to understand the singularity of global issues within the geopolitical context of the border. Globalization has implied an acceleration of the exchange of goods, services, cultural elements, as well as major movements between people around the globe who—as its been discussed—are affecting social imaginaries. This helps us understand the concept of "contact zones,"[2] as Ybarra-Frausto discusses when citing Pratt, that is, the construction of new sites—not necessarily geographically—in which multiple voices, negotiations, cultural borrowing, and exchanges are developed.

We also have sites that are precisely geographic and geopolitical spaces on the border, in which all the characteristics and tendencies related to globalization are expressed. The fact that it is a geographical space (territoriality) and not purely symbolic generates different and more intense social dynamics. It is precisely this dual border condition—geographic and symbolic—that allows it to become a true social laboratory. Nevertheless, it is important to point out that a geopolitical border does not always yield this type of heightened interaction. This depends on the level of exchange and interdependence that exist between each side, as well as the quantity or frequency, intensity, directionality, and the material, symbolic, social, and cultural crossings and interactions. This is what I call the *transfronteridad*/[*transbordering*] level. A higher level of *transfronteridad* presupposes a more intense degree of interactions, crossings, and responsibility to "the other side," which, in turn, also assumes a more intense cultural richness, contents, and identity-based complexity. In transborder and transnational milieus, relations of power, conflict, and domination result from multiple asymmetries that are inherent in them. Moreover, there are different ways in which subjects constitute themselves in, and because of, relations established with multiple "others." It is understood that a higher level of *transfronteridad* also generates a more complex way of understanding and representing the border. Any border subject will understand and represent this space in a more or less complex way depending on her/his level of *transfronteridad*. Another element that distinguishes that which is transborder from transnational is that in spite of the fact that both presuppose an international exchange, the former has a local or regional dimension that provokes a faster or more frequent and intense movement of people, material goods, and cultural elements between each cultural and national space that in turn generate an intense and quotidian symbolic dynamic.

For instance, a tendency in these transnational processes is their complexity in political and social practices, such as in the case of dual citizenship. This is about a dual practice of citizenship that is simultaneous and within the local-binational scale. For these commuters, the concepts of space and territory are one and the same; it is the practice of this dual transborder citizenship exercise that operates only in an "Urban Transborder Ecosystem," as defined by Larry Herzog,[3] among other writers. Despite enormous differences between the two areas, for these commuters, it is one space. These transborder subjects are absolutely competent and functional every day, on either side; their personal/social relations embody these transnational tendencies. This is one of many representations here; there are others who live a border (not a transborder) reality who have never gone across, but whose lives are still affected because they live there. At the same time, that which is transborder has actually taken us to the concept of "post-border," which, of course, is related to the wider discussion of "post-national" identities and its impact on the practice of citizenship by migrant peoples. Such practices assume theoretical discussions of postmodernity and postcolonialism, which I am not able to discuss in this short chapter.[4]

## Transborder Culture, Multiple Asymmetries, and their Relation to Social Representations

Social representations are a symbolic version of the relationship between the object that is represented (in this case the border) and the subject that interprets it. Therefore, it is crucial to analyze and contrast border social representations from different subjects and places that occupy the social and cultural border spaces. It is expected that the border signifies and represents different things for each social group depending on their levels of *transfronteridad*

In a comparative analysis between university students from Tijuana and San Diego,[5] we found some general tendencies related as much to the frequency and purpose of the border crossing as to the type of relationship that is established with the inhabitants of the neighboring city. In general, there are four types of relations found in border interactions (in each case we are looking at legal crossings through the international ports of entry), and from these, one derives the complexity of the discursive representational level that tends to go from the most basic, impersonal, and superficial to the most intense, and therefore complex.

First, there are the superficial, circumstantial, and impersonal relationships established due to sporadic interactions, commercial in nature between subjects who do not know each other and do not wish to go beyond the commercial relations. These are, fundamentally, relations established in micro-spaces in the city generally designed for tourism and consumption and that are done in a short amount of time.[6] In the case of Tijuana, we look especially at Avenida Revolución and three or four adjacent streets where there are bars, restaurants, and tourist souvenir shops. These stores are frequented by U.S. tourists, but not by Tijuana residents.

The border representations that U.S. tourists create under these types of interactions tend to remain in the graphic, superficial reality, that is, in the more visual characteristics of the border space. We are highlighting specifically the first impressions that surprise and impress the visitors, negatively or positively, possibly due to the difference from the usual. In this category of interaction, the U.S. visitor represents the border (specifically the Mexican side) in the following way: (1) in terms of negative descriptions or with problematic terms such as *dirty, busy, noisy, cold, jail, dark, dangerous, deadly, scary, unsafe, smelly, vendors, crowded, homeless, hungry, survival,* and *poverty.* In terms of feelings, the following words are used: *sad, frustrating, depressing, intimidating,* and *distasteful.* Some of the very few positive aspects of these representations are not centered on the characteristics of the city, its people, or its culture, but rather on the opportunities that Tijuana offers them as tourists; the common terms are: *chip, party, fun, bargain, good time, drinking, good food, friendly, colorful.* The discursive representations by this group tended to describe the view more than the culture or the people behind it.

In the case of Mexicans who cross the border to San Diego and establish basic commercial relations, these are conducted primarily in big business and recreational centers and in different parts of the city. These are spaces that are not exclusively for foreign tourists (such as Avenida Revolución in Tijuana) but rather for a wider clientele that includes residents as well as tourists. In general, these border representations made fewer references to the U.S. side, confirming the idea that the concept of "border" is associated much more with the Mexican side. In the cases where these were included, it was always by young people from Tijuana. These representations were centered on the advantages of Tijuana as a great consumer center, with terms such as *sales, warranties, quality, variety,* and *clothing*; in some cases they referred specifically to a label and store such as *Gap* and *Old Navy*. Therefore, a characterization of San Diego by Tijuana residents is as *The Shopping Center City*. In some instances there were some references to the U.S. border side in terms of its urban infrastructure, especially its *freeways*, to the *ordered and clean* city, and to the *quality of life* that this implies.

Second, there are interactions that require periodic visits and somehow personal, but not emotive, relations. This is about general crossings with the purpose of visiting doctors and dentists as well as to buy medicine and some food products. This type of interaction assumes a better knowledge of urban spaces in Tijuana, given that the doctor's offices and hospitals are located in various parts of the city. It assumes also a certain level of cultural understanding that, in turn, allows this interaction and trust on such medical services. Knowing how to speak Spanish is important but not essential since all of these businesses are bilingual. The consumption of prescription drugs in Tijuana by U.S. citizens does not necessarily follow an ethnic-cultural pattern, but more generally Mexican-origin population uses these medical services. This is why U.S. citizens characterize Tijuana as a *pharmacy* and *hospital city*.

This type of interaction happens on both sides of the border and presupposes a more sophisticated representation of the border in terms of a certain level of abstraction, such as *division, separation, racism, control,* but at the same time *opportunity, diversity, exchange, growth, connection, and development*. Or terms that point to specific border issues, such as *maquiladoras, tourism, drug trafficking, drugs, migration.*

Third, we have border relations that are characterized as being extremely warm and emotive, given that the main reason for crossing is to visit relatives, friends, or significant others, or to attend weddings and funerals; but generally these border relations happen more frequently and regularly. This group also does other activities such as tourism, attending cultural events, visiting restaurants, doctors, and consuming various products and services. These subjects have a vast command of urban spaces on both sides of the border where interaction happens in both directions. However, it is primarily from north to south and under a specific ethnic profile, given that, in the U.S. case, it is related primarily for Mexican Americans or Mexicans with legal residence in California. This major tendency to cross the border and enact *transfronteridad* is explained by the asymmetry of power characterizing the relationship between these two countries. Mexicans are more interested in crossing into the United States because their need is based on accessing a job pool (with better salaries), U.S. products (better prices and warranties), and services (better infrastructure). Therefore, the levels of transfronteridad are linked to the place one occupies in this border relation of power. The need to cross the border due to social, cultural, and economic reasons is bigger on the more disadvantaged side. On the Mexican side of the border, such dependency on the United States is acknowledged and it has become part of the everyday life as well as of the social and cultural imaginary; whereas on the other side, not only is this dependency on Mexico considered less important, but it is strategically negated as a way of maintaining power. The discursive characterizations of the border in this third type of interaction are varied and complex and quite similar to the ones discussed below.

Finally, there are emotive, intense, and varied relations between border subjects. In some cases they are people with both nationalities who have lived, studied, and worked on both sides, who are bilingual and bicultural and have these types of relations in each country. With frequent crossings, in some cases they do this daily. This is about subjects with an important amount of cultural capital and knowledge that allow them to move easily on both sides of the border. They embody the border's diversity and vitality. They, along with the previous group, are precisely the ones who represent the border in a more complex way.

First we have discursive representations that are centered on knowledge of the border as a fracture with words such as: *limit, separation, armor, wall, barrier, line, and river*. But at the same time, it is acknowledged that this can be crossed and then it is represented with terms such as: *bridge, window, door, or springboard*. Second, there are representations that allude to the economic dynamism of the border with terms such as *exportation, industry, technological investment, maquiladora, growth, development, work, dollars,* and *credit* as well as a place of *prosperity* and *opportunity*. The border is associated with a U.S. model and style and therefore it is represented in terms such as *comfortable, convenient, appliances, modernity*. In part, this U.S. style is linked to recognizing the border as a great center of *consumerism*, as the place of *sales* and *publicity*. It is also the place for *diversion, tacos, fiestas, nightlife, music, and beer*. Another positive aspect in which the border is represented is as a place with access to distinct cultural events, concerts, recreational areas, and sporting events. On the other hand, among these representations, the one highlighted is the acknowledgment of the border as a place of *fusion*, of *cultural encounters*. As a space characterized by *hybridity, diversity*, as a *pluricultural, international*, and *cosmopolitan place*. As a site *open to change, to difference*, and *cultural influences*. The place for English, Spanish, and especially Spanglish.

The discursive relations of the last two groups also included the problems related to asymmetry and power between the United States and Mexico. They recognized the *pain, racism*, and *injustice* lived daily on the border; this includes terms such as: *arrogance, trenches, authoritarianism, abuse, passports, searches, avarice, dispute, humiliation, marginalization, domination, exploitation*, and *inequality*.

In its complex representation, there are other social problems highlighted at the border; among them are lack of planning, hunger, ignorance, diseases, poverty, waste, prostitution, drug addiction, corruption, instability, thefts, overpopulation, disorder, chaos, and death. There are also ecological problems, such as toxic waste, smog, and pollution in general. Traffic, hurrying, long lines, and wasted time consistently represent the border due to these quotidian problems experienced by people who live on both cities.

Finally, one of the biggest headings of border representation was the one related to feelings, where once again the complexity and contrast of life and interaction on the border are represented. Some negative aspects were recognized: depression, sadness, impotence, pain, stupidity, loss, indifference, and fear. Also, some positive feelings like love, friendship, solidarity, tolerance, patience, desire, pride, forgiveness, satisfaction, and happiness. There were also other aspects such as beauty, liberty, unity, homeland, home, and life, which tend not to be recognized by people with a low level of transfronteridad. The subjects in the last two interaction profiles were the only ones who included in their representation of the border circumstances related to unity. For example, the militarization of the border was mentioned, as it has become more evident after the events of 9/11; also, the toughening of security measures that affect the daily reality of crossing and the relations between border dwellers on both sides; the intensification of insecurity on both sides was also mentioned, and also recognition of the different reasons for this. These groups are the ones whose daily lives have been most affected and who have felt especially vulnerable.

It is evident that the subjects with major interactions on both sides of the border develop more complex ways of representation. There is evidence also that there is a better level of criticism and responsibility toward the border milieu as there are stronger and more frequent interactions.

The border's complexity and its problems may be understood and comprehended in an easier way by those subjects who include the reality of transborder visions. This areas' potential exists precisely in the support and development of these transborder subjects. In this sense, visual artists in Tijuana are contributing, among other things, to understanding the transborder dynamics and phenomena as well as to questioning the border itself.

### Visual Arts, Tijuana, and Transborder Processes

How are we able to explain the fact that in a short amount of time the border city of Tijuana went from being considered a "cultural desert" to an "emergent art center" observed and analyzed from various cities in the world? Perhaps the most evident answer is that its complex and contrasting dynamics (not only between the U.S. and the Mexican sides but also toward the interior of the city itself), its multiple asymmetries, contradictions and deficiencies, its accelerated and constant shifts, its condition as a border or "in-between" space, as well as the quantity and intensity of its multiple border processes become an incentive to its creative attitude. In other words, Tijuana and its graphic, defying, and stimulating dynamics work as a critical muse and as an encouraging workshop. It is also important to point out that, unlike other places in Mexico and in other parts of the world (or during other historical moments) where art was born and maintained its ties to the nation-state, or was directly related to the economic market, in Tijuana art was born and has been maintained independent of both the state and the market. It is a "Do-it-yourself art," according to Claudia Sandoval,[7] given that in most cases it has been independent, not always due to conviction or strategy but due to necessity. Inspite of this, one cannot ignore other important factors that have intervened in the artistic development of Tijuana, such as the creation of multiple artistic spaces and projects (be they government sponsored or independent). One example is the Tijuana Cultural Center founded by the federal government in 1982 with the intention of attracting U.S. tourists. However, it has changed its orientation completely over the years and has become the principal art space for local artists, as well as become a producer of world-renown art shows. These exhibits—that show art by well-known local artists—have travelled throughout Mexico and other countries promoting the Tijuana artistic production and attracting the attention of new artists, curators, critics, and projects worldwide. One must also highlight the work of contemporary artistic projects such as *InSite* that, since 1992, has promoted and welcomed to Tijuana many recognized artists and their work from various countries in Latin America and Europe.

Other institutions that have promoted the growth of artistic productions and artistic professionalization in this city are: Art and Humanities Departments at the Autonomous University of Baja California (UABC), the Baja California Cultural Institute (IMAC), and other organizations and private projects such as the Tijuana Humanities Center. There are also other independent centers and galleries, such as El Lugar del Nopal, El Sótano del Río Rita, La Galería H&H, Galería Lui Velázquez, La Caja Galería, La Galería Arte 256, La Casa del Túnel, La Alianza Francesa de Tijuana, La Casa de la 9, La Antigua Bodega de Papel, Café Revólver, La Alborada, Café Latitud 32, El Centro Cultural Independiente La Escala, Distrito 10, and Galería Name, among others.

In Tijuana, creativity seems to emerge as a mechanism of resistance and of physical and spiritual survival. Here, a creative and creating activity, from an art piece to a stair made completely of tires, in a way humanizes and liberates the population and allows not only the resolution of major problems and challenges in their everyday life but also enables them to reimagine, to think of themselves, and to reexperience each other in a another way. In other words, Tijuana works as a magnifying glass that intensifies the social ills inscribed in the current development models, but it also magnifies the creative potential and alternative life styles and social relations.

Amidst the multiple problems that Tijuana suffers and in spite of being the de facto backyard of the United States, its artistic practice (as all creative activity) allows it to be rescued, to make it honorable, and to imagine it in a different way. In other words, the fact that it is a border between Mexico and the United States and that it occupies a smaller space of power in the asymmetric relationship between the two countries in a way limit or constrain the city and its people. Nevertheless, it is precisely this creative practice that questions and transcends its liminal condition. The city provides the environment, dynamics, themes, materials, and modes of production for its artistic production to flourish. Tijuana is the muse and also the workshop. This city, not only as a repertoire of objects and conditions but rather also as an accumulated social dynamics and reality, is characterized by its incredible capacity to aspire, a capacity that without a doubt exists also in other places in the world, but here it acquires specific tones as an exacerbated and transborder reality from which it emerges.

Here, visual artists survive in the same manner and with the same strategies as any other citizen does. Artists tend to produce in a collective way and under informal and flexible networks; they are, as are most in the city, "multi-taskers," who work in and with the community (as cocreators), for which they are questioned in a certain way as the artistic authority, and in this way creation is incentivized. Several artists do not define themselves as such, instead they feel more comfortable when they are recognized as "cultural producers," "communicators," or "art practitioners." This probably derives from the fact that the majority of these visual artists from Tijuana do not have formal art education but rather have degrees in communication, architecture, design, history, and philosophy, among other areas of study. They are self-taught artists who have learned art through networks of friends, informal lessons, workshops, parties, but above all, due to their own artistic practice.

It is important to highlight that in Tijuana there are local and foreign artists in residence who live together and collaborate in projects financed by big institutions or programs (such as InSite, for example), or in projects that are self-financed by the artists and their families. These are projects and artists that dialogue and collaborate with each other in spite of their origin or budgetary differences.

Visual artists in Tijuana, with a major or minor level of *transfronteridad* and who are acutely or lightly aware of it, through their creations/events reflect, and in fact alter and intervene, in their city and its uses. That is, visual arts not only modify the city's modes of representation but its reality itself. Their work, moreover, questions and denaturalizes national borders. Artists also contribute to questioning and changing local identities and collective memory. Art in Tijuana, as the city itself, is in a "do-it-yourself" style; it fundamentally emerges as a response to the most basic needs, as a scream in the face of a complex reality, as a product that recuperates the instinctive and the conceptual. It is an art form without schemes to tie it down or techniques or forms that limit it. It is a multimedia art form that also tends to be ephemeral, which does not always seek the production of an object but rather generate events with the objective of eliciting the audience's reaction. As the reality from which it emerges and inspires it, this art tends to utilize recycled or highly symbolic materials in terms of the interaction, interdependence, or asymmetry in relation to the *other side*. This is about an art that reconstructs and denaturalizes the most notable aspects of its transborder character: consumerism, waste, inequality, drug trafficking, violence, corruption, lack, abuse of power.

Another highly important aspect in Tijuana's artistic practice is that the art exhibits are curated in public city spaces—streets, parking lots, beaches, international border crossings, abandoned movie theaters, bars—places that are not institutionalized, and therefore liberate art and its cannons. Sometimes this is an artistic intervention strategy, but other times it is derived from the lack of museums and galleries. This is about public art exhibits that do not respond, like in other parts of the world, to a mechanism of production, questioning traditional and legitimate spaces like museums and galleries in a natural and spontaneous way of producing their art in the face of limited art exhibit spaces.

Undoubtedly, Tijuana's visual artists' contribution is the stimulation of the creative faculty in other social subjects. In moments when apparently we are running out of everything—the natural, material, spiritual, and symbolic—what we require is an enormous measure of creativity that allows us to construct a new civilizing order that returns to us future options. And in this area, Tijuana's visual artists are doing an outstanding job.

Some of the most obvious examples of this tendency are the artistic production by Marcos Ramírez "Erre," Jaime Ruiz Otis y de Tania Candiani.

### Marcos Ramírez "Erre:" The Exposed Power of Asymmetry

"Erre" comes, as many Tijuana artists, from a middle-class family. He received a B.A. in law, practiced his degree for a year and a half, but did not wish to continue in this line of work due to its corruption. Like many transborder subjects, he decided then to work in the United States with the support of some family members. As a commuter worker, he worked in construction, doing carpentry work for 17 years. For ten of those years he also dedicated himself to his artistic production.

Erre was one of the first local artists who received international fame. His fame began when he was invited to participate in the public binational art project by *InSite* in its 1994 edition. For this event, "Erre," as he is known, produced an installation ironically titled *Century 21*. This was a piece where, for the first time, he was able to utilize all of his experience: law, construction (carpentry), and art. The piece was constructed inside the Tijuana Cultural Center's (CeCut) plaza, which is considered the emblem of modernity and urban development in the city. This monumental construction is located in the Zona Río area, which is precisely one of the most modern and expensive areas of the city. This project confronted the reality of poverty for thousands of people in Tijuana. The *Century 21* house, outside of its actual context, evidenced and questioned not only the constant improvisational character of the city but also the social injustice from which the Zona Río area was consolidated. This area was inhabited by people with very few economic resources, with houses that were self-constructed with waste materials. On January 1980, the removal of this community was violent when—in the middle of the night—city officials ordered the Abelardo L. Rodríguez dam's gates open and the water current flooded and destroyed everything on its way (Valenzuela 1989). The artistic project *Century 21* included not only the construction and installation of this house but also the computerized elaboration of blueprints (which was a difficult part of the production because the computer software refused to create a plan for such an irregular home), as well as exhibits of these two objects. The blueprints were submitted to the municipal authorities for approval. They followed the same construction procedure as any other physical structure in Tijuana. The seals and multiple signatures authorizing its construction document and prove the high levels of corruptions by the authorities who, thanks to receiving their "cut," never verified its location or architectural characteristics. In its interior and exterior, *Century 21* followed the functional logic of the self-constructed houses in Tijuana; for example, it stole electricity from the museum, did not have running water but an outhouse, and it was furnished and decorated with second-hand products. The audience that visited the house began to appropriate it, and it created its own dynamic and nature. The guard who protected the house during the exhibit and who knew the tragic history of the eviction in the ZonaRío spontaneously answered a visitor's question by pointing out "that this house emerged from the earth because its roots were there."

In 1997, Marcos Ramírez "Erre" received an invitation to participate in *InSite97*. For this occasion, he constructed a wooden structure that was more than ten meters tall at the San Ysidro border crossing (the main port of entry between Tijuana and San Diego) in the middle of the area that divides the two cities. This was the installation entitled *Toy an Horse*, an enormous Trojan horse with two heads, one looking north and the other to the south. The horse represented the border as a shared transborder space that in order to progress, to move, requires negotiation, not walls. The horse also questioned the stereotypical one-directional impact of the border, "if it were considered an invasion, as it was the function of the Trojan horse, it would be an invasion, in this case, of both sides."[8] Unlike the original Trojan horse, this one had an empty, transparent body intended to be filled with a great amount of border gestures and relations. "This horse does not contain surprises, everyone knows what's at stake in the union of cultures, the good and the bad," stated the artist. Both pieces temporarily modified the original characteristics of two of the most symbolic city spaces—the CeCut esplanade and the international border crossing in San Ysidro. Both pieces intervened not only in the physical space but in its uses, dynamics, and symbolic value. There were these two artistic interventions imprinted in the mind of a great majority of Tijuana residents that helped to denaturalize the asymmetrical logic of this border.

**Figure 10.1** "Don't Be a Man for a Minute, Be a Man Your Whole Life," by Marcos Ramírez "Erre," 2007 (Archive: Norma Iglesias).

Another emblematic art piece by Marcos Ramírez was the enormous billboard along Interstate 5—immediately across the San Ysidro border crossing that read "Don't be a man for a minute, be a man your whole life." This piece questions not only the border but also the anti-immigrant groups like the Minutemen. This piece was part of the critical art exhibit entitled "Strange New World: Art and Design from Tijuana" in the Museum of Contemporary Art in San Diego. Elisabeth Malking from *The New York Times* wrote:

> So Marcos Ramírez's contribution to "Strange New World" is an off-site highway billboard for motorists driving south toward the border. It depicts a gray-haired man in camouflage—a reference to the Minutemen, as some American vigilantes patrolling the frontier call themselves—looking toward the wall and the cluttered Tijuana hillside beyond. (The model is actually Mike Davis, a Southern Californian urban theorist.) The billboard exhorts: "Don't be a man for just a minute, be a man your whole life." Only the back of his head is visible. Mr. Ramírez, known in the art world as Erre, said of his piece: "The fact is that man migrates. We all have to continue moving, and we will continue moving."[9]

For Marcos Ramírez,

> Borders are imposed by human beings [...]. It would be ideal for me if there were no borders anywhere in the world, although that is too idealistic [...]. That is never going to happen. But what I can do with my work is to

create bridges of understanding. I do believe, unlike other artists, that perceptions can be changed. It takes time, but it can be done. Art can change them. In that sense our job counterbalances all the negative influences that exist, with groups such as the *Minutemen*, that seek power and division between races and nationalities. We can do this work in another way. What we need to promote is the coming together of different cultures that in reality the only thing they do is benefit and enrich as they come into contact. Borders are an opportunity to get to know, to live together and to share. In an elementary way, the border is the opportunity to meet and get to know the other...[10]

### Jaime Ruiz Otis. Archeology and Industrial Waste Art

Another interesting example of art in Tijuana is the work of Jaime Ruiz Otis, who has questioned and symbolically changed the city's condition as a cheap labor provider and backyard to San Diego. For some years Jaime worked in a maquiladora, and this experience has marked his artistic work. His strategy and peculiarity resides in the fact that all of his pieces are created with industrial waste (especially from the maquiladoras). After getting out of work, Jaime would go into the huge trash containers at the factory, recuperating various materials for his art pieces, doing a type of archeological work that would allow him to rescue not only the elements, logic, and more profound character of industrial work but also the possibility of finding materials to transform them creatively. In this way, and similarly to the 1960s neorealists, industrial waste obtained new results when it became art pieces.[11] Industrial work is not only his topic of reflection but also main provider of art materials. As the city itself, Ruiz Otis appropriates trash, gives it an aesthetic sense, and generates a new use for it. He recuperates and questions various elements and characteristics of the work in these factories, such as assembly work, repetition, homogeneous global consumerism, pollution due to toxic chemical waste, and the urban industrial view that articulates and guides residential areas. Among his artistic pieces, the best examples are the prints entitled *Registros de labor/Trademarks* (2004), which are silk screenings done with industrial irons on paper. These iron pieces were originally used as protection for the tables where cloth, metals, and plastics were cut in different industries. These are artistic pieces that reveal the logic behind mass production of consumable articles, such as industrial time-space, a graphic demonstration of the hours invested in each of the industrial jobs.

Ruiz Otis' multiple pieces give meaning to industrial waste, dignifying the worker and the artist. In each of his pieces, the fax machine toners, the metal sheets, the cloth leftover pieces, and the leftover paper and plastic are shown as "blind, but not mute, witnesses of the routines of a microclimate of use, abuse, consumption, fabrication, time, duration, on top, underneath, that is an essay on the planetarium" (Pozuelo 2007). Another example is the *Caja de lluvia/Rain Box* (2001), where he resignifies the noisy and alienating repetition of industrial work, with its repetitive and relaxing rhythm created by the rain water, reproduced in a fountain made by industrial plastic pieces. One of his last pieces is a Zen garden created with plastic from shredded TV monitors and plastic boxes that are used as boulders. The Zen garden invites us to a space of reflection and calm, in opposition to the tension and stress experienced by the worker during its production time, or the isolation of the consumer subject in front of the TV screen who looks to escape from her/his routine. With this artistic piece, Tijuana goes from being—like its welcoming billboard states—"the Television Capital" (because it produces around 85 televisions per minute (Carrillo 2007)) to becoming the Capital of the production of dreams, hopes, and plastic poetry.

One of his most recent artistic interventions entitled "Trade marks" was part of the series "Ephemerals" in the Tijuana Cultural Center. His work consisted of using thousands of industrial discarded stickers, commonly used on a great variety of appliances assembled in Tijuana, affixed to the walls and floor of the center. With such material, Ruiz Otis formed a beautiful urban landscape with more hope than the one offered to the thousands of industrial workers.

Jaime Ruiz Otis has exhibited his work in important museums in Mexico, the United States, and Spain, such as Museum of Contemporary Art, Alameda Art Laboratory, ExTeresa Alternative Art, Tijuana Cultural Center, Museum of Contemporary Art San Diego, Museum of Latin American Art, Santa Monica Museum of Art, and Alcalá 31 Art Center, as well as in other famous galleries around the world. His critical art, created with urban waste, no doubt contributes to the resignification of the city when he creates a new sense of the industrial labor, which in turn help us to recover our and the environment's lost dignity:

> My work is an archeological type of work from supply and demand, from consumerism [...] when I pick up the materials from the dumpsters and recycling spaces I think about the workers, the labor behind it; I begin to think about the hours invested and about the repetitions, in each object there should be all type of stories [...] My creations are made with 95 percent trash and my intention is to transform this waste into something aesthetic[ally pleasing].[12]

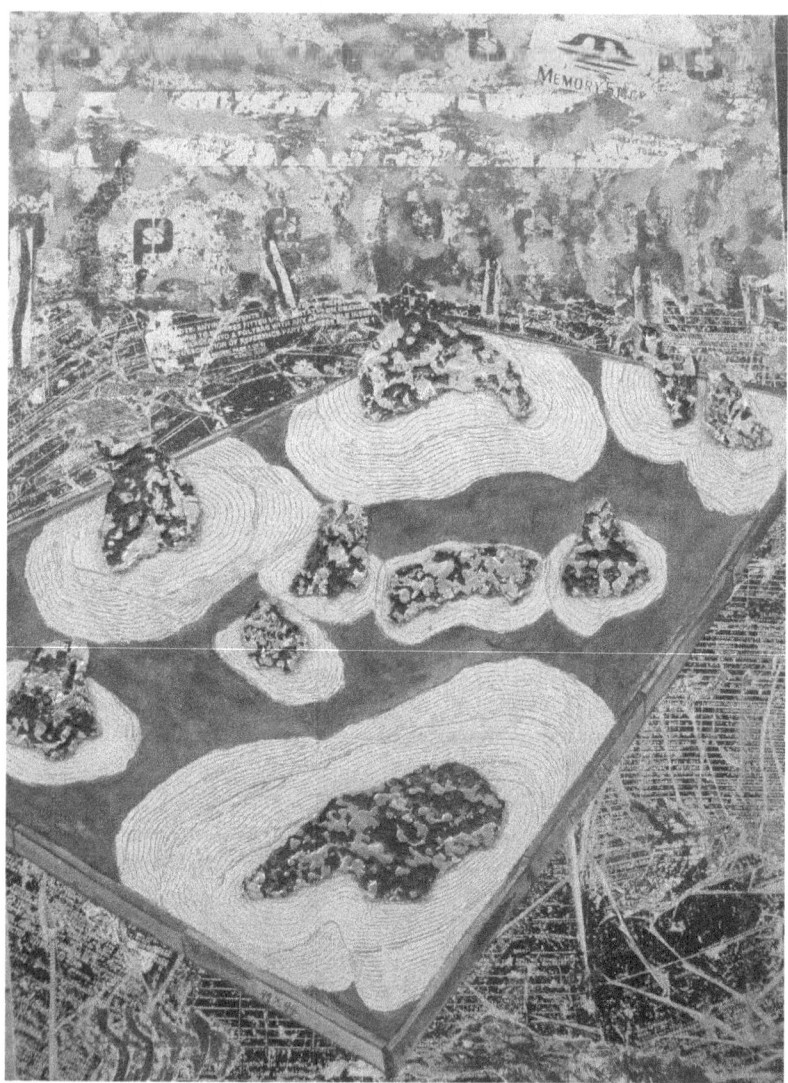

**Figure 10.2** "Proyecto Jardín Zen," by Jaime Ruiz Otis (Archive: Norma Iglesias-Prieto).

### Tania Candiani. Bodies and Souls Marked by Gender Borders

Tania Candiani, like many other Tijuana residents, was not born there; she arrived from Mexico City when she was young. She has increased her *transfronteridad* levels, but this has not been explicitly represented in her art. Candiani studied Hispanic Literature but discovered her real talent in visual art like Maros Ramírez "Erre" and Jaime Ruiz Otis. Like several visual artists from Tijuana, she is self-taught in this field. She has become a professional through workshops and especially through her own practice and artistic trajectory. She, like the two other artists, is internationally recognized.

Unlike the last two artists, Tania has worked less explicitly on topics related to the geopolitical border and the asymmetries of power derived from there. Instead, she concentrates her work on issues related to borders of gender, where the power structures are marked by sex and gender in our society. One of her first recognized creations was her series entitled *Gordas/Fat Women*. This is a group of huge pieces (most of them sewing on cloth) on the topic of the female body and the obsession with body types and diets. In her work, women's bodies became the territory of debates regarding which models to follow. Mass media has been in charge of showing feminine bodies that are incredibly svelte, that become models for women in general but that have become "a heavy cross to bare."[13] Tania's art, those enormous fat women, become the materialization of the multiple obsessions and everything that society does not want to see and tries, by all means, to hide. The interest on gender in Tania's work is not only expressed in her topic but also in the way and techniques with which she produces and works on them. The fat women are produced with cloth, in giant canvasses of a crude color, upon which the machine stitches and begins to shape enormous silhouettes, and the love handles and other body textures—such as wrinkles—are produced by areas filled up with cotton balls. Sewing—a traditionally feminine job—is not only used to mass-produce clothing to cover up the human body, but on the contrary, in this case it is also used to produce art that uncovers the feminine body.

Presenting her subjects in this manner, Tania Candiani tells the eye to pay a lot of attention to the form of the figure, its pose, its facial expression, and, at times, apparent supports, because there is no color or interior guide or view that attracts our attention in other directions. And what these faces and figures transmit, while we observe them, is the dark side of this ideal—the collective obsession with thinness that turns into an obsession with food and appetite.[14]

Another one of Tania's most recent and still in progress artistic projects involved "sweeping" artists' studios in London. This was an objective to pick up and trace what they have and what they discard during their artistic production process. This is a type of archeological work about the artist's tasks and also a type of artistic meta-discourse, since

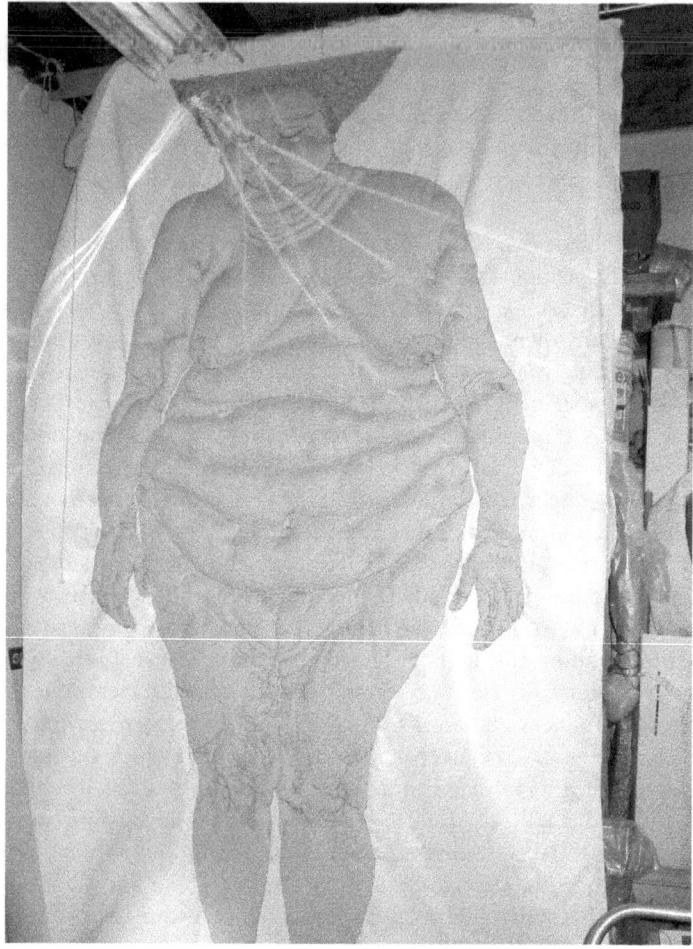

**Figure 10.3** "Gordas," by Tania Candiani (Archive: Norma Iglesias-Prieto).

Tania reflects upon her art through the artistic practice of other subjects. Regarding this, Tania states:

> This speaks about the creative moment; it is a register of that. In this case, I would go into the studio most of the time when the artists were not there. The studio administrator would authorize me to go in and he would open them. I would go inside to sweep them and to take pictures, not of the place, but of the things within them, of the order and disorder, things that were stuck to a wall, the materials used, thrown on the floor, in the trash,

of the clothing used to paint, the chair and materials. I did not know what richness I would find. It was incredible, very moving because it allowed me to enter into these people's universe because it was like being in their homes, in their world. I want, with this, to create an image of the painter without having seen her or him. I need to go again, I was only able to sweep eighty studios, and in London there are so many artists that this cannot be a good sample.[15]

Another one of her most recent projects that incorporates, in a more active way, the communities with which she works was the one entitled "The Intervened Visible: Inhabitants and Home fronts" (2007), where she temporarily intervened, through collaboration with the residents of homes with specific social interest, in their home fronts, materializing their aspirations and dreams. The home fronts created by Tania with different techniques (sewing, painting, digital art) covered the crude reality of the inhabitants creating a scene from the multiple interviews she conducted with them. Tania states that this project was about

> Interpretations of the reflections of the homes, of the people that live in them. [...] and it shows the relation that can exist between the emotional state of a character or her/his contexts while at the same time it proposes an exploration of the picturesque concept through the material used—the support and mode of exhibition. Each inhabitant constructs her/his own constellation of material and immaterial places to define multiple personal territories. The intimate inhabitants. This is why the process of making these pieces is linked to the vital exercise of sharing memories and emotive connections with strangers... [Such interventions] are inscribed in everyday life [...] without any other apparent purpose but to re-live experiences and make someone feel something again.[16]

In this way, one of those houses became a Japanese dream house, or a sophisticated New York beauty parlor, or a house of critical intellectual reflection, or a white house machine-sown like the work of the seamstress woman who lives there. Regarding the Japanese style house, Tania states:

> This was the home front for one of the first women who opened her house to us and wanted to participate in the project. It is Sonia's house; she is a *reggaetón* dance teacher, has three children and considers herself a Geisha. When we asked her in the questionnaire to draw her ideal home she told us: "I don't know how to draw, but do you see that miniature house over there, well that's my ideal house." Departing from this Asian house image, I brought her some designs and we starting working. She started requesting things to be included, like a dragon on top, things like that, and together we began to compose it. She asked me to create a Geisha who would be by

the door and who would greet each person when they got to her house. This home front will stay there until it falls because she wants it to stay there as long as possible. She is even thinking about permanently remodeling some aspects of her home.[17]

This project, like many other Tijuana artistic projects, shows one of the tendencies in contemporary art: a more specific attention to the creation process than to the art itself. The incorporation—as co-creators—of the communities with whom and for whom they work—urban interventions and the exhibit in public city spaces: the streets, the parking lot, the beach, the international border crossing, the abandoned movie theater, the bar, and places that are not institutionalized—liberate art and its cannons. Sometimes this is an artistic intervention strategy, but it also arises from the lack of museums and galleries. This is about public exhibits that do not respond, like in other places around the world, to a production mechanism that questions traditional and legitimized spaces like museums and galleries, but rather as a natural and spontaneous way of producing and exhibiting their work due to the lack of exhibit spaces.

Undoubtedly, Tijuana's visual artists' contribution is the stimulation of the creative faculty in other social subjects. In moments where we are apparently running out of everything, the natural, material, spiritual, and symbolic, what we require is an enormous measure of creativity that allows us to construct a new civilizing order that returns to us future options. And in this area, Tijuana's visual artists are doing an outstanding job. They work intensely in a process of reappropriating their city, the border condition, the search of new ways of creating and representing its relations, as well as a process of practical redefinition and what it means to be an artist. Their work, as well as their life trajectories, demonstrates the transborder character of their reality. They are artists that have a need to express themselves through any means at their disposal, because their multimedia formation does not recognize barriers between one medium and the other or one technique or another. These are unorthodox artists who participate in art and video installations, mixing video live, photography, sculpture, and so on. They direct their projects and support others. They are enormously creative people who have taken over forgotten spaces, making them theirs, reviving them for the benefit of a larger community. They are also subjects who have demonstrated new perspectives of the border inhabitants and their dynamics that have created their own life and work trajectories to create new border narratives, who have utilized everything within their reach for their artistic productions. They are a clear example of the border as a place of cultural encounters and clashes, as well as a generation that absorbs content from everywhere without losing sight of their deepest identity aspects, their experiences as transborder Tijuana subjects, their local and global character (glo-cal or its specificity in global contexts), their place in an asymmetrical relation, and their strength as the ones in charge of the creative potential in their communities. They are artists who do not fear cultural borders but take advantage of them instead, who question but at the same time offer something. They are artists with a vast potential who do not fear fusion and experimentation and have bet on behalf of the search for new ways to express their experiences as transborder artists. Artists who, with their work, revive the capacity for aspiration and change in the city and its people, who question and denaturalize the border and its inequalities. Artists who know they have a power: to imagine and generate a different society and city that is not circumscribed to accept their multiple limitations and shortages. Without a doubt, the way in which they have redefined and resignified the city, its dynamics, relations, and objects that comprise it has been what has allowed them to transcend and what has generated an international recognition of their work.

## Notes

1. See Appadurai's "Geography, Imagination, and the Traffic in the Everyday" (2004) and Bhabha's *The Location of Culture* (2004).
2. Pratt' concept is detailed in *Imperial Eyes* (1992), cited by Ybarra Frausto, "De Imágenes y Sueños" (2008).
3. Concept first developed by Herzog, *Where North Meets South* (1990), and, recently, *Shared Space* (2000).
4. See Dear and Leclerc's *Postborder* (2003); Del Castillo's "Illegal Status and Social Citizenship" (2007), and "Cultural Citizenship" (2005).
5. About 258 student surveys were conducted in San Diego State University, the Autonomous University of Baja California (UABC), and the National Pedagogical University (Tijuana Campus) between January 2002 and January 2003. Students had to describe briefly what the Mexico-U.S. border represented to them. Additional information was gathered to understand the subject's basic profile and the frequency/reasons for crossing the border. In some cases interviews were conducted to know the mechanisms that play a part in the representation of the border.
6. According to Tijuana's Business Bureau, the average U.S. tourist's visit in the city is for 3.5 hours. Tijuana's visitors to San Diego spend more time because their activities vary more and take longer to complete due to great distances between recreational places.
7. Sandoval López's "*Do-it-yourself art*" (2004).
8. Interview with Ramírez "Erre" (2007).
9. Malking, "Tijuana Transforms Into a Cultural Hotbed" (2008).

10. Interview with Ramírez "Erre" (2006).
11. Hertz's *Axis Mexico* (2002).
12. Interview with Ruiz Otis (2007).
13. Pincus, "El cuerpo toma muchas formas" (2003).
14. Ibid., 27.
15. Interview with Candiani (2006).
16. Candiani, Event invitation (2007).
17. Comments by Candiani during a guided visit to her project (2007).

Part V

# Young Voices at the Crossroads: Student Artistic and Scholarly Interventions

## II

# Petition

*Analicia Sotelo*

    Named pure, sans blemish,
*O Most Holy and Immaculate Virgin*
        of clean kitchens, bed sheets tinted
        a pale blue, and roses crushed, framing
        weary young necks—I must speak
        with you. For me to pray,
*Be my faithful companion*
*On this life's journey*
        would beg a logical impossibility, like
        the longing to be born wombless. A fruit
        can only contain itself, its ripened ovary
        dangling paradoxically from the principal tree.
        For this, should I
*Thank you?* For all *I have found*
*in this basilica* is the frigid tile, the fast
        flickering of flames, too many women
        wearing the crown of the lonely, watching
        each flame lick quietly in the dark from a solitary
        mark at the firm foot of your altar. This should be
*a place where I feel at home*
*with you and my brothers*
*and sisters*, a sanctuary for the lost, though sanctuaries are
        merely holding places, zeros caught in time, lacking
        natural progression. I've come here as a last resort,
        searching for a faith prescribed—one guaranteed sacred,
        for Faith was my father,
        in the days I believed he would return,
        and Doubt was my mother,

      seeing me wait for him by the window—
      then, in the evening, quietly tucking me
      beneath the covers. Please
*Mother, help me come closer to your Son,*
         as there are times when I cannot trust even Him. Once,
         I fell asleep on the grass of my garden, with the lilies encircling
         my arms, thinking only of Him and the life I could lead,
         when a series of men came knocking at my skirt,
         offering strange things to me.
         The thing is, I've no way of knowing
         which one to follow, the female
         or the male, body
         and soul.
*That I may find in Him the Way of Life*
      is what you've instructed, the way
*Which gives meaning to moments*
      you yourself once knew.
      Such moments
*of sorrow and happiness,*
      alternating without warning
      cause my endless petition
here *in this my earthly pilgrimage.*

# 12

# Self-Portrait

*Analicia Sotelo*

> Do what you are going to do, and I will tell about it.
> —Sharon Olds

He is twenty-six, humming to himself
in the studio. She is on her way to class,
touching her growing belly.

His plans to sculpt a baptismal dress
are set in place. There are: *Ironic infant
ruffles set in a breathless,*
*greening copper.*

She is in the grocery store, counting coupons.
Her palette is brighter, softer.

When I was twelve, there was an exhibition in New York
for rising artists. In my birthday phone call, my gift
was two questions: *How old are you?* and *Where
did your mother store the cast?*

In her bedroom, my mother sets silk on silk,
paints images of young girls balancing over cement
and water.

The mobile in my crib is a composite
of graphite and clay, turpentine and liquid glue.
The figures suspended in the air are naked, torn
at the torso, the wrist. From a desert Eden they rose,
far from innocent, so the world would see them
caught in mid-air and turning.

13

# Socialized into "Whiteness"

*Roxana J. Rojas*

The formation of identity is the product of geography and time, being born in a specific place at a specific time. This chapter will discuss the experience of racial formation and the influences that cause the development of the Latino identity from the perspective of a second-generation Mexican American woman. While citing documents on assimilation and the construction of Latino identity, the chapter will relate the personal experiences of the author and the formation of identity within a predominately white environment. The chapter will also discuss the repercussions (on both sides of the ethnic/race border) of socialization into "whiteness" while being ethnically Mexican American. This will allow for the discussion of the complexities of identity formation due to the challenges by both sides of the ethnic spectrum.

> "When I first met you I thought you were one of those *Hispanics*, you know? I mean, you seemed like stuck up, like a white wanna be"

When I heard my partner say this to me regarding the moment when we first met, it was not the romantic love story I expected to have him reconstruct. This simple line repeated itself in my head and in my subconscious. After hearing it, I adamantly tried to defend (and prove) my Latina-ness. It was the first time my authenticity as a Mexican American was challenged and questioned by another Mexican American. I found myself in a serious identity crisis, more so than I already was, having been thrown into a predominantly Anglo institution of higher education. I had little to prepare me for this environment. Besides the academic preparation, there was not much else, and I had to rely on my cultural and religious background to get me through. In the fall of 2006, I had come to Trinity University with a very strong sense of who I was and very conscious of my Mexican Americanness. I had learned since childhood that I was different from the rest ("the rest" being a white majority), so by the age of 20 I knew in what ways I was/am different. Yet, there was something disconcerting about my partner's comment that sent me into the exploration and examination of my perceived whiteness, considered a sort of privilege.

Mexican American women at predominately Anglo institutions of higher learning, like myself, define themselves as being perceived as the "other" and are marginalized as result of their differences (García, Alma 2004, 145). This makes the university experience much more difficult to navigate, because there is a constant negotiation with responsibilities that are expected of ourselves as daughters of traditional Mexican immigrant parents who often need our help in navigating the English-speaking world. As García states, "The lives of second generation individuals are ones characterized by tensions, conflicts, and negotiations between themselves and their immigrant parents and between themselves and the larger society" (2004, 15). This experience challenges the long-standing theory of assimilation and asserts that "adjustment to the new society does not necessarily erase all of their culture," and that assimilation is more a "process through which immigrant groups experience varying degrees of integration into American society" (García, Alma 2004, 15). Therefore any type of desire to advance is not the result of wanting to be perceived as white or to fit in as white, but rather as an attempt to reach personal and familial goals. I propose that the "you are selling out" attitude comes from third-generation Mexican Americans whose parents don't have immigrant experience and thus do not subscribe to the same set of values as do first and second generations. They tend to reject institutions and view social mobility as buying into the "white man's system," not as a way to do better and help other Latinos. Yet, even within the immigrant experience and desire to move upward, there are contradictions. There are barriers specifically for women as a result of machismo and marianismo that emphasize the idea that women should be mothers and concentrate their activities in the home; doing otherwise is considered deviant (Doob 1999, 197). The idea of an educated Latina aspiring for social mobility is like desecrating the sanctity of La Virgen María. Thus, the barriers are many, but the reasons to overcome them are even more numerous and outweigh them enormously.

The complexity of relations among Latinos considering themselves Hispanic or white and those Latinos who identify ethnically with their

Latino ancestry is such that there are schisms created among Latinos and on the personal level even between family members. There are many reasons why one may wish to pass for white or be seen as whiter. Additionally, there are certain "advantages" that allow for being perceived as white. Some of these so-called advantages include lighter skin color, no discernable accent in speaking standard English, a college degree, circle of friends that include many whites, a private school education, and even the manner of dressing. Eduardo Bonilla-Silva categorizes this type of Latinos into a group called "honorary whites." The Latinos that can gain admittance to this group are typically lighter-skinned, college educated, include those married to whites, those with higher income (higher class distinction), those who are half Latino-half white, and so forth. Generally, any Latino with characteristics that place him or her in a position that is "significantly better off than the collective black (the last group in Bonilla-Silva's proposed triracial order of racial stratification)" can be included in the "honorary white" category (Bonilla-Silva 2006, 194). This is where I come in: relatively light-skinned, no accent to give away my ethnicity, private schooled, and yes, most of my friends have been white. So, is it my fault that I grew up in a predominantly Anglo environment? My Latina cultural capital is questioned because of these features and I am often taken for a *Hispanic* or of non-Latino roots. Once I was asked if I was Italian, and the woman looked disappointed at having guessed wrong; she pursed her lips and squinted, in a perplexed sort of way, after I said I was Mexican. She followed by saying, "Well, you don't *look* Mexican." Well, of course, once again, she felt that I didn't have the stereotypical dark skin and the accent to give my ethnicity away.

There is significant privilege in being able to be classified as an "honorary white." But that same perceived privilege results in negative perceptions of who I am and what I stand for. My own extended family and other Mexican Americans tend to see my "privileged" status as a result of my lack of identification with my heritage. According to Bonilla-Silva, many Latinos who would be a part of the "honorary" group often classify themselves as "white"; in fact, 60 percent of them do so (2006, 187). Mexicans are not generally considered a part of the "honorary white" group, due to the high level of immigrant Mexican population in the United States, but, once again, certain exceptions can be made if the "prerequisites" have been met. As Bonilla-Silva states, those certain honorary whites may be "believing that they are different (better) than those [he] argue[s] likely to comprise the collective black category"; there is a notion that these "honorary whites" have a sense of haughtiness in them (2006, 186). Though this may be true for some, there are Latinos who are perceived as a part of the honorary white category but do not necessarily identify with that category. The fact that the Latinos considered a part of the honorary white category might be acquiring "white-like racial attitudes" and distancing themselves "from the members of the...collective black" (2006, 186) makes all possible honorary white Latinos suspect of having this same "I'm not one of *them*" attitude in regard to Latinos who would be considered as a part of the collective black group (recent Latino immigrants, darker-skinned Latinos, etc).

> **"That 'goody two shoes,' she thinks she's better than us because she goes to a private school. She thinks she's so smart; she's always correcting us. She even *dresses* like a white kid"**

As a result of this type of perception about honorary whites (the term I will use from here on to describe Latinos who do not necessarily identify with being Latino or identify more with white, suburban, middle-class America), there is a sense of scorn toward this group, or those perceived as part of this group, by those who don't identify as honorary whites. Common terms used to refer to these Latinos are "coconuts" and "sellouts." I have often been scorned by my family, who feel that I am stuck-up since I go to a four-year private college instead of Palo Alto, the community college of the *barrio*. I sometimes tend to use vocabulary not commonly used among them (which is seen as my way of showing off) and have even been looked down upon for the way I dress (seen as preppy and white). I don't have the "urban" look and therefore am not "in." All of these characteristics, though, are a result of the way I was brought up. I grew up in Addison, a small German town outside of Chicago. My father was able to purchase a house very cheaply as a result of connections his older brother had with a real estate agent, from whom he and three other brothers bought houses in the same area. I was always enrolled in a private school and thus always wore a uniform. My parents have always upheld the value of a good education because they saw it as a way for us to have a better life than they did, a way to reach the fulfillment of the American dream.[1] Mexican immigrant parents generally instill this "dream in their American-born daughters, grounding them in their immigrant world view—a belief in striving for a better life" (García, Alma 2004, 145). They made every sacrifice—even paying for a private Catholic education—necessary to ensure what they thought would be the best education for my siblings and me. Growing up, all my friends were always white; I never had any interactions with Mexicans except at home or at family parties. My entire personality, including language, dress, and attitude, was formed around this environment. The Mexican immigrant parents included in a study by ethnographer Alma García, as a norm, "gave their daughters solid roots they hoped would guide them as they navigated through American society," and my parents are no exception to this (García, Alma 2004, 145). Yet, the issue that arises here is the fact that "as the second generation progress[es] through higher education, their parent's universe compete[s] with their emerging one, playing an increasingly significant role in the unfolding of their ethnic identity" (García, Alma 2004, 145). Therefore the effect of having a white middle-class teacher throughout early identity formation causes the instilment of white middle-class values for a Mexican American child. Yet, the muddled experience of values and nuances call into analysis the process of assimilation that minorities are said to undergo. In my case, as in the case of all minorities seeking social mobility, there is scorn from our minority counterparts because of the "explicit linkage of social mobility with assimilation," but as in the studies of Ruben Rumbaut, the once perceived linear process of assimilation that lead to the "further dilution of ethnicity" is challenged as empirical data suggests a not so linear process (1997, 925). For example, Rumbaut states, "students whose parents are both immigrants outperform their counterparts whose mother or father is U.S.-born" (1997, 938). This empirical data reported by Rumbaut backs my experience in outperforming my cousins who had at least one U.S.-born parent, and his findings on the outperformance of white peers by children of immigrants also corresponds with this nontraditional interpretation of assimilation. So, contrary to what some Mexican American peers may say about my "assimilation" or selling-out to the dominant society, I am only falling within the normal performance of second-generation Mexicans.

The Mexican American family holds several distinct features different from the typical white family, and thus this identity development is much more conflicted and complex. Caldera, Fitzpatrick, and Wampler explain, "The Mexican American family has been identified, typically, as adhering to traditional values that include familism, traditional male/female roles, and extended family networks. Even with changes resulting from acculturation and socioeconomic pressures, the importance of family unity continues as a major characteristic among Mexican Americans to this day" (Caldera, Fitzpatrick, Wampler 2002, 112). As such, my parents always stressed the importance of good behavior or buen comportamiento to me as their young Mexican daughter. I was taught to do all the things expected of a woman: cook, clean, look after children (I have two younger siblings), be responsible, and, of course, be a good, traditional Mexican Catholic girl. According to González, "In response to subalternity, the emotion of minority status…Mexican-origin families selectively and strategically deploy certain cultural traits to differentiate themselves from the 'outside,' Anglo world" (González 2001, 64). In suburban America, playing these roles was not easy for me because of the environment I was in. What was valued and taught at home was usually not the same as what was valued by others in my surroundings outside my home. Yet, I was always taught about my ancestors and my family, and I heard stories of their journey from Mexico and often travelled to the town where my parents are from. These trips to Mexico usually occurred at the end of the year for Navidad and Las Posadas, which made what is Mexican directly connected with music, joy, food, and family, and thus created for me a positive identity construction. Yet, this positive connection with what is Mexican was often shunned in a predominantly white school. I learned to speak only Spanish before attending school, where English was the only acceptable means of communication. Who I was at home and who I was being taught to be at school was strikingly different and often clashed. According to González, "within a 'zone of proximal development' [children] receive each caregiver's personal rendition of the many macro forces in a society" (2001, 62). Some aspects of my behavior were favored or disdained depending on whether I was in my familiar (home) or public setting (school). Many times I found myself getting odd looks from others while crossing myself at school Mass. The way the sign of the cross was taught to me as the proper and appropriate way involved a longer prayer in Spanish. The way that was the "right" way at school was a shorter version in English. So while I continued through my motions at the benediction, I would see perplexed looks, and I was at one point approached by my teacher who asked me why I crossed myself that way if I had learned the "right" way. The two settings (private and public) pulled me in two very opposing directions, and according to González, "For the Mexican origin child, the issue of language and linguistic input is complicated by hegemonic structures that inhere in minority status. Language is not simply a vehicle for communication, but the site of a highly politicized and vitriolic debate concerning the nature of who speaks what language where and under what circumstances" (González 2001, 54). With González' statement in mind, the experience I narrated above is a good example of how language and what is acceptable in one language versus another can take on a very political meaning for both parties involved.

### "You can't speak Spanish here"

As mentioned before, I did not speak any English when I started school, and it was my experience that Spanish was not preferred there. My school did not have a bilingual education program or any type of language transition program for Spanish speakers. This made my learning experience within the classroom a distinct one. As Bonvillain states, "When Spanish-speaking children enter a traditional classroom where the teacher does not understand Spanish, the children often become silent, and are not expected to respond" (Bonvillain 2003, 320). This was the case for me, and I sat through a meeting with my parents and the teacher while the teacher explained her "concern" at my slow learning and suggested I be tutored or examined for mental incapacities. I was the only one in my class when I started school, and one of very few students in the entire school that spoke only Spanish. Language is one of the most important factors in identity formation, therefore when a child's native language is forbidden, something vital is taken away; in my case, communication was barred, and as I did not speak English, it was as if I didn't exist, "English was the currency of exchange for securing personhood" (González 2001, 50). Even after I learned English, the invisibility did not go away, it persisted as I was still not one of "them." English was still my second language, and a monolingual English student has privilege over a bilingual student if the first language is something other than English. On one occasion, after I was older and had learned to speak English, I conversed with another girl in Spanish, but I felt as if this action and just being myself were violations. Indeed it was. Shortly thereafter, the other girl and I were asked to report to the principal's office and were reprimanded for speaking Spanish in front of other students who could not understand us. We were asked to not converse in Spanish while in school from that point onward. Soto indicates that language is pivotal, "for children, especially younger children, issues of language and culture are intertwined and directly related to the formation of a healthy identity as members of a family and a nation" (Soto 2002, 2). Therefore, if there is a rejection of the mother language within the educative sphere, there is a rejection of identity. This feeling of rejection led me to try to become accepted, and as I got older I made it a point to have an extensive vocabulary and become the most avid reader. Yet, this same ambition and the resulting expansive vernacular was not well met by other Mexican Americans, who thought that my way of speaking meant I was attempting to be white. My feelings were captured by González, who stated, "It is an emotion that juxtaposes assimilation and alienation" (González 2001, 59). Children in my position find it difficult to navigate this "living heteroglossia" and thus a bicultural negotiation, "On one hand, such children evince a seep and fierce loyalty to the emotions that being Latino engenders. On the other, there is a desperate bid to belong to a totality that is greater than they, powerful and alluring in its domination of their lives (González 2001, 60). In the midst of this, my parents, like other Mexican immigrant parents, divulged "intergenerational transmission of useful knowledge in the quest for 'disambiguating' the paradoxes of Latino identity" (González 2001, 63). This "useful knowledge" was usually of a religious nature, but it often included anecdotes of their own experiences or that of my grandparents and extended family that could serve to help me in navigating my experiences.

## "So you gunna go to one of those white people schools n' shit?"

As a result of my language acquisition in combination with my non-Latino academic environment during my early identity formation, my upbringing as a conservative Catholic, strict traditional Mexican upbringing, and my continued private school education, I was not exposed to the rougher side of being a low-income, minority that is typically described in statistics. I was on the "servile" side of the spectrum of "high subordinated minorities." Brint describes that "if they [members of highly subordinated minorities] are agreeable they are scorned as servile. If they are assertive they are characterized as overbearing" (1998, 215). According to him, among "highly subordinated minorities...as a result of denied status in the terms valued by the larger society...develop an alternative status system based not on 'respectability' but on 'reputation' for eye catching behavior" (Brint 1998, 215). I was not allowed to follow into the typical rejection of institution, and because of this I had no other Mexican American friends who held the reported views of low expectation for social mobility. My father always said that pride in being Mexican comes from hard work and perseverance in reaching the American dream. There is a tendency among first- and second-generation immigrants that, as the result of a "highly traditional culture," they "had grown up believing that their children's success in an alien world required a disciplined, dedicated approach" (Doob 1999, 191). This tendency also partially explains the rate of college completion of Mexican Americans, which "peak[s] with the second generation and then decline[s] with the third generation (Doob 1999, 159).

I had no solidarity to build with my Mexican American peers. The alternative solidarity and ethnic pride that comes from "eye catching behavior" was not a part of my experience, thus I have no "street" credibility, and consequently I am considered less Latina, or not "down" like other Mexican Americans. Hegemonic institutions of education and social constructions of segregation cause these inequalities among Latinos. Studies by Murguia and Telles indicate a correlation between phenotype and educational attainment: it's not wanting to be white that has allowed me to more easily "fit in," and it is clear that there are other factors such as "generational status, religion, and predominant language of the neighborhood" that are also at play (1996, 276). There are factors beyond what I can control that allow certain Latinos to gain advancement over others, and it is not necessarily a selling out of the self to the white dominant society. The idea that any attempt at social mobility is seen as a movement toward whiteness is one with which I have become very familiar, but it is the statistics of low educational attainment and high poverty that my parents have tried to help me overcome. I do not aspire to gain a higher education because I want to be white, it is because I want to bring pride to my family and my people. I work against the odds to be accepted not for the sake of having a special privilege with white people, but for the sake of fulfilling an "American dream," which includes educational attainment at the highest degree possible. Contrary to the perceptions of some Mexican American peers and family members, my ambition is not for the purpose of self-achievement, it is solely for the purpose of bringing pride to, and being a tool for, the advancement of my family and my Latino community.

## Notes

1. For a thorough analytical reflection on this subject, see López, Josefina, *Simply Maria, or the American Dream* (1996).

# 14

# From My Street to Main Street

*Miguel Guerra*

Deep in the heart of South Texas is a place along the border where its people are often considered "ni de aquí ni de allá"—not Mexican, not American—the Rio Grande Valley. It is an area comprising nearly 90 percent Latino population where Spanish-speaking or bilingual households are common.[1] The majority of public schools offer bilingual or dual-language programs to meet the needs of the English-language learners in the area. The four counties that make up the Lower Rio Grande Valley—Starr, Hidalgo, Cameron, and Willacy—rank among the poorest in the nation. The McAllen-Edinburg-Mission Metropolitan area at the heart of the Rio Grande Valley has the lowest per capita income of any metropolitan area in the country.[2] Here, I formed ideas and opinions, reaffirmed my beliefs and values, and socialized as a member of the majority: a Latino.

With parents expecting me to go to college since I was born and cousins attending universities during my grade school years, I knew early on that I would attend an institution of higher learning. Friends dropping out of school to lead more unfortunate lives also reassured me I had to continue my education. So I did. Wanting to leave home but not be too far from my family, I traveled 250 miles north to Trinity University in San Antonio, Texas. Located in a city that is 61.3 percent Latino,[3] Trinity is an 11 percent Hispanic campus and finds itself as an anomaly in this city.[4] This is my new home.

After 18 years of being a Latino in the Rio Grande Valley, I was a Latino, literally overnight, at Trinity University—two very different worlds. Whereas there were a few white people in my high school, I now shared a suite with three white guys, and a hall with only one other Latino who identified more strongly with the non-Latino community—I quickly realized I was no longer in my element. For the first time in my life I socialized as the ethnic minority. Though I did not feel like myself around my peers, staying on this campus, this microcosm of what is considered "mainstream," would be the only way I would see firsthand what mainstream society thought of me. I had to stay. Facing the fire in my first couple of months at Trinity, I had to figure out how to socialize with the white majority—the dominant "in-group." How white did I have to be? How Latino could I be? How could I make my peers see that I belonged in the classroom next to them when most Latinos on this campus serve them food at lunch or clean their rooms every other week? I had to find a middle ground between my "Latino-ness" and my "white-ness." I had to balance myself on the Latino-white spectrum, but I was always weary not to assimilate into "white mainstream society" for fear of becoming part of the "out-group" among my Latino community at home. This is my story.

Growing up in the Rio Grande Valley is a unique experience. Sociologists define the term "habitus" as "a set of acquired patterns of thought, behavior, and taste as a result of internalization of culture or objective social structures through the experience of an individual or group."[5] The term, modified by sociologist Eduardo Bonilla-Silva to "white habitus," describes the result of residential and social hypersegregation of whites from blacks and other minorities.[6] Using Bonilla-Silva's definition of "white habitus," one could argue that the Rio Grande Valley forms a type of "Latino habitus." Bonilla-Silva posits, "White habitus geographically and psychologically limits whites' chances of developing meaningful relationships with blacks and other minorities."[7] Such is the situation for Latinos in the Lower Rio Grande Valley. Housing segregation established the Latino population as the overwhelming majority. Ninety percent of the 1.2 million residents of the Lower Rio Grande Valley are Latino.[8]

As a result of housing segregation, schools too were segregated. Approximately 98.7 percent of my classmates through grade school were Latino.[9] While I knew somewhere in my mind that this was not the norm, I did not completely understand it. In 2002, the U.S. Department of Education's National Center for Education Statistics determined that the best way to measure "better" from "worse" schools was class composition.[10] The average Hispanic child in the Texas metropolitan regions in the valley is in a school that is more than 95 percent Hispanic.[11] The NCES added, "much evidence...shows that high-poverty schools reduce the educational performance of children." The same report stated, "The average poor student in public schools attends a school that is 63 percent poor (the average Hispanic student attends a school that is 66 percent poor), as measured by the percent of students qualifying to receive a free school lunch."[12] Interestingly enough, there were so many students who qualified for a free lunch in the school district that officials decided that every student in the district would be eligible for a free lunch.

Students of the Rio Grande Valley are exposed to ethnic diversity when they travel out of the Valley to compete in athletics or academics. I recall the first time I traveled out of the Valley with our all-minority drama troupe to Regan High School in San Antonio, Texas. As we drove through the neighborhood surrounding the school, we noticed the majority of homes were relatively new and large in comparison to what we were used to seeing. "We're not in Kansas anymore," one of my friends said in an effort to fight off this feeling of uncertainty as we pulled up to the school. As we walked in, we saw the other teams unloading equipment and they turned to see us—silence. We had come to compete at a predominantly white school against predominantly white casts from the area. While some companies had a few ethnic minority cast members, we walked in with nearly 30 Latino students. We had never seen an all-white cast and it appeared they had never seen a nearly all-Latino cast. "Well, let's go find our dressing room," our director instructed in an effort to break the silence as he feared our company would lose focus. The rest of the day was full of comments to the tone of "Did you see the way they just stared at us?" and "Had they never seen that many dark-skinned persons before?" The following day our all-minority cast presented *Man of La Mancha*—the story of Don Quixote. We performed a Spanish play featuring Spanish characters, portrayed by Spanish surnamed people, at a predominately white school. After winning the competition, comments such as "The spics won?" and "How could we lose to the brown people?" were spoken by the other cast members. Our director had previously warned that if we heard such remarks, retaliation of any kind would lead to immediate removal from the company. This was, by far, one of the most uncomfortable moments of my life. This was my first "predominately white" school experience.

As high school came to a close, I decided I would have to leave the Valley to broaden my view of the world. Nearly 52 years after *Brown v. Board* was decided in our nation's Supreme Court, I left the comfort of segregation for the discomfort of integration at my new university in San Antonio. Trinity University is the first private school I have ever attended. My parents work for the Texas public school system. My mother, the Region One Director of Bilingual/Migrant/ESL Education for the Rio Grande Valley, believed the schools she vowed to better were good enough for her children.

It was on my second day at Trinity that I realized I was completely out of my element. Lunch that day was terrifying since I, like most others in my class, knew no one and had to join a table or sit by myself and pretend to read or hope someone would join me. I decided to take my greasy, dining hall pasta and sit with some people I recognized from my hall. They gladly made room for me and I joined the ritual "Hi, my name is…I am from…" conversation taking place. As I sat at the table, I thought, "Are these the people that will become my best friends for college? Are they smarter than me?" I also thought, "This is the first time I have ever had non-Latino peers; people who do not look like me, who did not grow up in the same neighborhood, and have very different experiences than me." After that I immediately thought, "What will my friends back home think when I tell them?" I was very excited and scared. As we were making small talk about interests and hobbies, one girl looked up and said, "Did anybody else get Mexican food? Is this how *quesadillas* are supposed to taste?" I did not respond and smiled to myself thinking about the Mexican food back home. "Well I don't know, ask Mike he's 'the Mexican.'" My heart dropped, head lifted, and eyes shot open. My suitemate of one full day felt comfortable enough to crack an ethnic joke at my expense in front of our now uncomfortable peers. I was called "a Mexican" in a pejorative tone to my face by someone of another race and for the first time, I was the only Latino in the group. Most at the table glared at me not knowing whether or not to laugh. Others, embarrassed by the comment, continued eating as though they had not heard anything. "Is this what it's like?" I thought. "Is this what life is really like for a minority? Is this "subtle racism" acceptable? Is this what I had been shielded from in my predominately Latino school system?" I did not know what a person in my position should say. "I am Mexican-American," I responded. Those thinking about laughing did not; those pretending to ignore, acknowledged; and my suitemate looked at me with a blank stare, speechless: "It means I was born in the United States and have Mexican ancestry. Also, the term 'Mexican' is usually applied to a person from Mexico and is not a pejorative term in my mind," I stated. I did not know how my statement would be received or how I would be perceived afterward, but I knew I could not just be silent. I had to say something, not to defend, but to inform. The rest of lunch was silent, but more importantly, I got respect the rest of the year.

Reaffirming my belief that I was part of the "out-group" was the fact that the only other Latino in the hall was a female from San Antonio with a Spanish surname who refused to admit to being Latino/a. For the first time in my life, I doubted myself, asking, "Is being Latino a bad thing?" "Am I wrong?" "Have I been wrong all my life?" On top of the fact that most college freshmen feel confused about life, I was concerned that I had grown up in the wrong place believing the wrong things. What if my parents were wrong? Doubting my parents in this way really scared me.

At Trinity University and in the United States in general "there is a fundamental denial that race is a central feature in a 'colorblind' America."[13] Colorblind racism is a racial ideology that very indirectly and subtly maintains inequality.[14] Many people at Trinity claim they are not racist and "don't see color." This aligns with the egalitarian values in our society. Still, when I arrived at Trinity I thought about why no one wanted to talk about race, especially whites. I argue that most students at Trinity keep an open mind and have no intention of being racist, but most practice colorblind racism.

A good friend once asked me about the Ronald E. McNair Program I participate in. I informed him that it is a government-funded program to help historically unrepresented people continue their college career. He responded with a grimace saying, "Oh ok, Mike, well I'm happy for you but that in no way helps me or anyone who looks like me." He continued, "I don't mean to offend you, but why is it that these programs are only for minorities? White people need help too, you know?" This was not the first time I had heard this question. "It has a lot to do with history of our country. Did your parents go to college?" He replied yes. "Did your grandparents go to college?" He replied, "No they were poor farmers." I continued, "Ok, my grandparents came to America illegally, were poor and uneducated farm workers, but my mother, like yours, went to college. If your grandparents wanted to become educated and earn more money, what was stopping them was poverty. What prevented my grandparents from being educated and earning more money was mostly their ethnicity." At this point my friend began to look at me as though I was making sense, but he did not necessarily want to hear it. I continued, "even if your grandparents had not been poor and mine not undocumented, compared side by side, yours would have had an advantage in this country because of the color of their skin. You may not realize it, but they did have more opportunities than mine did. Now, I'm getting the opportunity my grandparents never had. It's not that I'm advancing past you; I'm still playing catch up. In a perfect world, these programs wouldn't exist." My friend looked at me and nodded as though to say, "I understand." We never discussed it again.

While some people on campus do not want to recognize color, others are looking forward it. It's a running joke between all students—particularly those of color—how Trinity tries to promote diversity and make it seem like there are more people of color than there actually are. I am considered a fair-skinned Latino. Once at a luncheon my friends and

I were next to the guest of honor. The photographer there found a shot he liked and asked everyone to freeze and smile for the camera. When we posed for the picture, he stopped, looked around, and called the attention of an African student nearby and asked him to step into the photo. He then asked me to step away. Somewhat disgruntled by his request, I stepped out of the photo, but then he asked me, "Well, where are you from?" When I responded the Rio Grande Valley, the photographer said, "The Valley! That's great! Step in right there." I was part of the photo that included two white students, two black students, and a Latino.

Another occasion when my ethnicity was sought after was when I decided to audition for Trinity's first play of the semester—Romeo and Juliet. This allowed me to find my niche and follow my passion for theater. The adaptation to be performed was a modern-day version set in San Antonio with the Montague/Capulet feud alluding to the northside-white/southside-people-of-color dichotomy of the city. As a result, whites were cast as part of the Montague family and "more ethnic-looking" people, or minorities, were cast as members of the Capulet family. I was cast as Juliet's fiery cousin, Tybalt.

As we sat down for our first company meeting, questions and comments began to fly. "Don't you think people of the community will be offended with the fact Whites and minorities are cast as two opposing groups?" "Why would they be offended? We're not saying anything bad about any one group." As the conversation continued and tension grew, I noticed people of all races used the word "Mexican" to encompass all Latinos regardless of nationality. I raised my hand and added, "I just want to point out that not all Latinos are Mexicans. While it may be that the majority of Latinos in San Antonio, due to its geographical location and historical ties, are of Mexican descent, not all Latinos are 'Mexicans.'" The group was completely silent. I just wanted to point that out because I consistently hear people saying "Whites," "Blacks," and "Mexicans." Everyone in the group looked at me with curiosity. The rest of the meeting carried on with some people catching themselves when about to say "Mexican" and change it to "Latino" or "Hispanic." After the heated meeting, I remember a friend approached me and said, "I've never really thought about what you said. In my high school, there was always the White group, the Black group, and the Mexican group. It never occurred to me to say Hispanic or Latino. Thanks." After this, I realized that regardless of how uncomfortable I felt addressing my peers about race, I had to do so. Notwithstanding the curious and confused looks and the encouraging and annoyed glances I received, I felt it was my responsibility to inform.

Despite the meeting and the ongoing debate about whether or not we should really perform the adaptation of Shakespeare's classic, the show went on. Since it was set in the present day, my costume consisted of tight pants, button-down shirt, and a goatee, to which people thought I looked "very Latin." Also, knives and guns were used instead of rapiers and daggers. So in my first performance on stage in front of a Trinity audience, my dark boot-shaped sideburns, moustache, and beard, along with the tight pants, depicted the "Latinidad" of the character. As if the costume was not enough of a stereotype, I carried a knife and gun, stabbed a man (Mercutio), and was beaten to death, all before the first act ended.

To this day, my best friends at Trinity joke about how they did not approach me at first because they were afraid of me, saying, "We thought you were a mean person. Think about it, the first time we saw you, you had a knife and gun." One might argue that this could have happened to anyone regardless of race. Still, the point is that I was cast in the role because of my ethnicity.

Growing up in my proposed "Latino habitus" has given me a unique perspective to view the world, the people in it, and the problems they faced. While my point of view was not formed in a "mainstream white society," it is important, valid, and essential as we, society, continue to shape the future. Latinos are currently the largest ethnic minority and the fastest growing one in the United States. Latinos are an important part of our country's history and will be essential to its future. Bonilla-Silva states, "light-skinned" Latinos will be "honorary white" or white in the future.[15] I feel it is my responsibility as a light-skinned, upper-middle-class Latino who grew up in a low-income, working-class community to inform the uneducated and always ensure that the voices of the poor, the non-English speaking—the unheard in this country—are heard.

## Notes

1. United States Census Bureau, *Census Demographic: Cameron, Hidalgo, Starr, and Willacy Counties.* (2007).
2. Bureau of Economic Analysis, *Per Capita Personal Income for Metropolitan Statistical Areas* (2004).
3. United States Census Bureau, *Census Demographic: San Antonio, Texas Metropolitan Statistical Area.* (2007).
4. Trinity University, "Trinity University: Fast Facts" (2007).
5. Scott and Marshall, *A Dictionary of Sociology* (1988).
6. Bonilla-Silva et. al., "When Whites Flock Together" (2006).
7. Ibid.

8. United States Census Bureau, *Census Demographic: Cameron, Hidalgo, Starr, and Willacy Counties* (2007).
9. Pharr-San Juan-Alamo Independent School District, *History* (2009).
10. Logan, John R., Jacob Stowell, and Deirdre Qakley, "Choosing Segregation" (2002).
11. Ibid.
12. Ibid.
13. Fluher-Lobban, *Race and Racism* (2005).
14. Bonilla Silva, *Racism without Racists* (2006).
15. Ibid.

# Part VI

# Interviews with Transnational Mexican Artists

# 15

# Interview with Yolanda Cruz, April 16, 2008, San Antonio, Texas

*Rosana Blanco-Cano*

(Translated from Spanish by the editors)

Yolanda Cruz is a Chatino filmmaker from Oaxaca, Mexico, and a Sundance Screenwriters Lab Fellow with her first feature script *La Raya*. Cruz has produced seven documentaries on native people in the Americas. Her work was screened worldwide at the Sundance Film Festival, The Guggenheim Museum, The Smithsonian National Museum of the American Indian, and the National Institute of Cinema in Mexico City. Cruz's honors include an Audience and Best Feature Documentary award from The National Geographic All Roads Film Project 2005 and The Expresión en Corto International Film Festival 2009. Before becoming a filmmaker, Cruz worked as a community organizer.

> RBC (Rosana Blanco-Cano): Thank you for being here. I'll start with your transnational work. When did you start producing documentaries? And why do you use visual production?
> YC (Yolanda Cruz): I have always had an interest in narrating stories; as a child I was curious, I listened to gossip, anecdotes, and I had a good ear. I was raised bilingually but it was hard for me to separate Chatino and Spanish. That is why I think I spent my childhood observing in silence before I was five. But when I started to talk, I talked too much. I always had stories to share. I made up the end of each story, to create some new ones.

Also, my father was a community organizer. He loved writing and talking to his friends; many of them were anthropologists and sociologists; I was raised in that environment. When I migrated to the United States, I thought I would be a lawyer, but I also liked journalism and radio. But in the United States I started to work in theater; I participated in public events and lectures discussing the living condition of indigenous Mexican communities and got tired of that rhetoric. So I began studying photography, but I felt it was not enough; I was missing the use of words and this is when I discovered Russian film and loved it. I thought, "here is the way to communicate politics efficiently." So I decided to study media production. I attended Evergreen State College and when I found visual production I recovered my memories as a girl in Oaxaca. I never had a problem finding a story; it was easy to find a message. My first theme was about the experience of living in multilingual environments. Exploring language and its use was very interesting to me; what I found more difficult was the issue of language politics. Everybody was impressed at school. It was very easy to produce this material. This experience also helped me realize that I was not ready for all the topics; I was not mature enough to develop more complex stories. I decided to get an academic background to develop the perspective I wanted to use in my films. Later I applied to the film studies program at UCLA, but I was torn about my decision. I wanted to study film and also go back to Mexico. I was not aware of the academic prestige associated with this program; I just started in it with my strong voice. I had much to say. I still remember my interview. I wanted to start a revolution. They told me they wanted students capable of making shots of five or six minutes. I felt I could do everything then. Film school was a challenging experience. You are nobody there. You have to prove yourself, and the professors are the ones with the knowledge. I was in shock. I felt I was a master's student, and I wanted respect. I also lacked experience in technical production. That was very difficult; I felt that the program was trying to conform us to the traditional concepts of authorship and cinematic direction. But you have to be a strong authoritative voice if you want to survive within the world of cinema. I learned the formal aspects of film and I developed stories from my personal perspective. Those past stories are different from the ones I'm developing now.

RBC: Could you say more about those old stories?

YC: What I really wanted to do was to portray social movements through fiction. I never considered the documentary perspective because I never felt I was good at conducting research. In that sense, I think I was more dramatic in my early years as a film producer. But all the stories were located in Mexico. What brought a new perspective to my work was finding a binational organization of communities from Oaxaca (Frente Indígena de Organizaciones Binacionales, FIOB) in Los Angeles, and it is then when I recover my sense of home. There are intellectuals from

Oaxaca, indigenous people who worked as activists. In Los Angeles, I had a vital experience, which was opposite to my isolated life in the state of Washington.

The burden of being confused—about staying in the Unite States or returning to Mexico—started to be less significant. Many of the *compañeras* and *compañeros* in Los Angeles experienced a multilocal life without having to explain that to themselves every single day; I felt very comfortable. I decided then to focus my work on the transnational Oaxacan communities by using my experiences as a filmmaker. In other words, I was not looking at the past but at our current transnational experiences. This has not been easy due to the expectations one has as a member of an indigenous community; often people want to see the traditional anthropological study looking at our communities from the outside, not from within them.

I wanted to create something that could be presented and analyzed within the indigenous communities. I thought I was the only one with that particular perspective, but I have met other artists and filmmakers who are adopting the same standpoint in their work. And it was from that perspective that I created my first documentary, a UCLA's requirement to graduate. I went to Oaxaca and created an experimental film entitled *Entre sueños*. That film represents the explosion of the emotions I experienced while in graduate school. My film went to Sundance. I am very practical. I decided to send the film while other peers were obsessively working on aspects like sound; they kept working because they have a strong sense of technical aspects; I just wanted to "send a message." I used a mixture of Super 8 and Super 16, I added color, and also used black-and-white. I wanted to mix everything. Everybody was very surprised when the film was accepted because it was a difficult film to understand. I got support from UCLA since they actually printed the film, and Sundance paid my travel expenses to the festival. But the experience with Sundance was a little confusing in relation to my career. I saw many possibilities and after that I did not want to participate in any other festival. I thought I did not need other types of venues for my films. What is interesting is that I actually submitted the film to indigenous film festivals and they rejected it. I suppose it is because it was a crazy film from a traditional perspective. So the whole experience with that first film was, as I said, confusing.

RBC: The main character is a woman, and the film deals with issues of gender. That is one of the most fascinating aspects of your work.

YC: Yes, this is the story of a woman. It starts with the memories of a girl who goes to the cemetery to a community ceremony. She is struggling with images and sounds that tell her that indigenous people are lazy, and other negative things. She also struggles with spirits who are trying to communicate with her through dance and other interventions.

At the end it is a dream, and the negative connotations were messages she got from television. It is then, explicitly, that it is hard for the girl to separate what is a dream from reality and the TV messages. That is basically the story. After having that dream she decides to go to the mountain to leave a lit candle as a purifying experience. This allows her to reconnect with herself. I like the film. It is very simple but very complex. Simplifying is a goal I have in my work. But being able to transmit a simple and effective message is accomplished only through experience at work, especially in the editing room. I hope my current work is clearer for the public.

RBC: Would this enable you to reach a broader audience and be better received among indigenous communities in both countries?

YC: I like films that are simple. But when a filmmaker discovers all the different techniques, we can overexploit them. For example, when I decided to play with Super 8 in my first film I did not do it because of aesthetic reasons. I think many of my peers did not dare to mix formats because they knew it would not work. For me it was more like "it has to work." Now I plan more; the final outcome is not a product of mere coincidence. I am very demanding of myself; I also have more time, more money, and more experience to produce my films. Before, I did not care about the audience, I used to say, "if they do not understand it is not my problem." I felt that my strong effort as a filmmaker was enough. Nowadays, I feel more responsible for creating an accessible story. And that is also difficult, because I do not want to create the ABC of what I want to say. I still want to create simple ideas that can be complex at the same time. It will only depend on the viewer: if you are looking for profundity you will find it; if you prefer something less complicated you can also access that aspect in my films.

RBC: Why do you use interviews in your films?

RBC: *Sueños Binacionales* was my first film after I graduated from UCLA. As I said before, my first film created a lot of confusion. My professors were also confused because they did not understand the film. It was a watershed moment for me, you are graduating, professors are less and less attached to your work, and you need to take a direction. After that difficult experience with my first film, I worked with my friend Maureen [Gosling] who helped me clarify some aspects in my work. I wanted to develop an expression that reflected an indigenous identity. I was concerned with the issue of migration. For example, anthropologists did not know what to do with their "migrant subjects," those who decided to leave their original communities. I wanted to talk about that particular shift, because it was my own experience. When I started to work on *Sueños*, that perspective was underexplored in film. I decided it would be my niche. Indigenous film festivals screened documentaries about the cultural traditions of elders, but I wanted to defend my voice and visual standpoint. I received a Rockefeller's Foundation grant to produce *Sueños*. The project was exhausting. I had to travel for about two years. I did not know how to proceed. The communities I was visiting in Oaxaca are far from each other, around ten hours by bus. When you travel you feel very tired and there is no energy to continue working that day. Because the history of Mixtec communities is fascinating; I wanted to include the perspective of towns that were organized and those that were not. I also was not sure if I had enough money to cover both perspectives, so I emphasized the organized towns. As a filmmaker you never know when you will finish your projects, but something was clear: I wanted to defend my point of view, my voice.

RBC: Can you talk about your project on Alejandro Santiago, the 2501 migratory statues?

YC: Just to end with *Sueños*. The film is still traveling. I presented it at many venues; I traveled for almost a year. Then, I started to ask myself "And now, what am I going to do?" The [Rockefeller] Foundation told me about the project with Alejandro [Santiago]. But working with foundations is a slow process, so I decided to work on other projects for a while. I worked on the direction and production of three documentaries in a time frame of six months. I had always worked by myself, but this time I had a team working with the camera, the sound, editing; and I also had a production and a research assistant. Four people were supervising the work, and I was supervising four other colleagues. We produced documentaries on relevant issues, such as gay marriage, among others. The difficult part for me was to put aside politics and just work as if you were in a maquiladora production line. Around that time, the funds for the documentary on Alejandro Santiago became available and he was in the final stage of making his sculptures. I thought, "Alejandro is crazy," because while he works and talks about art, he also drinks and talks about mezcal. And there I was, with my political awareness, promoting organization and agency for marginalized people, and Alejandro is simply talking about his sculptures. It was until I was done with the documentaries that I was really able to know more about him and his work. Sometimes he talked about immigration using a nostalgic perspective that is also related to his work as an artist. But I saw that he was creating a fantasy about immigration; he was also repeating a script he used with me and other filmmakers; I think I was the sixth filmmaker trying to document his work. I told him I did not need his fabricated answers, I was looking for something more. I thought I needed to clarify that I was very familiar with this topic. That was difficult in the beginning, but after knowing each other for a while, accepting that communication is a process and it needs time to evolve, we were able to get some interesting ideas. The foundation suggested doing a documentary about the creative experience. However, I also wanted to portray the reasons behind Santiago's work. So I followed him for six months, with all the ups and downs that a person experiences in that period of time. I am happy with the project. I feel more mature and capable of creating a complex message, but I am still defining the final outcome. I study my projects carefully. For me it is like baking bread, I feel out what is needed in each moment of the process. But I also need to delegate, instead of intervening in every aspect of the production. I think this as a part of growing and maturing. We released a trailer for the documentary and it was well received. It is an attractive piece, because the sculptures seduce you. [Laughs]. I remember that the first time I looked at Santiago's sculptures I thought, "They are ugly! Because some look crooked or imperfect. Should I work on this?" But after you spend time with them they represent a presence-absence that is sad. I see the power of dialogue that they inspire. You will find diverse populations talking about immigration after looking at the sculptures; not only Mexicans but also foreigners. We all are talking about a subject that is silenced in many ways; when you see it as an "object" it is easier to define it and understand it. And for me it is the most powerful aspect of Santiago's work. Producing this documentary has been a beautiful process because I have worked with many people. I also had funds to produce it, and this is a new experience for me. But I also feel the pressure because I am working fulltime; I work 10–12 hours per day, every day. I have a salary, but working like that is very difficult; you cannot separate yourself from your project. Now I am more conscious about the power of the image; therefore, I try to do my best because the visual work we make will survive us. It is one's own creation, but once it is released one cannot defend it. It is where I am now. After I finish the project, I will be living another transition. I would like to explore fiction as a genre. I also need to train more people and expand my company.

RBC: What fictional projects do you have in mind?

YC: I already have a script on "microeconomics." It is about a small town that gets a fridge, and how everybody wants to own it. It also talks about how people try to find means to survive, little business, and so on. I believe it is ridiculous to try to survive with [Vicente] Fox's idea of "micro changarros [stores]," little convenience stores, mini businesses. But I have other projects in mind too. I just need to see if they are feasible.

RBC: How do you conjugate your work as a creator and cultural promoter?

YC: I try to keep both roles separate. Sometimes I am a cultural producer; other times I am a cultural promoter. I think now I represent an alternative voice in the field of visual production. There is also the fact that there are only a few women filmmakers, and for me that is unfair. I fight against discrimination in all the areas; I also advocate for labor rights not only for immigrants but also for women. I still participate, though not as much, in social-activist initiatives. This comes from my family, my past, my academic and social formation; it is impossible for me to stop being an activist. But now I am more selective. My participation as an activist is in conjunction with my work as a filmmaker. I also want to mentor young voices, because I would not like to be 70 years old and be watching my own films. I want to see films made by others.

RBC: Yes, it is urgent to open spaces for other creators, like you, who are strong models for young people growing up transnationally. When young women see your work they will think: "If she can to do it, I can do it too."

YC: Exactly. I have also been very fortunate because I had the chance to study both in Mexican and Chicano academia. It is easier to read the book than create it.

16

# Interview with Rosina Conde, March 10, 2008, San Antonio, Texas

*Rosana Blanco-Cano and Rita E. Urquijo-Ruiz*

(Translated from Spanish by the editors)

Rosina Conde (Mexicali, Baja California, Mexico, 1954) is a writer, singer, poet, performance artist, designer, and creative-writing professor. Among others, in Mexico, she has won two National Prizes for Literature—the "Gilberto Owen" (1993) and "Carlos Monsiváis" (2010)— and she was nominated Creadora Emérita 2010 of Baja California. With a BA in Hispanic Language and Literature, and an MA in Spanish Literature from the National University of Mexico (UNAM), she is the founder of literary magazines such as *El Vaivén*, and *La línea rota/The Broken Line*. Some of her publications are: *Poemas de seducción* (1981), *De infancia y adolescencia* (1982), *El agente secreto* (1990), *Bolereando el llanto* (1993), *Arrieras somos* (1994), *La Genara* (1998), *En la tarima* (2001), *Como cashora al sol* (2007), and *Desnudamente roja* (2010). Conde is also the author of performance art pieces such as "Señorita maquiladora," "Cilicios de amor," and "Those were the days." She has been translated into English and German.

 RUR (Rita Urquijo-Ruiz): I would like to start the interview by asking you about your family history in relation to your work. I understand some members of your family participated on the 20s, 30s, and even 50s Mexican cultural industry.

RC (Rosina Conde): Both my parents were artists. The artistic tradition in my family started even before. My grandmother on mother's side is the most immediate reference I have. She and her first husband worked during the era of "las carpas" (itinerant popular theatre) presenting comic sketches as a couple. My mother also started to sing very young, but she dropped her artistic side to be a wife and mother. She was successful. She sang for the XEW (Radio) in Mexico during the 40s, and she also worked with the Follies Berger Company. We still have some images of my mother from those times, but you have to think that my grandmother was my mother's agent; she was very protective of her daughter. My mother was invited to participate in cinema, but my grandmother never allowed her to do it.

RUR: I am very interested in women artists of that period. Do you remember some artists or performers that shared the stage with your mother?

RC: Yes. I have pictures of my mother with Tin Tan and with other famous figures of that period. María Victoria was starting her career at that time; my grandmother was a very good friend of Agustín Lara.

RUR: What can you tell us about your father, was he a musician?

RC: My father played all the instruments, but he never devoted himself to the artistic life. He played guitar, piano, accordion, flute, and all kinds of percussions. My grandmother on my father's also played piano, and was a singer. What is interesting is that when she discovered my father was very talented as a musician she stopped teaching him. She did not want him to be an artist. He had a lot of talent.

RUR: And in what way this factor is an influence during your childhood?

RC: All my siblings and I also got a musical education at home. At home, my father played the guitar or the piano in our living room. And, of course, as usual, the children showed their talents in family gatherings and even during official celebrations of the city. I started to play a banjo my father kept. I was very small. What is also interesting about this story is that my father suffered a mimesis; one day he discovered I was very good at playing the banjo, and he took it away. That banjo simply disappeared from home. After I finished middle school, I was sent to the United States where I was able to take music lessons as a high school student.

RUR: How many kids were in the family?

RC: We are six siblings. My father was a wonderful father and from the moment we started to talk he taught us to recite poetry. He even wrote little pieces, poems, for us. So each kid had a little number to perform.

RUR: It seems to be the starting point for your career in theatre and performance. Even being in your living room, you were on a stage already.

RC: And the stage was also available at school, community gatherings, among other spaces. My father also taught me poetry rhyme. In fact, when I started to write I used to consider rhyme as an important aspect of my poetry. I wrote my first poems when I was in middle school and high school. Evidently, I got rid of those poems a long time ago (LAUGHS).

RUR: When did you feel that you wanted to be a writer?

RC: I decided to be a writer when I was at the university studying literature. I wrote when I was a teenager but I formally assumed to be a writer when I was 22 or 23. As a child, I considered writing a game. I used to write TV scripts, since I was in love with many famous actors (LAUGHS).

RBC (Rosana Blanco-Cano): Now that we are talking about your literary work, could you tell us about your contributions as a cultural promoter?

RC: I had to migrate to Mexico City because I wanted to study literature. When I got to Mexico City, I became aware of the many options you have in the area of the arts. It was incredible for me to see so many activities in comparison to the scarce schedule of events you could see in Tijuana at that time. I thought it was unfair. Baja California had a university already in place during the 70s, but you could only choose among five careers. Living in Mexico City opened my eyes to the great disparity between the country's capital and the rest of the states in Mexico. I have to say that Tijuana was recognized worldwide as the Mecca of cabaret. During the 60s and 70s, Tijuana was also known for being the Mecca of Rock. However, we did not have enough spaces for promoting local and young artists. Fortunately, while living in Mexico City I learned some of the techniques to work in literary production, edition, and publication. Then I decided to open an independent publishing house and I started to work at the Mexican Ministry of Education in the area of book production. My intention was to open a space for young writers that were trying to publish their work. There were other independent publishing houses already in place, but they functioned with very strict publishing criteria. I wanted to work in a space in which everybody could see her/his work published. I thought that the only person that could legitimate a literary work was the reader. While being in Mexico City I started to publish authors from Monterrey, Cuernavaca, or Tijuana.

RUR: So, you were creating that bridge during your years in Mexico City.

RC: And I kept working on that bridge in Tijuana.

RBC: An excellent example of your bridging work in Tijuana is the experimental project *The Broken Line*.

RC: I created that project with Guillermo Gómez Peña. He was also working intensively in the area of cultural promotion. He used to collect materials to be published, and also did some work on editing those materials. We were a big group that worked on the production, impression, and distribution, all the areas. A key element for the success of *The Broken Line* was to create a big distribution circuit. I had many contacts both in Tijuana and Mexico City. Gómez Peña and Marco Vinicio González had several contacts in the other side of the border, in the United States. We were able to distribute *The Broken Line* locally, nationally, and transnationally.

RUR: So, you open new spaces in the northwest of Mexico, and beyond the line.

RC: There is another element on this line. When I decided to be a writer, I also wanted to be a good reader. By reading, I discovered there was a missing voice in the Mexican literary realms: the female voice. We had a few visible women writers; but most of them were invisible.

RBC: And when you decided to write, did you consider embodying the experience of living in the border?

RC: Yes. On the one hand, I realize that when I was a teenager I only had access to books written by men, with a majority of male characters. The few female characters were designed by the masculine-patriarchal architecture. They are like a man in the body of a woman. I could not see myself reflected in any of those characters; either women were evil and murderers or they were weak and fragile. Of course, they were either a prostitute or a virgin. Of course, I am not against prostitutes. Actually, I have tried to portray them using a multifaceted perspective. I want to create characters that break with traditional patterns of representation. Therefore, I try to play with characters that live in quotidian spaces, and have both virtues and defects. They must reflect on their lives, attitudes, and they are the only ones that can judge themselves. But I enjoy seeing them valuing themselves; always trying to find a life project with alternative life paths.

RBC: I am thinking about "Sonatina," *La Genara*, and "De infancia a adolescencia," where you provide readers with an open ending.

RC: Something fascinating happened to me recently. As you may know, the Universidad Autónoma de la Ciudad de México just reprinted my novel *La Genara*. I went to the distribution center and a guy from the warehouse tells me: "So, maestra, when are you publishing the second part of *La Genara*?" I just answered that the second part was not in my agenda. A significant aspect of my literary production has been the establishment of a close relation with my readers. As I said before, as a Tijuanense you have a lot of access to literature written in English; you name it. I remember finding a lot of publications in Spanish but all of them used a Spanish that was not familiar. It was either Chilango [from Mexico City], or Uruguayan, Argentinian, or Castilian. So I wanted to see characters that talked like I talk. In addition, I wanted my characters to move in the streets and spaces that were also recognizable, familiar. Then, I decided to create characters either from Tijuana or Baja California that could go to the same cinema I used to go; that visited the stores I liked, and that had fun in the same spaces I had fun. I wanted readers who could recognize their lives in my literary works.

RUR: And what did you expect from your Mexico City's readers?

RC: Actually, some of my short stories like "Sonatina" are located in Mexico City. What I thought then was that the central area of Mexico had already developed a big body of literary works. I had a very clear goal in mind. I wanted to contribute to the development of a Baja California literary identity. I also wanted to encourage young writers from the northwest of Mexico to publish their work. Fortunately, I was not alone in the endeavor. And the result has been amazing. In relation to my audience in Mexico City, I feel very fortunate. For example, there is this feminist group that was formed a few years ago. They decided to create a magazine entitled *Las Genaras*. Of course, they were inspired by the title of my novel. This is when I say that good things are happening as a result of my work.

RBC: As you said before, there are geographic references, but other references help readers to recognize themselves in your work. A key element is your focus on sentimental education. Music and the feelings that come with it are abundant in your texts.

RC: I can see that clearly. It comes from my own musical formation. On top of that, rock and counterculture music was very important for my generation. Women singers were a big influence in my work; Baez's political discourse, on the one hand, and Nina Simone's critical attitude on race issues. I liked many Afro American women singers when I was a child, but most of them sang as if they were white, to be accepted in the mainstream. Simone decides to sing as an African American. That strong vindictive attitude in Simone was extremely important for me. She was also the first one in introducing African outfits to the stage. I believe some of the topics she addresses are very relevant; historical and social issues pertaining to the conditions of African Americans in the United States.

RUR: And is it from Simone that jazz and blues styles are central in your musical work?

RC: I grew up in Tijuana, a border city. In Tijuana we used to listen to all the popular American music. Actually, when I went to Mexico City, people criticized me because I sang in English. I was like a Molotov bomb for many: woman, student, from Tijuana, rock singer, and an English speaker. I was very fond of counterculture music, Zappa, Dylan, Rolling Stones, all those musicians were contesting the system through their work.

RUR: And did you sing songs by those artists in English? Or did you write your own songs in English?

RC: At first we just sang songs by the famous bands. It was later that Mexican bands started to write their own music in Spanish. I think rock and alternative music written in Spanish is just starting to be accepted by society. Because it was believed that if opera must be in Italian, rock should be in English. My attitude in relation to language was very different. I sang in English because I was interested in the lyrics. The genre was secondary for me. I also wanted to keep in touch with my second language, which is English. Now I write my own songs in Spanish. Actually I have elaborated on that aspect in some of my texts. One needs to take positive aspects from other cultures in order to be a better human being. I also reject negative aspects of all cultures including mine. For example, I do not function with domestic violence and masculine dominance that are common aspects of my culture.

RBC: Going back to your literary trends. There are many images of travel and space in your texts. In fact, most of your female characters are yearning for space. I am talking about physical and metaphoric spaces of power.

RC: Yes, I agree with that. The aspect you point out also comes from my own experience as a child and as an adult. During my childhood, my siblings and I were considered equal. When I left home and decided to live in Mexico City with my baby son I saw how men and women are in fact not considered equals. It was very shocking for me to see that my idealist upbringing was just a fantasy. In addition, do not forget that in the 70s, working women, the ones who went to the streets everyday, were pretty much considered prostitutes. It was the beginning of the 70s. It was then when I saw that, in Mexico, women did not have the right to have a space. The only space they had access to was the kitchen, and the bedroom for service. They could not even own the rest of the house. And kitchens in Mexico City are, in general, minuscule. So, the only place where a woman can be in control is inside that tiny space. When I saw that, I was horrified. That is the reason why my characters are yearning for space; they try to find spaces in which they can move themselves and be the one in charge of their own destiny.

RBC: I also see in your work a reference to the body, and it seems to be connected to the notion of space.

RC: Yes, that is another layer in women's constrained experiences. I remember that, in the 70s, when I started to work in Mexico City, it was very shocking to see that many women did not even know they had a vagina. Some women actually thought that babies came from the rectum. They did not know how their babies were going to be born! In addition, they did not own their sexuality because they felt in constant surveillance by the "big eye." Women could not think about adoring themselves or masturbating. All those experiences were part of my grave cultural shock when I left home. My characters are trying to break with all those notions. And this is not only a personal quest, but they are actually investigating a broader female experience.

RBC: I would like to point out the aspect of quotidian struggles; about those private everyday spaces that contribute to women's invisibility in society.

RC: Right. And I want to add that invisibility is also perpetuated by the lack of connection and solidarity among those women who are confined. There is a profound sense of loneliness. Those who have a job are in a better position, but women who stay at home everyday do not have enough support to overcome the confinement. If only they have a mother, a sister, an aunt that might be experienced in the same constrained life. All of them live afraid of god and their husbands' punishment.

RBC: In that respect, I particularly enjoy the ways in which your female characters dare to be different in spite of the fear they can feel.

RC: We always ask ourselves, what is going to happen if I cross the line I am not supposed to cross? There is a transgression in that crossing. I think that society has very clear ways to make that line explicit. I remember when I arrived in Mexico City there were waiters in restaurants that ignored me blatantly if I wanted to eat there by myself. They acted as if they did not see me. If I was not with a man that talked for me and paid for my food, I just had to leave the restaurant.

RUR: I have the image of you with your baby arriving in Mexico City in the 70s. What other struggles were part of your everyday life?

RC: Many things happened to us. And I think all those experiences marked my style of writing. I arrived in Mexico City as a single mother in 1971. I was 17 years old. The most difficult part was finding a job. There was a moment in which I decided to hide my son in order to find a job. People told me things like "you have excellent qualifications in the area of business, you are bilingual but you have a son." I did all kinds of jobs: doing laundry for other people, baking cakes, working as a receptionist, as a dressmaker, or as an accounting assistant. After a few years, I started to work in jobs related to my career in editing or publishing houses, or as an instructor. Finding an apartment was very difficult as well. Everywhere people saw the "P" [for prostitute] on my forehead. Fortunately, I had a solid education and values. On top of that they thought: and she is not from Mexico City she is from Tijuana, and she must be a drug addict and a slut. That was the stereotype of young single women from the north.

RUR: Due to the multiple nature of the jobs you have done, I would like to see how that is somewhat connected to your work as a performance artist and costume designer for artists like Astrid Hadad. You will present tonight "Señorita Maquiladora" at Trinity University; we are thrilled to know more about the character you created.

RC: In 1996, I was invited to participate at the International Writers' Congress in Monterrey. The key topic was the city. We were supposed to read a text, and a literary essay. I remember I was working on a dress for Astrid Hadad. I had, on the same table, a sewing machine and a computer. I had just finished the reading of a thesis on industrial pollution in areas like Tijuana. We are talking about pollution produced by the electronic industry in Tijuana, maquiladoras. Then it came to me, the fact that I was going to complete a metaphoric trip from a maquiladora city—Tijuana—to an industrial city—Monterrey. And then I got the image of the character of "Señorita Maquiladora": I was going to be Tijuana's ambassador. Furthermore, Monterrey was just starting to have several health problems related to the construction of new residential developments. At the time health problems were reported, all of them seemed to be effects of chemical pollution. The Maquiladora industry treaties among countries establish that imported materials that are part of the production of electronics must be returned to the country of origin. However, that is not the case between Mexico and the United States. It is well known that there is an enormous quantity of clandestine industrial cemeteries. The Maquiladora industry was brought to Mexico to serve as a palliative, directed to supposedly resolve the economic inequalities in Mexico. But it will take many years to reverse the damages those Maquilas has brought to both the environment and society.

RUR: And, do you think your project has made an impact on the implications of treaties like NAFTA?

RC: Unfortunately, performance art is considered only in small intellectual realms. Performance does not have a social impact as literature can have. Performance is ephemeral. You attend a performance today, and tomorrow it is gone. That does not make performance less important. I have to say that other performances have had bigger audiences than "Señorita Maquiladora." I would love to perform it more often, but it is expensive due to the costs of the dress, makeup, hairdo, nails…being a Miss is not an easy endeavor (LAUGHS)…

RBC: We would like to conclude this interview by asking you about your current and future projects.

RC: Right now I am working on the development and implementation of a five-year BA in creative writing in the Autonomous University of Mexico City. As it is a new career in Spanish-speaking countries, you can imagine we have to start from scratch. We are compiling and organizing texts and useful exercises that will be included in a textbook. We want to create class offerings that will benefit and agree with the program. I also work for the Publications Department of the National Institute for Public Health in Cuernavaca, and I keep working on my singing and my writing.

RBC and RUR: Thank you so much for your time.

RC: Thank you.

# Bibliography

*16 en la lista.* Dir. Rodolfo Rodobertti. Cine Producciones Molinar, S. A. de C. V., 1998.
Acuña, Rodolfo. *Occupied America: The Chicano's Struggle Toward Liberation.* San Francisco: Canfield Press, 1972.
Aguilar, Ricardo. "Life as Fiction, Fiction as Life." Unpublished Manuscript. ND.
Aguilar Melantzón, Ricardo. *¿Qué es un soplo la vida? Trilogía de la frontera.* México: Ediciones Eón, 2003.
Alarcón, Norma. "Anzaldua's Frontera: Inscribing Gynetics." *Chicana Feminisms: A Critical Reader.* Ed. Gabriella Arredondo, Aída Hurtado, Norma Klahn, and Olga Nájera-Ramírez. Durham: Duke University Press, 2003. 354–369
Alvarez, Julia. *Once Upon a Quinceañera: Coming of Age in the USA.* New York: Viking Press, 2007.
Anzaldúa, Gloria. *Borderlands/La Frontera: The New Mestiza.* San Francisco: Aunt Lute Press, 1987, 1999.
Anzaldúa, Gloria and Ana Louise Keating. *This Bridge We Call Home.* New York: Routledge, 2002.
Aparicio, Frances R. "Jennifer as Selena: Rethinking Latinidad in Media and Popular Culture." *Latino Studies* 1. 1 (2003): 90–105.
———. "La Lupe, La India, and Celia: Toward a Feminist Genealogy of Salsa." *Situating Salsa: Global Markets and Local Meaning in Latin Popular Music.* Ed. Lisa Waxer. New York: Routledge, 2000. 135–160.
———. *Listening to Salsa: Gender, Latin American Popular Music, and Puerto Rican Cultures.* Hanover: Wesleyan University Press, 1998.
Aparicio, Frances R. and Wilson A. Valentín-Escobar. "Memorializing La Lupe and Lavoe." *CENTRO Journal* 16. 2 (2004): 79–101.
Appadurai, Arjun. "Geography, Imagination, and the Traffic in the Everyday." *InSite05 Conversations.* San Diego: Institute of the Américas, University of California, InSite05, 2004.
Arreola, Daniel. *Tejano South Texas: A Mexican American Cultural Province.* Austin: University of Texas Press, 2002.
Arriola, Elvia. "Difference, Solidarity and Law: Building Latina/o Communities through LatCrit theory." *Chicano-Latino Law Review* 19 (1998): 1–612.
Arrizón, Alicia. *Latina Performance: Traversing the Stage.* Indianapolis: Indiana University Press, 1999.

"Art works." Nao Bustamante. www.naobustamante.com.
Avalos, David. "A Wag Dogging a Tale." *La Frontera/The Border: Art about the Mexico/United States Border*. San Diego: Centro Cultural de la Raza and the Museum of Contemporary Art, 1993.
Avilés Luis A. *Health and Human Rights Violations at the US-Mexico Border.* Washington, DC: American Association of Public Health, 1999.
Barr, Alwyn. *Black Texans: A History of African Americans in Texas, 1528–1995.* Norman: University of Oklahoma Press, 1995.
Barrera, Cordelia. "Border Places, Frontier Spaces: Deconstruction Ideologies of the Southwest." Diss. University of Texas at San Antonio, 2009.
Barrera, Eduardo. "Apropiación y tutelaje de la frontera norte." *Puente Libre, Revista de Cultura* 4 (1995): 13–17.
Barthes, Roland. "The Grain of the Voice." *Image Music Text*. Trans. Stephen Heath. New York: Hill and Wang, 1977. 188.
Berelowitz, Jo-Anne. "Border Art Since 1965." *Post Border City*. Ed. Dear Michael and Leclerc Gustavo. New York: Routledge, 2003. 143–182.
Bernardi, Daniel. *Classic Hollywood, Classic Whiteness*. Minnesota: University of Minnesota Press, 2001.
———ed. *The Birth of Whiteness: Race and the Emergence of U.S. Cinema Classic.* New Brunswick: Rutgers University Press, 1996.
Bhabha, Homi. *The Location of Culture*. New York: Routledge, 1994; 2004.
Birringer, Johannes. "Border Media: Performing Postcolonial History." *Gestos* (April 1996): 49–65.
———. "La melancolía de la jaula." *Performing Arts Journal* 52. 18. 1 (1996): 103–128.
Blanco-Cano, Rosana. "Dissident Mexican Women: Textual and Performative Reconfigurations of National Models of Gender Since 1970." Diss. Tulane University, 2006.
———. *Cuerpos disidentes del México imaginado: Cultura, género, etnia y nación más allá del proyecto posrevolucionario*. Madrid/Frankfurt: Editorial Iberoamericana-Vervuert, 2010.
Bolaño, Roberto. *2666*. Barcelona: Editorial Anagrama. 2004.
Bonilla Silva, Eduardo. *Racism without Racists: Color-blind Racism and the Persistance of Racial Inequality in the United States*. Lanham: Rowman and Littlefield Publishers, 2006.
Bonilla-Silva, Eduardo,, Carla Goar, and David Embrick. "When Whites Flock Together: The Social Psychology of White Habitus." *Critical Sociology* 32 (2006): 229–353.
Bonvillain, Nancy. *Language, Culture and Communication*. Upper Saddle River: Prentice Hall, 2003.
*Bordertown*. Director Gregory Nava. Möbis Entertainment, El Norte Productions, Nuyorican Productions and Mosaic Media Group. 2006.
Bowden, Charles. *Juárez: The Laboratory of Our Future*. New York: Aperture Foundation, 1998.
———. "While you were Sleeping: In Juárez, Mexico, Photographers Expose the Violent Realities of Free Trade." *Harper's Magazine* (December 1996): 44–52.

# BIBLIOGRAPHY 241

Brandes, Stanely. *Skulls to the Living, Bread to the Dead: The Day of the Dead in Mexico and Beyond*. Malden: Blackwell Publishing, 2006.
Brint, Steven. *Schools and Societies*. Thousand Oaks: Pine Forge Press, 1998.
Bureau of Economic Anlysis. *Per Capita Personal Income for Metropolitan Statistical Areas, 2004*. Washington D.C.: U.S. Department of Commerce. http://www.bea.gov/newsreleases/regional/lapi/2006/mpi0406.htm.
Bustamante, Maris. "Non-Objective Art in Mexico 1963–1983." *Corpus Delecti: Performance Art of the Americas*. Ed. Coco Fusco. London: Routledge, 2000. 204–217.
Bustamante, Nao and Miguel Calderón. *The Chain South*. Hemispheric Institute of Performance and Politics' video library: http://hidvl.nyu.edu/video/000509596.html.
Calavita, Kitty. *Inside the State: The Bracero Program, Immigration, and the I.N.S.* New York: Routledge, 1992.
Caldera, Yvonne, Jacki Fitzpatrick, and Karen Wampler. "Coparenting in Intact Mexican American Families: Mothers' and Fathers' Perceptions." *Latino Children and Families in the United States*. Westport: Praeger Publishers, 2002. 107–131.
Calderón, Héctor. *Narratives of Greater Mexico. Essays on Chicano Literary History, Genre, and Borders*. Austin: University of Texas Press, 2004.
Campbell, Howard and Josiah Heyman Slantwise. "Beyond Domination and Resistance on the Border." *Journal of Contemporary Ethnography* 36. 1 (February 2007): 1–28.
Cancian, Frank. *The Decline of Community in Zinacantan*. Stanford: Stanford University Press, 1992.
———. *Economics and Prestige in a Maya Community: The Religious Cargo System in Zinacantan*. Stanford: Stanford University Press, 1965.
Canclini, Néstor, and José Manuel Valenzuela Arce. *Intromisiones compartidas, arte y sociedad en la frontera México/Estados Unidos*. México: Fondo Nacional para la Cultura y las Artes, 2000.
Cantú, Norma E. "Los Matachines de la Santa Cruz de la Ladrillera: Notes Toward a Socioliterary Analysis." *Feasts and Celebrations in the North American Ethnic Communities*. Ed. Ramón A. Gutiérrez and Geneviève Fabre. Albuqueque: University of New Mexico Press, 1995. 57–67.
———. "The Semiotics of Land and Space: Matachines Dancing in Laredo, Texas." *Dancing Across Borders: Danzas y Bailes Mexicanos*. Ed. Olga Nájera-Ramírez, Aída Hurtado, Norma Klahn, and Olga Nájera-Ramírez. Urbana Champaign: University of Illinois Press, 2009. 97–115.
———. "Chicana Life-Cycle Rituals." *Chicana Traditons: Continuity and Change*. Ed. Norma E. Cantú and Olga Nájera-Ramírez. Urbana Champaign: University of Illinois Press, 2009. 15–34.
———. *Canícula: Snapshots of a Girlhood en la Frontera*. Albuqueque: University of New Mexico Press. 1995.
Carmichael, Elizabeth and Chloe Sayer. *The Skeleton at the Feast: The Day of the Dead in Mexico*. Austin: University of Texas Press, 1992.

Carrasco, Gilbert Paul. "Latinos in the United States: Invitation and Exile." *The Latino Condition: A Critical Reader*. Ed. Richard Delgado and Jean Stefancic. New York: New York University Press, 1998. 77–85.

Carrillo, Jorge. "La industria maquiladora en México: ¿Evolución o agotamiento?" *Comercio Exterior* 57.8 (Agosto 2007): 668–681.

Castañeda, Antonia. "Sexual Violence in the Politics and Policies of Conquest." *Building with Our Hands: New Directions in Chicana Studies*. Ed. Adela de la Torre and Beatriz M. Pesquera. Berkeley: University of California Press, 1993. 15–33.

Castellanos, Octavio and Omar Pimienta. *The Bookleggers*. Tijuana, BC. CalTranzit Productions, 2004.

Castillo, Debra and María Socorro Tabuenca. *Border Women: Writing from La Frontera*. Minneapolis: University of Minnesota Press. 2002.

Cepeda, María Elena. "'Columbus Effect(s)': Chronology and Crossover in the Latin(o) Music 'Boom.'" *Discourse* 23. 1 (2001): 63–81.

_____. "*Mucho Loco* for Ricky Martin; or The Politics of Chronology, Crossover, and Language within the Latin Music 'Boom.'" *Popular Music and Society* 24. 3 (2000): 55–71.

Chagoya, Enrique. "Artist Statement/2002." *Art of Engagement: Visual Politics in California and Beyond*. Ed. Peter Selz. Berkeley: University of California Press, 2006.

Chance, John K. and William B. Taylor. "Cofradías and Cargos: An Historical Perspective on the Mesoamerican Civil-Religious Hierarchy." *American Ethnologist* 12. 1 (1985): 1–26.

Chang, Heewon. "The Heartland Chronicles, Book Review." *Journal of Contemporary Ethnography* 26. 3 (1997): 382–385.

Chávez-Silverman, Susana and Frances R. Aparicio. *Tropicalizations: Transcultural Representations of Latinidad*. Hanover: University of New England Press, 1997.

Chavoya, C. Ondine. "Collaborative Public Art and Multimedia Installation: David Avalos, Louic Hock and Elizabeth Sisco's 'Welcome to America's Finest Tourist Plantation' (1988)." *The Ethnic Eye, Latino Media Arts*. Ed. Chon A. Noriega and Ana M. López. Minneapolis: University of Minnesota Press, 1996.

_____. "Orphans of Modernism: The Performance Art of Asco." *Corpus Delecti*. Ed. Coco Fusco. London: Routledge. 218–240.

Clifford, James. *The Predicament of Culture*. Cambridge, MA: Harvard University Press, 1988.

"Culinary Union Local 226." *Culinary Union Local 226*. http://www.culinaryunion226.org/.

Dávila, Arlene. *Latinos Inc. The Marketing and Making of the People*. California: University of California Press, 2001.

Davy, Kate. "Constructing the Spectator." *Performing Arts Journal* 29. 2 (1986): 43–52.

Dear, Michael and Gustavo Leclerc. *The Postborder City. Cultural Spaces of Bajalta California*. New York: Routledge, 2003.

Del Castillo, Adelaida R. "Illegal Status and Social Citizenship: Thoughts on Mexican Immigrants in a Postnational World." *Women in The U.S.-Mexico Borderlands: Structural Violence and Agency in Everyday Life*. Ed. Denise A. Segura and Patricia Zavella. Durham: Duke University Press, 2007. 92–105.

———. "Cultural Citizenship." *The New Dictionary of the History of Ideas*. Ed. Maryanne Cline Horowitz. Vol. 1. New York: Scribner and Sons, 2005. 338–339.

Deleuze, Gilles and Félix Guattari. "What is a Minor Literature?" *Poetry and Cultural Studies: A Reader*. Ed. Maria Damon and Ira Livingston. Champaign: University of Illinois Press, 2009. 56–60.

Delgado, Richard and Jean Stefancic, eds. *Critical White Studies: Looking Behind the Mirror*. Philadelphia: Temple University Press, 1977.

Deloria, Vine. *Red Earth, White Lies: Native Americans and the Myth of Scientific Fact*. New York: Scribner, 1995.

DeSippio, Louis et. al. *Immigrant Politics at Home and Abroad: How Latino Immigrants Engage the Politics of Their Home Communities and the United States*. Claremont: The Tomás Rivera Policy Institute, 2003.

Dolan, Jill. *Utopia in Performance: Finding Hope at the Theater*. Ann Arbor: University of Michigan, 2005.

Doob, Christopher Bates. *Racism: An American Couldron*. New York: Addison Wesley Longman, 1999.

Durán, Javier. "Los Wet Minds." *LASA Conference*. Puerto Rico, March 16, 2006.

Du Bois, W. E. B. *The Souls of Black Folk*. Ed. Ewing, Katherine Pratt. New York: Oxford Press, 2007.

Esquibel, Catrióna Rueda. "Memories of Girlhood: Chicana Lesbian Fictions." *SIGNS: Journal of Women in Culture and Society* 23.3 (Spring 1998): 644–681.

Ewing, Katherine Pratt. "Crossing Borders and Transgressing Boundaries: Metaphor for Negotiating Multiple Identities." *Ethos* 26. 2 (1998): 262–267.

*Espejo retrovisor*. Dir. Héctor Molinar. Cine Producciones Molinar, S. A. de C. V., 2002.

*Flashdance*. Dir. Adrian Lyne. Perf. Jennifer Beals. Paramount Pictures, 1983.

Florescano, Enrique. *Etnia, estado y nación: ensayo sobre las identidades colectivas en México*. México: Aguilar, 1997.

Fluher-Lobban, Carolyn. *Race and Racism: An Introduction*. Lanham: Rowman and Littlefield Publishers, 2005.

Foley, Douglas. E. *The Heartland Chronicles*. Philadelphia: University of Pennsylvania, 1995.

Foucault, Michel. "Of Other Spaces." *Diacritics* 16 (Spring 1986): 22–27.

Fox, Claire F. *The Fence and the River*. Minneapolis: University of Minnesota Press, 1999.

Fregoso, Rosalinda. *MeXicana Encounters: The Making of Social Identities on the Borderlands*. Berkeley: University of California Press, 2003.

Fulana website. February 13, 2009. http://fulana.org/origins.html.

Fusco, Coco. "Introduction: Latin American Performance and the Reconquista of Civil Space." *Corpus Delecti: Performance Art of the Americas.* Ed. Coco Fusco. London: Routledge, 2000.

———. "The Other History of International Performance." *The Drama Review* 38.1 (Spring 1994): 143-167.

García, Alma M. *Narratives of Mexican American Women: Emergent Identities of the Second Generation.* Walnut Creek: AltaMira Press, 2004.

García Canclini, Néstor. *Diferentes, desiguales y desconectados. Mapas de la interculturalidad.* Barcelona: Gedisa, 2004.

García, Ramón. "Against *Rasquache*: Chicano Identity and the Politics of Popular Culture in Los Angeles." Ed. Rosaura Sánchez. *Crítica: A Journal of Critical Essays* (1998): 1-26.

García Riera, Emilio. *México visto por el cine extranjero.* Guadalajara: Ediciones Era, 1987.

Garofalo, Reebee. *Rockin' Out: Popular Music in the USA.* Boston: Allyn and Bacon, 1997.

Gaspar de Alba, Alicia. *Desert Blood: The Juárez Murders.* Houston: Arte Público Press, 2005.

———. "The Maquiladora Murders 1993-2003." *Aztlán: A Journal of Chicano Studies* 28. 2 (Fall 2003): 1-17.

"Gay-Owned Resort in Cuernavaca, Morales, Mexico - La Villa Hidalgo Resort." *Purple Roofs Gay & Lesbian Travel Directory - Bed & Breakfasts/Hotels/Travel Agents/Tour Operators & More.* http://www.purpleroofs.com/lavillahidalgo-mx.html.

George Yancy. *What White Looks Like: African American Philosophers on the Whiteness Question.* New York: Routledge, 2004.

Gilly, Adolfo, Arnoldo Córdova, Armando Barta, Manuel Aguilar Mora, and Enrique Semo. *Interpretaciones de la revolución mexicana.* México: Editorial Nueva Imagen, 1979.

Goodenough, Ward H. *Culture, Language, and Society.* Menlo Park: The Benjamin/Cummings Publishing Company, 1981.

Gómez-Peña, Guillermo. "The Multicultural Paradigm: An Open Letter to the National Arts Community." *Beyond the Fantastic: Contemporary Art Criticism from Latin America.* Ed. Gerardo Mosquera. London: INIVA, 1995. 183-194.

———."La Pocha Nostra: Manifesto." *La Pocha Nostra.* www.pochanostra.com.

———. "A Binational Performance Pilgrimage." *The Drama Review* 35. 3 (Autumn, 1991): 22-45.

González, Juan. *Harvest of Empire: A History of Latinos in America.* New York: Penguin Books, 2000.

González, Norma. *I am my Language: Discourses of Women and Children in the Borderlands.* Tucson: University of Arizona Press, 2001.

Green, Stanley, ed. *A History of the Washington Birthday Celebration.* Laredo: Border Studies Publishing, 1999.

Grossberg, Lawrence. "Is there a Fan in the House?: The Affective Sensibility of Fandom." *The Adoring Audience: Fan Culture and Popular Media.* Ed. Lisa Lewis. New York: Routledge, 1992. 50-65.

Gutiérrez, David. *Walls and Mirrors: Mexican Americans, Mexican Immigrants, and the Politics of Ethnicity.* Berkeley: University of California Press, 1995.

Gutiérrez, Laura G. *Performing Mexicanidad: Vendidas y Cabareteras on the Transnational Stage.* Austin: University of Texas Press, 2010.

_____. "Sneaking into the Media: Judi Werthein's *Brinco* Shoes and Post-Border Art, Illegal Immigration, Global Labor, and Mass Media." *Spectator*, special issue "Building Walls in a Borderless World: Media, Violence and Human (im)Mobility" 29.1 (Spring 2009): 11–22.

Handegneu-Sotelo, Pierrette. *Gendered Transitions: Mexican Experiences of Immigration.* Berkeley: University of California Press, 1994.

Henze, Rosemary C. and Lauren Vanett. "To Walk in Two Worlds-or More?: Challenging a Common Metaphor of Native Education." *Anthropology & Education Quarterly* 24 (1993): 116–134.

Hertz, Betti-Sue. *Axis Mexico: Common Objects & Cosmopolitan Actions.* San Diego: San Diego Museum of Art, 2002.

Herzog, Lawrence. *Where North Meets South. Cities, Space and Politics on the U.S.-Mexico Border.* Austin: CMAS, University of Texas at Austin, 1990.

_____. *Shared Space. Rethinking the U.S.-Mexico Border Environment.* San Diego: Center for U.S.-Mexican Studies. University of California, 2000.

Hickson, Patricia. "Borderlandia Unbound: An Abbreviated Guide to the Visual Anthropology of Enrique Chagoya." *Enrique Chagoya Borderlandia.* Exhibition Catalog. Des Moines: Des Moines Art Center, 2007.

Hill, Mike. *After Whiteness: Unmaking an American Majority.* New York: New York University Press, 2004.

Huerta, Elisa Diana, "Embodied Recuperations: Performance, Indigeneity, and Danza Azteca." *Dancing across Borders: Danzas y Bailes Mexicanos.* Eds. Olga Nájera-Ramírez, Norma E. Cantú, and Brenda M. Romero. Urbana: University of Illinois Press, 2009. 3–18.

Hughes, Walter. "In the Empire of the Beat: Discipline and Disco." *Microphone Fiends: Youth Music & Youth Culture.* Ed. Andrew Ross and Tricia Rose. New York: Routledge, 1994. 147–157.

Hytten, Kathy. "Postcritical Ethnography: Research as a Pedagogical Encounter." *Postcritical Ethnography: Reinscribing Critique.* Ed. George Noblit, Susana Y. Flores, and Enrique G. Jr. Murillo. CressKill: Hampton Press, 2004. 95–105.

Iglesias Prieto, Norma. *Emergencias las artes visuales en Tijuana. Volume I. Los contextos glo-cales y la creatividad.* Tijuana: Consejo Nacional para la Cultura y las Artes, Centro Cultural Tijuana y Universidad Autónoma de Baja California, 2008.

_____. "New Social Agents, New Urban Spaces, and the Possibilities for Change: Visual Arts in Tijuana." *Berkeley Planning Journal* 21 (2008): 47–74.

_____. "Le mur a la frontière entre le Mexique et les États-Unis: Flux, contrôle et créativité de l'esthétique géopolitique." *Outre-Terre. Revue Francaise de Geopolitique* 07.1.180 (2007): 123–141.

_____."En pocas palabras: Representaciones discursivas de la frontera México-Estados Unidos." *Aztlán: A Journal of Chicano Studies* 29. 1 (Spring 2004): 145–153.

_____. *Entre polvo, yerba y plomo. Lo fronterizo visto por el cine mexicano.* Vol 1. Tijuana B.C.: El Colegio de la Frontera Norte, 1994.

Itzigsohn, José, Carlos Dore Cabral, Esther Hernández Medina and Obed Vásquez. "Mapping Dominican Transnationalism: Narrow and Broad Transnational Practices." *Ethnic and Racial Studies* 22. 2 (1999): 316–339.

"Immigration and Human Rights on the U.S./Mexico Border. Interview in four parts with Roberto Martínez." http://www.inmotionmagazine.com/border.html.

Jensen, Robert. *The Heart of Whiteness: Confronting Race, Racism and White Privilege.* San Francisco: City Lights, 2005.

*Juárez, México.* Dir. J. Cahilh. Dodging Bullets. 2005.

*Juárez: Stages of Fear.* Dir. César Alejandro. Stages of Fear Joint Venture, 2005.

Kim, Eleana. "Wedding Citizenship and Culture: Korean Adoptees and the Global Family of Korea." *Cultures of Transnational Adoption.* Ed. Toby Volkman. Durham: University Press, 2005.

Klahn, Norma."Writing the Border: The Languages and Limits of Representation." *Travesía: Journal of Latin American Cultural Studies* 3. 1–2 (1994).

Knights, Vanessa. "Tears and Screams: Performances of Pleasure and Pain in the Bolero." *Queering the Popular Pitch.* Ed. Shiela Whiteley and Jennifer Rycenga. New York: Routledge, 2006. 87.

Koestenbaum, Wayne. *The Queen's Throat: Opera, Homosexuality, and the Mystery of Desire.* New York: Poseidon Press, 1993.

Kun, Josh. *Audiotopia: Music, Race, and America.* Berkeley: University of California Press, 2005.

Lalinde, Ana. "La otra migración: 100 mexicanos que enseñan en universidades de Estados Unidos." *Poder y Negocios* 3. 22 (2007): 24–64.

Leonardi, Susan J. and Rebecca A. Pope. *The Diva's Mouth: Body, Voice, Prima Donna Politics.* New Brunswick: Rutgers University Press, 1996.

Levitt, Peggy and Nina Glick Schiller. "Conceptualizing Simultaneity: A Transnational Social Field Perspective on Society." *International Migration Review* 38. 3 (2004): 3–4 and 1002–1039.

Linton, Ralph. "The one hundred percent American." *The American Mercury* 40 (1937): 427–429.

Lipsitz, George. *Dangerous Crossroads: Popular Music, Postmodernism and the Poetics of Place.* New York: Verso Press, 1994.

Logan, John, Jacob Stowell, and Deirdre Oakley. "Choosing Segregation: Racial Imbalance in American Public Schools, 1990–2000." Lewis Mumford Center for Comparative Urban and Regional Research. Albany: University at Albany, 2002.

López, Gerald P. "How Much Responsibility Does the U.S. Bear for Undocumented Mexican Migration?" *The Latino/a Condition: A Critical Reader.* Ed. R. Delgado and J. Stefancic. New York: New York University Press, 1998.

López, Josefina. *Simply Maria, or The American Dream.* Woodstock, IL: Dramatic Publishing, 1996.

Lorca, Federico García. "Play and Theory of the Duende." *In Search of Duende.* Trans and Ed. Christopher Maurer. New York: New Directions, 1998. 55.

*Lou Dobbs Tonight: Broken Borders.* CNN. Hazelton. May 2, 2007.
Lugones, María. "Purity, Impurity, and Separation." *Signs* 19. 2 (1994): 458–479.
Mahler, Sarah J. and Patricia R. Pessar. "Gender Matters: Ethnographers Bring Gender from the Periphery toward the Core of Migration Studies." *International Migration Review* 40. 1 (2006): 27–63.
Malagamba-Ansótegui, Amelia. Personal interview. September 5, 2006.
Malking, Elisabeth. "Tijuana Transforms Into a Cultural Hotbed." *New York Times.* June 8, 2006. http://www.nytimes.com/2006/06/08/arts/design/08bord.html.
McCaughan, Edward J. "Navigating the Labyrinth of Silence: Feminist Artists in Mexico." *Social Justice* 34. 1 (2007): 44–62.
McKinney, Karyn D. *Being White: Stories of Race and Racism.* New York: Routledge, 2005.
Méndez, Luis H. "Neoliberalismo y Derechización en México (1983-2000)." *El cotidiano* 23 (2008): 5–15.
Monárrez Fragoso, Julia. "Serial Sexual Femicide in Ciudad Juárez: 1993–2001." *Debate Feminista* 12. 25 (April 2002): 81–98.
Monsiváis, Carlos. "A dónde vas que más valgas." *El Universal.* February 18, 2007.
_____. "De la industria académica." *LASA Conference.* Puerto Rico. March 16, 2006.
Montejano, David. *Anglos and Mexicans in the Making of Texas 1836–1986.* Austin: UT Press, 1987.
Moraga, Cherríe and Gloria Anzaldúa, eds. *This Bridge Called My Back: Writings by Radical Women of Color.* Berkeley: Third Woman Press, 1981.
Morawska, Ewa, "Immigrants, Transnationalism, and Ethnicization: A Comparison of this Great Wave and the Last." *E Pluribus Unum? Contemporary and Historical Perspectives on Immigrant Political Incorporation.* Ed. Gary Gerstle and John Mollenkopf. New York: Russel Sage Foundation, 2001. 175–176.
Morse, Jane, "U.S.-Mexico Border Officials Balance Security, Commerce Needs: Technology Helps Minimize Delays, Detect Contraband." United States Department of State, Washington D.C. http://usinfo.state.gov/usinfo/products/washfile.html. September 7, 2007.
Muñoz, José Esteban. *Disidentifications.* Minneapolis: University of Minnesota, 1999.
_____. "Ephemera as Evidence: Introductory Notes to Queer Acts." *Women and Performance* 16 (1996): 5–16.
Murillo, Enrique. "Mojado Crossings." *Postcritical Ethnography: Reinscribing Critique.* Ed. George Noblit, Susana Y. Flores, and Enrique G. Jr. Murillo. CressKill: Hampton Press, 2004. 155–179.
Nájera-Ramírez, Olga. "Unruly Passions: Poetics, Performance, and Gender in the Ranchera Song." *Chicana Feminisms: A Critical Reader.* Ed. Gabriella Arredondo, Aída Hurtado, Norma Klahn, and Olga Nájera-Ramírez. Durham: Duke University Press, 2003. 184–210.
Nash, June. *Mayan Visions: The Quest for Autonomy in an Age of Globalization.* New York: Routledge Press, 2001.

"National Exit Polls - Election Center 2008 - Elections & Politics from CNN. com." *CNN.com - Breaking News, U.S., World, Weather, Entertainment & Video News.* http://www.cnn.com/ELECTION/2008/results/polls.main/.

Nericcio, William Anthony. *Tex[t]-Mex: Seductive Hallucinations of the "Mexican" in America.* Austin: University of Texas Press, 2007.

*Ni de aquí ni de allá.* Dir and Perf. María Elena Velasco. Bladys Filmes, 1988.

*No Country for Old Men.* Dirs. E. Coen and J. Coen, J. Miramax Films and Paramount Vantage. 2007.

Noblit, George, et. al. eds. *Postcritical Ethnography. Reinscribing Critique.* CressKill: Hampton Press, 2004.

Noriega, Chon. ed. *Urban Exile: Collective Writings by Henry Gamboa Jr.* Minneapolis: University of Minessotta Press, 1998.

Núñez-Mchiri, Guillermina G. "The Political Ecology of The Colonias on The U.S.-Mexico Border: Human-Environmental Challenges and Community Responses in Southern New Mexico." *Southern Rural Sociology* 24. 1 (2009): 67-91.

Ong, Aihwa. *Flexible Citizenship: The Cultural Logics and Transnationality.* Durham: Duke Univeristy Press, 1999.

Palacios, Monica. "Greetings from a Queer Señorita." Unpublished videotape and manuscript. Performed at Arizona State University in Tempe, Arizona. November 2, 2007.

———. "Describe Your Work." *Puro Teatro: A Latina Anthology.* Ed. Alberto Sandoval-Sánchez and Nancy Saporta Sternbach. Tucson: University of Arizona Press, 2000. 281-284.

———. "Greetings from a Queer Señorita." *Out of the Fringe: Contemporary Latina/Latino Theater and Performance.* Ed. Caridad Svich and María Teresa Marrero. New York: Theatre Communications Group, 2000. 365-390.

Paredes, Américo. *A Texas-Mexican Cancionero.* Urbana: University of Illinois Press, 1976.

———. *With His Pistol in His Hand: A Border Ballad and Its Hero.* Austin: University of Texas Press, 1958.

Patoski, Joe Nick. *Selena: Como La Flor.* Boston: Little, Brown and Company, 1996.

Peña, Manuel. *Música Tejana: The Cultural Economy of Artistic Transformation.* College Station: Texas A & M Press, 1999.

Pérez, Emma. *The Decolonial Imaginary: Writing Chicanas into History.* Bloomington: Indiana University Press, 1999.

Pharr-San Juan-Alamo Independent School District. *History.* Pharr, TX: PSJA ISD. http://psja.schoolfusion.us/modules/cms/pages.phtml?pageid=26834.

Portes, Alejandro. "NAFTA and Mexican Immigration: 'Border Battles: The U.S. Immigration Debates.'" Social Science Research Council Website. http://borderbattles.ssrc.org/Portes. July 31, 2006.

———. "Theoretical Convergences and Empirical Evidence in the Study of Immigrant Transnationalism." *International Migration Review* 37 (Fall 2002): 814-892.

———. "The Debates and Significance of Immigrant Transnationalism." *Global Networks* 1 (July 2001): 181–193.

Pozuelo, Abel H. "Jaime Ruiz Otis." *El cultural*. 15 March 2007. http://www.elcultural.es/version_papel/ARTE/20022/Jaime_Ruiz_Otis

Pratt, Mary Louise. *Imperial Eyes: Travel Writing and Transculturation*. New York: Routledge, 1992.

Ramírez-Cancio, Marlène. Personal interview. April 10, 2008 and February 13, 2009.

Rivas, Jorge. "U.S. Census Figures Show that Hispanics are Increasing their Clout." http://www.associatedcontent.com/article/318538/us_census_figures_ show_that_hispanics.html. 2007.

Rivera, Tomás. *Y no se lo tragó la tierra/ And The Earth Did Not Devour Him*. Houston: Arte Público Press, 1987.

Rivero, Eliana S. "Colored Ambiguities: Theorizing U.S. Latina Consciousness." Unpublished article, 2000.

———. "Fronterisleña: Border Islander." *Bridges to Cuba*. Ed. Ruth Behar. Ann Arbor: University of Michigan Press, 1996. 339–344.

Rocco, Raymond A. "Reframing Postmodernist Construction of Difference: Subaltern Spaces, Power, and Citizenship." *Transnational Latina/o Communities. Politics, Processes and Cultures*. Ed. Carlos G. Vélez-Ibáñez and Anna Sampaio. Lanham: Rowman and Littlefield Publishers, 2002.

Rodríguez, Nelson M. and Leila E. Villaverde. *Dismantling White Privilege: Pedagogy, Politics, and Whiteness*. New York: Peter Lang Publishing, 2000.

Rodriguez, Richard. *Hunger of Memory: The Education of Richard Rodriguez. An Autobiography*. New York: Bantam Books, 1984.

Rodríguez, Sylvia. *The Matachines Dance: Ritual Symbolism and Interethnic Relations in the Upper Rio Grande Valley*. Albuquerque: University of New Mexico Press, 1996.

Rohter, Larry. "A Legend Grows and So Does an Industry," *New York times*, 12 January 1997, H39.

Román, David. *Acts of Intervention: Performance, Gay Culture, and AIDS*. Bloomington: Indiana University Press, 1998.

Romero, Brenda M. "The Matachines Danza as Intercultural Discourse." *Dancing Across Borders: Danzas y Bailes Mexicanos*. Ed. Olga Nájera-Ramírez, Norma E. Cantú, and Brenda M. Romero. Chicago: University of Illinois Press, 2009. 185–205.

Romero, Rolando. "Troublemakers." *As We Are Now: Mixblood Essays on Race and Identity*. Ed. William S. Penn. Berkeley: University of California Press, 1997.

Romo, David Dorado. *Ringside Seat to a Revolution: An Underground Cultural History of El Paso and Juárez: 1893–1923*. El Paso: Cinco Punto Press, 2005.

Rosaldo, Renato. *Culture and Truth: The Remaking of Social Analysis*. Boston, MA: Beacon Press, 1989.

Ruiz, Vicki. *From Out of the Shadows: Mexican Women in Twentieth-Century America*. New York: Oxford University Press, 1998.

Rumbaut, Ruben. "Assimilation and Its Discontents: Between Rhetoric and Reality." *International Migration Review* 31. 4 (1997): 923–960.
Sáenz, Benjamin Alire. "In the Borderland of Chicano Identity, There are only Fragments." *Border Theory*. Ed. D. E. Johnson and S. Michaelson. Minneapolis: University of Minnesota, 1997. 68–96.
Saldívar, Ramón. *The Borderlands of Culture. Américo Paredes and the Transnational Imaginary*. Durham: Duke University Press, 2006.
Saldívar-Hull, Sonia. *Feminism on the Border*. Berkeley: University of California Press, 2000.
Sampaio, Anna. "Transforming Chicana/o and Latina/o Politics: Globalization and the Formation of Transnational Resistance in the United States and Chiapas." *Transnational Latina/o Communities. Politics, Processes and Cultures*. Ed. Carlos G. Vélez-Ibáñez and Anna Sampaio. Lanham: Rowman and Littlefield Publishers, 2002.
Sánchez, George J. *Becoming Mexican American: Ethnicity, Culture and Identity in Chicano Los Angeles, 1900–1945*. New York: Oxford University Press, 1993.
Sánchez, Patricia. "Adopting Transnationalism Theory and Discourse: Making Space for a Transnational Chicana." *Discourse: Studies in the Cultural Politics of Education* 22. 3 (2001): 375–381.
Sandoval, Chela. "Third World Feminism: The Theory and Method of Oppositional Consciousness in the Postmodern World." *Genders* 10 (Spring 1991): 1–24.
———. *Methodology of the Oppressed*. Minneapolis: University of Minnesota Press, 2000.
Sandoval López, Claudia Verónica. "'Do-it-yourself art.' Estudio de la producción artística y las redes sociales de cuatro grupos de artistas de Tijuana." Tesis de Maestría en Desarrollo Regional, El Colegio de la Frontera Norte. 2004.
Sandoval-Sánchez, Alberto, and Nancy Saporta Sternbach. *Stages of Life: Transcultural Performance and Identity in U.S. Latina Theater*. Tucson: The University of Arizona Press, 2001.
Santiago, Alejandro. Personal interview. June, 2001.
Sassen, Saskia. "The Reposition of Citizenship: Emergent Subjects and Spaces for Politics." *CR: The New Centennial Review* 3. 2 (2003): 41–66.
———. "Citizenship Destabilized." *Liberal Education* 89. 2 (Spring 2003): 2–19.
Saxton, Alexander. *The Indispensable Enemy: Labor and the Anti-Chinese Movement in California*. Berkeley: University of California Press, 1971.
Schiller, Nina Glick. "Transnational Theory and Beyond." *A Companion to the Anthropology of Politics*. Ed. D. Nugent and V. Joan. Malden: Blackwell, 2003.
Scmidt Camacho, Alicia. "Ciudadana X. Gender Violence and Denationalization of Women's Rights in Ciudad Juárez, México." *CR: The New Centennial Review* 5. 1 (Spring 2005): 255–292.
Scott, James C. *Domination and the Arts of Resistance: Hidden Transcripts*. New Haven: Yale University Press, 1990.
Scott, James C. and Gordon Marshall, eds. *A Dictionary of Sociology*. Oxford: Oxford University Press, 1998.

Smith, Robert C. *Mexican New York: Transnational Lives of New Immigrants.* Berkeley: University of California Press, 2006.

Smith, Sidonie and Julia Watson. *Reading Autobiography. A Guide for Interpreting Life Narratives.* Minneapolis: University of Minnesota Press, 2001.

Soto, Lourdes Díaz. "Young Bilingual Children's Perceptions of Bilingualism and Biliteracy Altrisitic Possibilities." *Bilingual Research Journal* 26. 3 (2002).

Svich, Caridad and María Teresa Marrero, eds. *Out of the Fringe: Contemporary Latina/Latino Theatre and Performance.* New York: Theater Communications Group, Inc., 2000.

Swain, Regina. *Señorita Supermán y otras danzas.* México: Fondo Editorial Tierra Adentro, 1993.

Tabuenca, María Socorro. "Reflexiones sobre los estudios culturales desde el norte de México." Presentation. Instituto Mora, Mexico, DF. March 31, 2007.

———. *Mujeres y fronteras. Una perspectiva de género.* Chihuahua: Instituto Chihuahuense de la Cultura: Fondo Estatal para la Cultura y las Artes, 1998.

Taylor, Diana. *The Archive and the Repertoire: Performing Cultural Memory In The Americas.* Durham: Duke University Press, 2007.

Telles, Edward E. and Edward Murguia. "Phenotype and Schooling among Mexican Americans." *Sociology of Education* 69. 4 (1996): 276–289.

*The Assumption of Lupe Vélez.* Dir. Rita González. Subcine, 1999.

*The Virgin of Juárez.* Dir. Kevin James Dobson. Las Mujeres LCC, 2005

Thompson, Jerry. *Laredo: A Pictoral History.* Norfolk: The Donning Company Publishers, 1986.

———. *Saberes on the Rio Grande.* Austin: Presidential Press, 1974.

Trinity University. "Trinity University: Fast Facts." 2007. http://www.trinity.edu/departments/admissions/mz3/fastfacts.shtml.

United States Census Bureau. *Census Demographic: Cameron, Hidalgo, Starr, and Willacy Counties.* Washington D.C: U.S. Census Bureau, 2007. http://factfinder.census.gov/home/en/official_estimates_2007.html.

———. *Census Demographic: San Antonio, Texas Metropolitan Statistical Area.* Washington D.C: U.S. Census Bureau, 2007. http://factfinder.census.gov/servlet/ADPTable?_bm=y&-qr_name=ACS_2007_3YR_G00_DP3YR5&-geo_id=31200US417004865000&-context=adp&-ds_name=&-tree_id=3307&-_lang=en&-redoLog=false&-format.

Urrea, Luis Alberto. *Nobody's Son: Notes from an American Life.* Tucson: University of Arizona Press, 1999.

Valenzuela Arce, José Manuel. *Paso del Nortec: This is Tijuana.* México: Trilce Ediciones, 2004.

———. "Introducción." *Por las fronteras del Norte.* Coord. José Manuel Valenzuela Arce. México: CONACULTA/ Fondo de Cultura Económica, 2003.

Varese, Stephano and Sylvia Escárcega. "Introducción." *La ruta mixteca.* México: Universidad Nacional Autónoma de México, 2004.

Vargas, Deborah R. "Bidi Bidi Bom Bom: Selena and Tejano Music in the Making of *Tejas.*" *Latina/o Popular Culture.* Ed. Michelle Habell-Pállan and Mary Romero. New York: New York University Press, 2002.

———. "Cruzando Frontejas: Re-mapping Selena's Tejano Music Crossover." *Chicana Traditions: Continuity and Change*. Ed. Norma Cantú and Olga Nájera-Ramírez. Urbana: University of Illinois Press, 2002.

———. "*Las Tracaleras*: Texas-Mexican Women, Music, and Place." PhD. diss. University of California, Santa Cruz, 2003.

Vélez-Ibáñez, Carlos G. *An Impossible Living in a Transborder World: Culture, Confianza, and Economy among Mexican-Origin Populations*. Tucson: University of Arizona Press, 2010.

———. *Border Visions: Mexican Cultures of the Southwest United States*. Tucson: University of Arizona Press, 1996.

Vélez-Ibáñez, Carlos G. and Anna Sampaio, eds. *Transnational Latina/o Communities: Politics, Processes and Cultures*. Boulder: Rowan and Littlefield Publishers, 2002.

Vélez-Ibáñez, Carlos. G., Paul Espinosa, James García, Marta Sánchez, and Michelle Martínez. "Genesis and Development of Latino/a Expressive Culture in Arizona: Theater, Literature, Film, Music, and Art." *State of Latino Arizona*. Phoenix: Arizona State University, 2009. 76–87.

Villareal, Jaime Moreno. "Alejandro Santiago: Convocar a los Ausentes." *2501 Migrantes*. Exhibition Catalog. Oaxaca: Museo de Arte Contemporáneo de Oaxaca, 2006.

Villaseñor, Antonia. "Dos Lenguas Listas: An Interview with Monica Palacios." *Latinas on Stage*. Ed. Alicia Arrizón and Lillian Manzor. Berkeley: Third Woman Press, 2000. 234–247.

Washington Valdez, Diana. *Harvest of Women: Safari in Mexico*. Los Angeles: Peace at the Border, 2006.

Wax, Murray. L. "How Culture Misdirects Multiculturalism." *Anthropology and Education Quarterly* 24. 2 (1993): 99–115.

Wolff, Janet. *The Social Production of Art: Second Edition*. New York: New York University Press, 1993.

Wright, Melissa W. *Disposable Women and Other Myths of Global Capitalism*. New York: Routledge, 2006.

Yarbro-Bejarano, Yvonne. "Crossing the Border with Chabela Vargas: A Chicana Femme's Tribute." *Sex and Sexuality in Latin America*. Ed. Daniel Balderston and Donna J. Guy. New York: New York University Press, 1997. 33–43.

Yépez, Heriberto. *Made in Tijuana*. Tijuana: Instituto de Cultura de Baja California, 2005.

Zamudio-Taylor, Víctor. "Living in Nepantla: Martín Ramírez's Complex Journey to Becoming Mexican American." *Martín Ramírez*. Ed. Davis Anderson Brooke. Seattle: Marquard Books and American Folk Art Museum, 2007.

Zirker, Joseph. "Malaquías Montoya." Exhibition Catalog. San Francisco: Walter McBean Gallery/San Francisco Art Institute, 1997.

Zúñiga, Víctor. "The Changing Face of Border Culture Studies." *NCLA Report on the Americas* 23. 3 (1999).

# Contributors

**Rosana Blanco-Cano** is Assistant Professor of Spanish and codirector of the Women's and Gender Studies Program at Trinity University. Her research interests are (trans)national Mexican cultural and performance studies, Latin American and Spanish cinema.

**Norma E. Cantú** is Professor of English and U.S. Latina/o literatures, cultures at UTSA. She is the author of *Canícula Snapshots of a Girlhood en la Frontera*.

**Marivel T. Danielson** is Assistant Professor of transborder Chicana/o and Latina/o studies at Arizona State University. Her research interests are Chicana/Latina literature, sexuality, gender, performance, race/border/diaspora theory.

**Javier Durán** is Associate Professor of Spanish and border Studies at the University of Arizona. He is the author of works on cultural studies and literary and cultural themes related to the U.S.-Mexico border.

**Miguel Guerra,** BA, graduated from Trinity University, is pursuing career interests in law and politics as well as film and television. He will represent the Rio Grand Valley in all endeavors for the opportunity to voice the needs of his community at the state and national levels.

**Laura G. Gutiérrez** is Associate Professor of Spanish at the University of Arizona. Her areas of research are Latin American and Latina/o media studies, performance studies, cultural studies, and popular culture.

**Ellie D. Hernández** is Associate Professor of Feminist Studies at the UC Santa Barbara. Her academic interests are feminist theory, transnational border studies, Chicana/o Literature, and LGBTQ studies.

**Norma Iglesias-Prieto** is Associate Professor of Chicana/o Studies at San Diego State University. Her research interests are Mexican cinema, cultural studies, border studies, and border art.

## CONTRIBUTORS

**Arturo Madrid** is the Norine R. and T. Frank Murchison Distinguished Professor of Humanities at Trinity University. Founding President of the Tomas Rivera Center in California, his areas of research and service are education, Latino studies, and Chicano studies.

**Deborah Parédez** is Associate Professor of theatre, race, and performance at UT Austin. She has published several works on U.S. Latina/o performance and popular culture.

**Roxana J. Rojas** is a graduate student of Latin American Studies at UT Austin. Her research includes deportation, migration, and issues of gender. Upon completion of graduation, she intends on continuing her education as a doctoral student and fulfilling aspirations of becoming an activist scholar.

**Analicia Sotelo** is an MFA in Poetry at the University of Houston. Her poems have been published in *DIAGRAM* and *Ink Node*. She also teaches for Writers in the Schools, a non-profit organization that brings creative writing into area schools.

**María Socorro Tabuenca Córdoba,** Professor of Spanish at the University of Texas at El Paso, is also the Academic Director for the Center for Inter American and Border Studies. Her research focuses on northern Mexican literature, feminism, cinema, and gender violence.

**Rita E. Urquijo-Ruiz** is Associate Professor of Spanish and codirector or the Women's and Gender Studies Program at Trinity University. Her research deals with Mexican and Chicana/o literatures and cultures, gender and sexuality studies, theater, and performance studies.

**Carlos G. Vélez-Ibáñez** is a specialist in migration and transnational communities, and Professor of transborder Chicana/o and Latina/o studies at Arizona State University. He is also the Chair of the School of Human Evolution and Social Change at Arizona State University, and Professor Emeritus of Anthropology, UC Riverside.

**Tomás Ybarra-Frausto** was the Associate Director for Creativity and Culture at the Rockefeller Foundation and participant of the Humanities Residency Fellowship Program, Museum Program, and U.S.-Mexico Fund for Culture. He also served as chair of the Board of the Mexican Museum, San Francisco, and chair of the Smithsonian Council.

# Index

academia 1, 19
'acculturation' 36
Acuña, Rudolfo 4
African Americans 145, 218, 235
Alarcón, Norma 51–52
American civil life 32
American culture 33, 139, 157
Anglo-Americans 34, 139, 203, 204
Anzaldúa, Gloria 9, 51, 52, 53, 119, 121, 161
Aparicio, Frances 141
Arizona 34, 35, 79
Arrizón, Alicia 126
Asco 103–105
'assimilation' 207
*Assumption of Lupe Vélez, The* (González) 98
Aztlán 158

barrios 23
Bhabha, Homi 29
bilingual households 213
binational indigenous communities 11, 31, 225
Blanco-Cano, Rosana 99
bolero music 141
Bonilla-Silva, Eduardo 205, 214, 219
Bookleggers 22, 25
border
  culture 53
  representations of 178–181
  as a third space 50
  U.S.-Mexico region 27, 32, 49, 86, 97, 99, 103, 121, 161, 167

Border Art Workshop/Taller de Arte Fronterizo (BAW/TAF) 108–110, 162
Border Industrialization Program
  *see* maquiladoras
*Bordertown* (Nava) 77, 83–88
Bracero Program 35, 160
*Broken Line, The* 233
Bowden, Charles 88
Bustamante, Maris 103–105
  *see also* Polvo de Gallina Negra
Bustamante, Nao 99–100

Cabrera, Margarita 167
California 31, 35, 37, 39, 45, 47, 58, 124, 127, 131, 151, 162, 163, 164, 180, 183, 187, 235
Caltranzit 22, 25
Candiani, Tania 191–192
Cantú, Norma 13
capitalism 50, 56, 58, 81, 102, 189
carpas (itinerant theater) 232
Castañeda, Antonia 3
Catholicism xv, 64, 65, 66, 165, 207, 210
Chagoya, Enrique 164–165
*Chain South, The* (Bustamante) 100
Chatino 223
Chávez-Silverman, Susana 117
Chicago 206
Chicana Feminisms 51, 118
Chicano Art 103–105
Chicano Movement xiv–xv, 69, 103–105, 161
*Cinépolis* (Cuevas) 101–102

citizenship 76
  binational 11, 31, 225
  cultural 32
  flexible 20
  non-ideal 9
  transborder 32, 34
  unilineal 33
Ciudad Juárez 7, 75, 168
class
  middle 206
  working 98
  working class music 141
Clinton, Hillary 57
colonialism (U.S.) 83
colonias in the U.S. 39
colonization 68
*Como la Flor* (Selena) 141, 142–146
  *see also* Selena
Conde, Rosina 15, 231–258
'contact zones' (Pratt) 10, 158
corporeality 129
coyotes 27
'crossing over' 139
Cruz, Yolanda 11, 15, 223–229
Cuevas, Ximena 101–102
'cultural boundaries' 54
'cultural citizenship' 2, 10, 11, 13, 20,
    32, 33, 76, 177, 195
'cultural performance' 62
'cultural practices' 66
culture
  fluxes of 159
  transborder *see* 'transborder
    culture'

Dávila, Arlene 115
deportation 41, 254
diasporic identity 12, 19, 86, 98, 145,
    253
differences 10
discrimination 5, 160
Dobbs, Lou 54
domestic abuse 86
  *see also* violence
Durán, Javier 19, 26, 28

economy 6, 13, 38, 43, 50, 51, 57, 58,
    77, 80, 166, 171
Ejército Zapatista de Liberación
    Nacional (EZLN) 7
El Paso, TX 169
EMI Records 140, 146
Escárcega, Sylvia 11
Esquibel, Catriona Rueda 138
ethnicity 86, 205, 207, 214
'ethnobiographic' 20
'ethnography, mojado' 21

family 204, 206, 207
femicide 75, 76, 77
feminisms
  Chicana *see* Chicana Feminisms
  Third World Feminism 52
folklore 64, 67
Fregoso, Rosalinda 76
Frente Indígena de Organizaciones
    Binacionales (FIOB) 224
fronterizo
  *see* border
Fulana Artistic Collective 171
Fusco, Coco 108, 109, 115

Gamboa, Harry Jr. 103–105
García-Canclini, Néstor 9, 170, 176
Gaspar de Alba, Alicia 76, 89
*Genara, La* (Conde) 234–235
gender 1, 2, 3, 7, 9, 10, 12, 13, 14, 15,
    49, 51, 52, 55, 57, 58, 77, 91, 107,
    109, 117, 120, 121, 126, 129, 130,
    131, 135, 136, 137, 149, 150, 151,
    190, 191, 209, 225, 254
globalization xv, 1, 2, 7, 8, 9, 10, 13,
    14, 21, 49, 51, 52, 54, 56, 58, 76,
    77, 85, 90, 102, 112, 113, 121, 163,
    167, 171, 175–176, 188, 195
Gómez, Marga 124
Gómez-Peña, Guillermo 109–110,
    162, 233
*Greetings From a Queer Señorita*
    (Palacios) 119, 123, 125, 127–128
grupos/groups artistic 103–108

Guadalupe Hidalgo Treaty xiv, 29, 63
Gutiérrez, Laura G. 122–123

Handegnau-Sotelo, Pierrette 56
hegemony 72, 78, 79, 83
heterosexuality/heteronormativity 10, 130, 135
hibridity 9, 147
human rights 75, 78

immigration 3, 4, 5, 6, 7, 8, 11, 15, 18, 36, 44, 50, 54, 56, 65, 112, 113, 127, 130, 131, 139, 150, 158, 160, 163, 165, 166, 167, 168, 172, 173, 174, 187, 205, 206, 207, 209, 210, 227, 228, 229, 261
'India María, La' 98
indigenous groups 72, 223, 224
InSite 111, 182, 185, 186

*Juárez, Stages of Fear* (Alejandro) 77, 88–91

Keating, Ana Louise 51

labor
  demand for Mexican workers 4
  domestic 167
  gender and 34
  manual vs. intellectual 23, 26
Laredo, TX 61, 62, 67, 73
'Latin Music Boom' 141
Latina Feminisms 171
'Latiness'
  *see* 'Latinidad'
'Latinidad' 102, 139, 140–142, 157–158, 214
Lesbians 128
  *see also* queer culture
López, Josefina 211
Los Ángeles, CA 225

*Made in Tijuana* (Yépez) 125
maquiladoras 6, 31, 76–77, 113, 167

Matachines de la Santa Cruz 61, 62, 63–68
Mayer, Mónica 103–105
  *see also* Polvo de Gallina Negra
McCaughan, Edward 115
'megascripts' 33, 42
Méndez, Luis H. 6, 16
'mestizaje' 51, 52, 53, 63, 66, 70, 71, 112, 121, 168, 173
Mexican American War 33
Mexican Americans 145, 149, 159, 203–210
Mexican Revolution 158–159
'mexicanization' 36
Mexicans
  culture 149
  elite 44
  identity xiii
  illegal crossings 217
  "illegals" *see* immigration
  undocumented immigrants 43, 163–164, 169
Mexico City 233
Mixes 31, 32
Monsiváis, Carlos 19–26, 28, 29
Monterrey, Mexico 143
Montoya, Malaquías 162–163
motherhood 236–237
Muñoz, José Esteban 21, 28, 126, 127

Nájera-Ramírez, Olga 153
Nash, June 7
national identities 102
nationalism 51, 102, 176
Nava, Gregory 142–143
*Ni de aquí ni de allá* (Velasco) 97
*No Country for Old Men* (Coen) 50
Noriega, Chon 115
Nortec 25
North American Free Trade Agreement (NAFTA) 6, 7, 32, 83, 112, 238

Oaxaca, Mexico 163–164, 223, 224
Obama, Barack 57

Ong, Aihwa 20

Palacios, Mónica 119, 120, 123–125
Pan-Latina/o 140, 147
Paredes, Américo xiv, 68, 161, 162
Partido Acción Nacional (PAN) 6
patriarchy 3, 9, 13, 77, 78, 79, 82, 234
people of color 217
Pérez, Emma 62, 138
Performance art 97, 99, 102, 119
'performative practices' 161, 169
'performativity' 97, 102
Pinzón, Dulce 165–167
Pocahontas 66, 68
Polvo de Gallina Negra 106–108
poverty 5, 23, 41, 58, 178, 181, 185, 211, 214, 217
power 49, 79
Pratt, Mary Louise 10, 120, 158
Puebla, Mexico 165–167
'Pueblatitlan' (Mexicans in NY) 165–167

queer culture 51, 52, 57, 121, 124, 135, 136, 149–150
queer performance 107, 119, 123, 124, 136, 153
queer tourism 58
queering 126, 128, 150
Quintanilla, A.B. 144–145
Quintanilla Pérez Selena
 *see* Selena

'racialized success' 42–43
racism 217
Ramírez, Marcos "Erre" 111, 112, 170, 185–188
Ramírez-Cancio, Marlene 171
Ramírez-Pimienta, Juan Carlos 22, 26, 28
ranchera music 141
repatriation 41
Rivera, Tomás 157, 174
Rocco, Raymond 8, 10–11
Romero, Brenda 64

Romero, Rolando 28
Rosaldo, Renato 55
Ruiz-Otis, Jaime 188–190
Rumbaut, Rubén 207

Saldívar, Ramón 10, 32
Saldívar-Hull, Sonia 52
Sampaio, Anna 8
San Antonio, TX 1, 6, 69, 71, 145, 152, 159, 213, 215, 216, 218, 219, 223, 231
San Diego 15, 111, 113, 170, 176, 179, 186, 187, 188
Sandoval-Sánchez, Alberto 116, 127–128
Santiago, Alejandro 163–169, 227
Saporta-Sternbach, Nancy 116, 127–128
Selena 139–154
*Selena—Live—The Last Concert* 142, 152
*Señorita Maquiladora* (Conde) 237–238
sex workers 88–89
sexual orientation
 *see* queer culture
*Sonatina* (Conde) 234–235
Sonora, Mexico 34, 35, 36
Spanish language 208–209, 213, 223
Swain, Regina 93

Tabuenca Córdoba, María Socorro 24
Taylor, Diana 161
Tejano music 140, 141, 150
Texas 35, 79, 213–215
Third World Feminism
 *see* feminisms
*This Bridge Called My Back* (Anzaldúa/Moraga) 51
Tigres del Norte, Los 19, 25
Tijuana 162–163, 169, 170, 175, 178, 182, 183, 184, 194, 233, 235
'transborder culture' 36, 37, 176–177, 178, 184, 191

'transborder exchanges' 38, 43, 175, 177
'transborder identity' 2, 119
'transborder subjects' 136
'transborder visual culture' 155–169, 175, 182
'transcultural exchanges' 1
'transculturality' 9, 168
'transnational capital' 49
'transnational exchanges' 1, 2, 26–27, 31, 49, 56, 158, 175, 177
'transnational history' 3
'transnational identity' 2, 140, 147
'transnational narratives' 75, 171
    see also globalization
'transnational networks' 32, 159
Trinity University, San Antonio 97, 98, 204, 213, 214, 215, 216, 217, 218, 219, 231, 237

'undocumented migrants'
    see immigration

Valenzuela Arce, José 12
Varese, Stephano 11
Vargas, Deborah 145
Vélez, Lupe 98
Vélez-Ibáñez, Carlos 56, 57, 58
violence
    against Latinas/os 3, 77, 91, 171–172
    on the border 50, 63, 67, 83, 89, 90, 92, 93, 120, 121, 184, 236
    domestic 86, 87
*Virgin of Juarez, The* (Dobson) 77, 80–83

Washington, George Birthday 61, 62, 68, 70
'wet backs' 19, 21, 27
'wet minds' 19, 21, 27
'whiteness' 43, 203, 205–206, 214
women
    art 107, 191
    of color 52, 76, 134, 187, 229
    oppression of 7, 13, 76, 78, 80, 81, 83, 84, 89, 167, 204, 236–237
    rights of 7, 76, 78, 80, 107

XEW 232

*Y no se lo tragó la tierra* (Rivera) 157, 174
Yabro-Bejarano, Ivonne 153
Ybarra-Frausto, Tomás 175
Yépez, Heriberto 25
*You Scared* (Palacios) 128–130

**GPSR Compliance**

The European Union's (EU) General Product Safety Regulation (GPSR) is a set of rules that requires consumer products to be safe and our obligations to ensure this.

If you have any concerns about our products, you can contact us on

ProductSafety@springernature.com

In case Publisher is established outside the EU, the EU authorized representative is:

Springer Nature Customer Service Center GmbH
Europaplatz 3
69115 Heidelberg, Germany

www.ingramcontent.com/pod-product-compliance
Lightning Source LLC
LaVergne TN
LVHW051914060526
838200LV00004B/134